LIFE CYCLES

LIFE
CYCLES

The Influence of Planetary
Cycles on our Lives

ROSE ELLIOT

M
MACMILLAN
LONDON

The publishers gratefully acknowledge permission granted by Age Concern to quote from *Famous Ways to Grow Old* by Philip Bristow.

Every effort has been made to trace all copyright holders but if any inadvertent omission has been made, please contact the publishers.

First published 1993 by Macmillan London
a division of Pan Macmillan Publishers Limited
Cavaye Place London SW10 9PG
and Basingstoke

Associated companies throughout the world

ISBN 0 333 59256 5

1 3 5 7 9 8 6 4 2
A CIP catalogue record for this book is available from
the British Library

Phototypeset by Intype, London
Printed and bound in Great Britain by
Mackays of Chatham PLC, Chatham, Kent.

To my mother, Joan Hodgson – my
first astrology teacher and my
friend – with great love

CONTENTS

APPENDICES

GLOSSARY   227

BIBLIOGRAPHY   236

LIST OF TABLES

CONTENTS

ACKNOWLEDGEMENTS

My warmest thanks to all the people who have contributed to this book; to those who generously allowed me to use their case histories, and to quote from their books; to my editors at Pan Macmillan, Catherine Hurley and Judith Hannam, with a special 'thank you' to Judith for her sensitive and precise editing of the manuscript; to my agent, Barbara Levy, who has been, as ever, supportive, helpful and encouraging throughout; to astrologers Sasha Fenton, Joan Hodgson and Simon Bentley for sharing their experiences with me, especially Simon who provided me with a number of case histories from his files. Most of all I'd like to thank my husband, Robert, for believing in me when I doubted myself; for patiently reading, re-reading and discussing the manuscript with me, and making many useful suggestions; for calculating the charts and creating the graphs, and for particular help with the astronomical and psychological aspects of the book.

ABOUT THIS BOOK

I've been interested in astrology for as long as I can remember. My mother is an astrologer, so talk of horoscopes was a natural part of the conversation in our home and something that always fascinated me. My mother taught me how to calculate and interpret a birth chart when I was just 13, using her correspondence course (the first in the UK). After that I went on to get the diploma of the Faculty of Astrological Studies, and I've been practising ever since.

The idea for writing *Life Cycles* came to me several years ago when I read the book *Passages*. In this book Gail Sheehy shows that there is a predictable pattern of crisis and change which we all experience during our lives. This interested me, because as an astrologer I knew that the cyclical movement of the planets means that they also affect each one of us strongly at certain ages. The actual dates may vary by a year or so – several years in the case of Neptune and Pluto – but I realized that the timing fitted, with remarkable accuracy, the life-changes described by Gail Sheehy. I began to study the charts of friends, family, clients and well-known people, calculating the times which, according to the planetary cycles, were significant, and noting what was happening in their lives. The results were uncanny. Not only did the crisis points shown by the planets tie in with the patterns described by Gail Sheehy, but the events which took place were in accordance with the nature of the planets involved. I feel that not only is this very strong evidence that astrology works, but it also means that by looking up their planetary cycles, everyone can understand why certain things are happening, or happened, to them at a particular time. Knowing the astrological reason for the 'predictable crises', as Gail Sheehy calls them, makes them easier to understand and accept, and also makes it possible to pinpoint the critical periods. As each birth chart is unique, and the speed of the planets is not completely regular, the exact timing of the crisis periods varies, while the details are as individual as the person concerned – as you'll realize when you read about them.

Having spent many years studying and practising astrology, working on hundreds of birth charts, I am totally convinced not only that it works, but also that it can be of great value. For reasons that we do not understand, the pattern of the planets in the sky at the moment of our birth – our birth chart – and their subsequent movement in relation to it correlate, in some extraordinary way, with our character and destiny.

I do not believe that astrology takes away our free will. An astrologer can tell you about possible trends in your life, in much the same way as a forecaster predicts the weather. But an astrologer cannot force you to take notice of what he or she says, just as a weatherman cannot make you take your umbrella with you if he says it's going to rain. If I advise a client to take extra care because Mars is active in his horoscope and he may act over-hastily, lose his temper or have an accident as a result, he still has a choice as to whether to heed the advice or not. And if, as he feels the energy rising, he remembers my words and deflects the energy elsewhere, I think that can only be good.

In my experience, a knowledge of our birth chart, and those of our loved ones, certainly enables us to understand ourselves, and them, and what is happening in our lives, better. One of my clients is a psychotherapist who regularly asks for personality profiles for her patients because, she says, 'One of your horoscopes can tell me in a few minutes what it would take me months and months to uncover.' Certainly I know many psychologists who use astrology to help them in their work, as indeed Jung did. Alice O. Howell, in *Jungian Synchronicity in Astrological Signs and Ages*, says that she has 'found it helpful that the chart properly used can give the client permission and later a sacred mandate to be who he or she is'. I see life as a journey which involves our physical, mental and emotional development, and the experiences which come to us during our life as neither 'good' nor 'bad', but opportunities for us to learn more about ourselves, and thus to grow and develop further. A knowledge of our birth chart, and our planetary cycles, can be a great help in understanding this process of growth.

This book consists of an introduction and three parts. The introduction explains the principles of astrology and of the planetary cycles and how they relate to the nature of our personality and its growth and development during our lives. Part 1 describes the planets and their cycles; what they stand for in the birth chart and how their movements link up with events in our lives. Part 2 explains the planetary crisis-points which affect us all from birth onwards, with examples taken from my casebook and from those of other astrologers who have kindly shared them with me (with names and details changed as necessary to preserve anonymity), as well as from the lives of many well-known people. Part 3 consists of graphs of the planetary movements from 1900 to 2050, and explains how you can look up the position of your own planets and work out your own cycles and those of your family and friends. There's also a glossary of the astrological and psychological terms used in this book.

I do hope that, whatever stage you've reached in your own journey through life, you'll find this book interesting and helpful.

INTRODUCTION

ASTROLOGY AND THE

PLANETARY CYCLES

For thousands of years people have looked at the starry sky and seen the planets moving against the constellations. Gradually they noticed that events on earth seemed to coincide with the positions of the planets. One planet would bring expansion and beneficence while another appeared to be connected with hard work and difficulty; one planet brought harmony while another brought discord and war. Over many years they correlated the different planets with qualities, events and attributes of life. They gave the five visible planets names: Mercury, Venus, Mars, Jupiter and Saturn. They also noticed that the effect of the planets seemed to be modified by the part of the sky they were seen against. There appeared to be twelve major divisions of activity and influence, and they gave names to each part of the zodiac (the path the planets followed through the sky): Aries, Taurus, Gemini, Cancer, Leo, Virgo, Libra, Scorpio, Sagittarius, Capricorn, Aquarius and Pisces. By convention the zodiac is said to start with the sign of Aries, and 0 degrees Aries is taken as the position of the Sun when it crosses the equator on the first day of spring. It marks the vernal equinox.

So astrology was, and is, a science of observation and correlation. It observes the patterns of the planets and correlates them with the patterns of our lives. Astrology is primarily, but not totally, concerned with human life, which is extraordinarily complicated and diffuse, with many different strands interwoven together. We may act rationally one moment and emotionally the next. We have moods, desires, passions, hopes, fears, needs, thoughts, beliefs, hates and loves, all mixed together in constantly changing ways. Through astrology we can begin to see the major influences which affect each person, why

1

one person is rational and another emotional; why one is stubborn and another flexible.

Every science needs to have a language of words or symbols to convey information quickly and conveniently, so that students understand one another and the ideas that are being expressed. Astrology uses symbols for each of the planets and the signs of the zodiac. It has symbols to represent special angular relationships (aspects) between planets, and also the twelve areas of a chart which each have particular significance and relevance (houses).

The symbols can sometimes represent things or people, but mostly they stand for principles of life which enrich us and enable us to develop as human beings. These are qualities, energies, emotional tendencies, mental activity, aspirations and inspirations, passions, sensitivities and so on. They provide the raw material from which our personalities are created and which drive our activities and steer us through the many experiences of our lives.

Each planet has an influence on our lives. Some, like Mercury, which orbits the Sun, change very quickly, introducing rapid but short-lived effects, while the slower planets, such as Jupiter and Pluto, take much longer to circle round us and their effects are therefore much longer lasting. This book is primarily about the effects on our lives of the cycles of these slow but powerful planets.

Picture our solar system. At the centre is the Sun; around the Sun revolves the tiny planet Mercury; a little further away is Venus, then the Earth, orbited by the Moon, with Mars, Jupiter, Saturn, Uranus, Neptune and Pluto beyond. They are all moving anticlockwise round the Sun, on much the same plane, like a flat plate, but at different speeds: it takes Mercury just 88 days to complete the journey, while Pluto takes 248.4 years.

Our solar system is one of some 100,000 million which are collected together in our galaxy. The other suns in our galaxy are seen as the stars in the night sky. The patterns of these stars have, over the centuries, been named – the Ram, the Bull, the Heavenly Twins – and have given us the signs of the zodiac. If we were able to stand on the top of the Earth, and if we could also eliminate the glare of the Sun, we would see the background of stars all around us in a

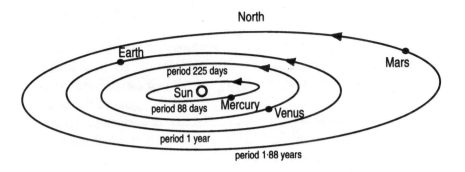

1 The orbits of the terrestrial planets of the solar system

circle, 360 degrees, each sign following the next. Each planet would be seen against the background of one of these signs, or, as astrologers say, 'in' that sign. This picture is represented in the birth chart. The Earth is at the centre of the chart; the twelve signs of the zodiac, each occupying 30 degrees, are round the outer circle; and the planets are plotted in their correct positions within that circle.

However, as we do not live at the poles of the Earth but nearer the equator, the view we get of the planets and signs is not of a flat, horizontal plate, but a tilted one. We see only a part of the zodiac at a time; the rest is hidden by the Earth under our feet. The part we can see is the path which the Sun and the planets appear to follow as they rise in the east, reach the zenith and then set in the west. Actually, this apparent motion is due not to the movement of the planets but to the Earth's rotation on its axis, and during each day every sign of the zodiac takes its turn to rise in the east and set in the west. The sign which is rising over the eastern horizon at the moment of birth is called the rising sign, or the ascendant. This is one of the major features of the horoscope and is as important as the sign the Sun is in – the Sun sign.

The personal chart which maps the positions of the planets at the time of birth, known as the birth chart or horoscope, is always set out so that the rising sign is on the left-hand side of the chart, at the '9 o'clock' position, as you will see if you look at the chart given as an example in Diagram 3 (page 5). From that point the rest of the signs of the zodiac, following the rising sign, are written round

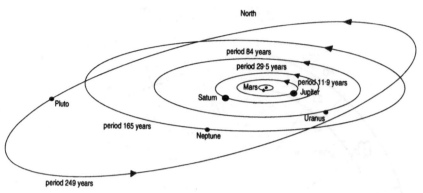

North

period 84 years
period 29·5 years
period 11·9 years
Jupiter
Mars
Saturn
Pluto
Uranus
period 165 years
Neptune
period 249 years

2   *The orbits of the outer planets of the solar system*

the chart in an anticlockwise direction, each occupying a 30-degree section of the circle. The planets are written into their correct places, depending on which sign of the zodiac they are in. In Diagram 3, for instance, the Sun and Mercury are in the 30-degree section which belongs to Cancer, with Mercury at 3 degrees of the section, and the Sun a little further on, at 9 degrees; the Moon is in the section belonging to Aquarius at 25 degrees, as is Jupiter, though nearer the beginning, at 5 degrees, and so on.

If you look at this birth chart diagram, and also at Diagram 4 (page 6), you will notice that the circle is divided into twelve sections. These are called 'houses' and, unlike the signs of the zodiac, are not necessarily of equal size. While some astrologers divide the chart into twelve 30-degree sections starting with the ascendant – called the equal house system – many, myself included, find we get more accurate results using one of the other methods of house division which does not result in houses of equal size. In these systems, the space around the place of birth is considered to be marked by two planes. One is the flat horizon banded by the N, S, E and W points, and the other is a plane which is imagined to pass through the N and S points and also directly above the place through the zenith point. It will also pass through the point directly underneath, the nadir. A circle drawn from the place through the E and W points and the zenith and nadir will thus be divided into four quadrants or equal parts. Because there are twelve houses, each quadrant has to be divided into three. Near the equator this is no problem because the ecliptic, or

BIRTH CHART

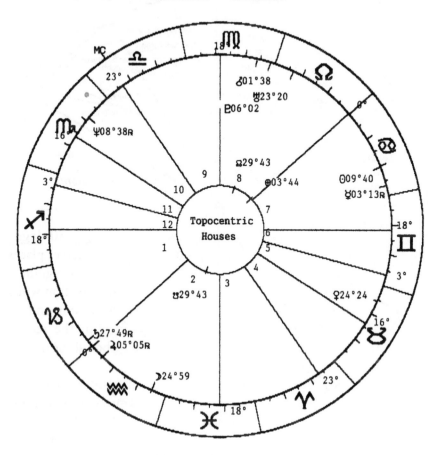

Name Diana Princess of Wales
Born Saturday 1st July 1961 at
Sandringham 52°50n   0°30e
Time 7.45pm

3   Birth chart of the Princess of Wales (see also page 203)

path of the zodiac, follows very closely the great circle through the zenith. This results in houses of fairly equal size, similar to those produced by the equal house system. As we move further away from the equator the ecliptic gets lower in the sky and the houses become more uneven in size. Over the years astrologers and mathematicians have worked out different systems for calculating exactly where to draw the houses, and there are a number of these house systems

5

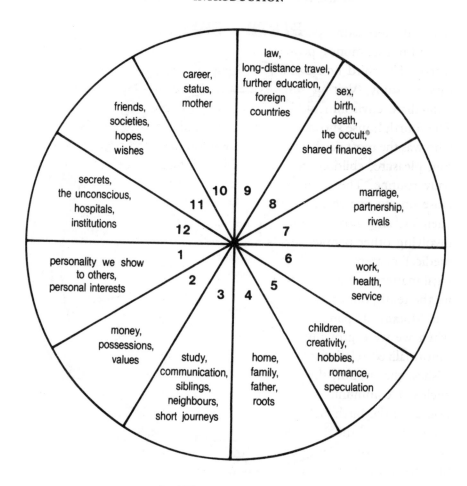

4   What the houses mean

which are used by astrologers. The quadrant system which I use for personal astrological work is actually one of the most modern. It was developed in the early 1960s by Wendel Polich and Nelson Page, who studied the effect of the planets through the houses of birth charts calculated from very accurate data and constructed a method of house division based on their findings. This is called the Topocentric House System, and I have found it to be very reliable in practice.

Whichever method of house division you use, however, each house is linked to a particular area of life. For example, the first house shows our outward personality, the face we like to show the world, our self-expression, personal plans and physical appearance; the second house, money, possessions and sense of values, including self-worth. The third house shows attitude and approach to communication, study, writing and correspondence; short journeys and immediate environment, brothers, sisters, cousins and neighbours. The fourth house shows our home, base and security, and the parent who was the most passive in our upbringing; the fifth house, creativity, fun, pleasure, children and love; the sixth house, health, work and daily routine. The seventh house shows marriage, partnership and close one-to-one relationships, including those with rivals and open enemies, and also the public; the eighth house, financial matters involving other people, inherited wealth, sex, birth and death, plus medical matters. The ninth house shows travel, higher education, legal matters, religion, widening of our horizons and what we believe in; the tenth, our career and success in the world, people in authority, our 'dominant' parent, that is, the one who was most in evidence when we were growing up. The eleventh house shows friends and unformalized relationships, groups, societies, ideals, aims, hopes and wishes; the twelfth, the unconscious, prisons, hospitals, retreats and enclosed communities, secret enemies. The fact that some of the houses of the birth chart do not contain planets does not mean that these areas of the life will be empty or unsatisfactory, although, conversely, more than one planet in a house means that the aspect of life shown by that house will be particularly important. When there is no planet in the house, the astrologer looks closely at the sign on that house cusp – the start of the house – and also at the position of the planet which is linked with that sign, or, in astrological terms, said to 'rule' it.

No one yet understands why, but this chart, when interpreted, shows the potential of that moment of time, whether it coincides with the birth of a baby, the launch of a ship or the opening of a restaurant. Whatever begins at that moment will express the characteristics shown in that moment. It is as if that moment is a 'seed', and by looking at it in the symbolic form of a birth chart, an astrologer can tell what kind of plant it will grow into. The symbols can be interpreted according to whatever it is that has begun at that moment: for example, if it is the start of a business, the first house will show the image which that business presents to the public, the second house will show its finances, the third its communications, and so on.

A personal birth chart, calculated for the moment of birth – considered to be when the first breath is taken – shows a person's character and potential, likes and dislikes, abilities, stresses, challenges and likely development. There are many factors which an astrologer would take into account to get a full picture both of character and of the likely development of the life, but you can learn quite a lot by simply considering the planets and the signs and houses in which they are placed, together with the rising sign.

Each planet stands for certain aspects of life, or for life-principles. For example, the Sun shows essential personality and symbolizes men, power and vitality, while the Moon shows feelings, our mother and the kind of mothering we had, and our own ability to nurture others and symbolizes women, domestic matters, emotional security and home and family life. It also symbolizes the general public, and is prominent in the charts of people who have a special rapport with the public. Mercury shows our way of learning and communicating; its house position reveals an important area of communication for us. Venus shows our way of loving and relating to others; its house position indicates what gives us pleasure. Mars shows our way of taking action and getting things done; its house position shows where we use our energy and initiative and what makes us angry. Jupiter shows expansion, opportunities; its house position demonstrates where we may find these; Saturn shows limitation, organizational ability and discipline; its house position indicates where our limitations, duties and responsibilities will lie. Uranus shows individuality, independence, change, rebellion, unconventionality, erratic behaviour, sudden and unexpected events; the house in which it is placed shows the area of life where these are likely to occur. Neptune shows nebulousness, impressionability, imagination, dissolution, self-sacrifice, escape, confusion; and, again, the house in which it is placed indicates where we are most likely to experience these. Pluto shows power and power-struggles, profound emotional experiences, elimination, renewal, regeneration, and its house-position tells us the area of life in which these will occur.

Each sign of the zodiac stands for certain characteristics, some of which are familiar to many people through popular astrology. There are many books which give descriptions of the signs, so I won't write about them here at length. Instead, I'll give you a few key words which express the essence of each sign:

Aries is assertive, energetic, always seeking the new

Taurus is possessive, practical, sensual

Gemini is versatile, communicative, changeable

Cancer is sensitive, caring, responsive, home-loving, conventional

Leo is proud, dramatic, passionate, generous

Virgo is critical, intelligent, realistic, with a keen sense of detail

Libra is harmony-loving, balanced, companionable, fair

Scorpio is passionate, secretive, intense, and has great determination

Sagittarius is freedom-loving, enthusiastic, optimistic

Capricorn is prudent, cool, ambitious, calculating, with high standards and respect for tradition

Aquarius is detached but friendly, quirky, erratic

Pisces is imaginative, gentle, kind, sometimes confused and deceptive.

The principle of a planet will function in the manner of the sign in which it is placed, and in the area of life shown by its house position. I must explain here that each planet has certain 'favourite signs' and houses, or ones in which it can function most fully, and, conversely, others in which it finds the going tough. For instance, Venus is happy in the signs of Taurus and Libra, which, in astrological terms, it is said to rule, and also in Pisces, in which it is said to be 'dignified' or 'exalted'. It is not so comfortable, however, in the opposite signs of Scorpio and Aries, in which it is said to be 'detriment', and Virgo, in which it is in its fall. On page 223 you will find a list of all the planets, together with the signs they rule and in which they are exalted, and the opposite, and the houses in which they function most comfortably.

When a planet is placed in a sign in which it is happy, it is said to

9

be 'strong', and this strength is increased if it is also in a compatible house and making a number of important aspects. The planet which rules the sign which is rising is naturally 'strong' and important in the birth chart; and strength is added to a planet if a number of other planets are placed in one of the signs which it rules. For example, the influence of Venus in a chart will be strengthened if there are two or more planets (not necessarily Venus itself) in Taurus or Libra, or in the houses with which Venus is naturally harmonious, the second and seventh. So, when I refer later in this book to a planet being 'strong' in a chart, or to someone having a 'strongly Martian' or 'strongly Uranian' chart, for example, you will understand what I mean.

Now let's demonstrate how some of this works out in practice by building up a simple interpretation of our example chart, that of the Princess of Wales, by noting the rising sign, and the sign and house position of the Sun, Moon, Mercury, Venus and Mars, the planets which correspond to the most personal factors in the horoscope.

If you look at the horoscope of the Princess of Wales on page 5, you will see that it shows:

Sagittarius rising

Sun in Cancer in the seventh house

Moon in Aquarius in the second house

Mercury in Cancer in the seventh house

Venus in Taurus in the fifth house

Mars in Virgo in the eighth house

Now, referring to the descriptions which I have given of the planets, signs and houses on pages 8, 9 and 6–7, we find we can interpret these positions as follows:

Sagittarius rising means the Princess's *outward personality* comes across as *freedom-loving, enthusiastic, optimistic.*

Sun in Cancer in the seventh house means that her *essential personality* is *sensitive, caring, responsive, home-loving and conventional,* with *a strong focus on her marriage and close one-to-one relationships, including those with rivals, open enemies and the public.*

10

Moon in Aquarius in the second house shows that *emotionally* the Princess is *detached but friendly, quirky and erratic* and that she finds emotional security in *money, possessions, her sense of values, including her self-worth.*

Mercury in Cancer in the seventh house shows that her *way of learning and communicating* is *sensitive, caring, responsive, home-loving and conventional* and that her *marriage and close one-to-one relationships, including those with rivals and open enemies and the public,* are *important areas of communication.*

Venus in the sign of Taurus in the fifth house shows that her *way of loving and relating to others* is *possessive, practical and sensual* and that *she finds pleasure* through *creativity, fun, children and love.*

Mars in Virgo in the eighth house shows that the Princess's *way of taking action and getting things done* is *critical, intelligent, realistic, with attention to detail,* and that areas where it is natural for her to use her energy are *financial matters involving other people, inherited wealth, sex, birth and death; medical matters.*

This is chart-interpretation in a very simple form, but I think you will agree that it ties in with what we know of Princess Diana's character. In her book *Princess,* Ann Morrow describes her as

outgoing but not outrageous . . . loyal, kind, tactful, warm, discreet, firm . . . she remains quirky, irreverent, dignified, motherly, skittish, sweet, hopeful, wistful, sexy, determined yet soft . . . She conveys warmth and is tactile in a way no other member of the royal family has found possible . . . Her care is for the unemployed, the elderly and the homeless . . . The reality is she is a down-to-earth well-born girl, conventional, cheerful, wanting to be liked, who has made a huge success of one of the most difficult jobs in the world.

Another very important factor in a birth chart is the network of aspects, or links, between the planets. These are rather like lines of communication which occur between the planets when they make certain angles together. If they are at the same point in the zodiac, their influences blend; if they are at opposite points (180 degrees apart), they pull in opposite directions and are said to be 'tense' aspects; if they are 120 degrees apart, they work together harmoniously; if they are 90 degrees apart the influences conflict with each other. Astrologers often draw lines on the birth chart to show these links between the planets. The tense aspects show conflicts in the personality and challenges to be met; they also show strength of character and the ability to overcome difficulties. The harmonious aspects show that the energies of the planets combine without friction to bring ease, opportunities and happy outcomes. The house positions of the planets involved show the areas of life where the conflicts or opportunities occur. The full list of aspects which astrologers normally use is as follows:

The conjunction ☌ is the term used when planets are very close to each other – usually 0–8 degrees apart – and thus usually in the same sign, although a conjunction can occur when one planet is at the end of a sign and another at the beginning of the next sign. This is a strong aspect and means that the two planets work together, their influences always blending. This may or may not be easy, depending on how compatible the planets are. For instance, if Venus, which shows our way of loving and relating to others, is in conjunction with the Moon, which symbolizes feelings and emotional security, our relationships are likely to be quite harmonious, if a little over-emotional and possessive (because of the Moon) at times. However, if Venus were in conjunction, say, with Uranus, which shows independence, individuality and an inability to conform, then our Venusian ability to relate is likely to be upset by our Uranian desire to be different, to go our own way and not to give way to anyone.

The semi-sextile ⚺ occurs when planets are 30 degrees, or one sign, apart. This aspect is traditionally said to be 'mildly harmonious', although as consecutive signs are often incompatible in a niggly kind of way, I've never understood the logic of this. This is such a minor aspect that if there are other, stronger aspects, many astrologers ignore it when doing character interpretation.

The semi-square ∠ occurs when planets are 45 degrees, or a sign and a half, apart, which means that the influences work together with difficulty and tension.

The sextile ⚹ occurs when planets are around 60 degrees, or two signs, apart. This is a harmonious aspect in which we can use the two influences productively together.

The square ☐ occurs when planets are 90 degrees, or three signs, apart, and it seems as if they are always at loggerheads to each other, pulling in different directions. If the part of our life symbolized by one planet is happy, then the part symbolized by the other is not! For example, if Mars, which shows our energy, drive, courage and desire to take a risk, is in square aspect, thus pulling in another direction from Saturn, which stands for organizational ability, discipline, fear, limitation and caution, then whenever we want to take action, one part of us wants to move forward with courage, but the other part is extremely fearful, wanting to work out all the details. So whenever any action is required, there is always an inner conflict.

The trine △ occurs when planets are around 120 degrees, or four signs, apart. In this position their energies function smoothly together, unlike when they are in square aspect, the limiting quality of Saturn being used in a positive way to organize and discipline our Martian drive and energy.

The quincunx ⚻ , which occurs when planets are 150 degrees, or five signs, apart, is another tense aspect. The signs involved are fairly incompatible, and trying to combine the influences of the two planets is like being in a three-legged race: difficult! I have a number of quincunxes in my birth chart, so I speak from experience. There isn't the tension created by a square; the feeling is more one of restlessness and of never being able to find complete harmony between the planets concerned.

The opposition ☍ occurs when two planets are at opposite sides of the zodiac circle, 180 degrees apart, or thereabouts. Here the energies tend to pull in opposite directions, although they can balance each other like a pair of scales or a see-saw with equal weights on either side.

To see how some of these aspects work out in real life, look again at the birth chart of the Princess of Wales (page 5): you will see that Venus makes tense aspects with both the Moon and Uranus, and that the Moon and Uranus are also in opposition, or at opposite sides of her chart. So the part of the Princess's nature symbolized by the Moon – *emotion, feelings, that which is important to our emotional security, the mother and important women in our life, home and family life* – is opposed to that symbolized by Uranus – *individuality, independence, change, rebellion, unconventionality, erratic behaviour,*

13

sudden and unexpected events – indicating that it is difficult for her to find emotional security; no sooner does she think she's found it than something comes along to disrupt it. This shows her early and sudden separation from her mother. Venus – *the way of loving and relating to others* – in tense aspect to both the Moon and Uranus shows similar difficulties in love, problems in the expression of feelings in close loving relationships, and, again, the possibility of breaks and separations. The Princess has probably learnt to live with these difficult emotions (the Moon and Venus) by becoming quite self-contained and independent (Uranus), and her Moon in detached Aquarius shows that there is a part of her which feels suffocated by too much closeness and emotion. However, the Sun and Mercury in sensitive Cancer, and Venus in loving Taurus (in tense aspect to Uranus), show that there is an important side to her which feels repressed by too much enforced independence. The ideal for her would be a mature relationship in which there was plenty of love and mutual support but also a healthy respect for each partner's independence and individual interests, allowing plenty of space. With the strong Cancer influence and Venus in Taurus, the Princess of Wales could, for all her detachment and independence, be quite possessive, especially as she has some emotional insecurity shown by the difficult Moon and Venus aspects.

There is also a strong harmonious aspect, a trine, in the Princess's chart, between Venus and Saturn – *organizational ability, limitation, duty and responsibility, practical solutions to problems, patience* – which shows that matters are likely to improve with time and with sensible, practical solutions. Another trine aspect between the Sun, which is in the house of marriage, and Neptune – *nebulousness, impressionability, imagination, dissolution, self-sacrifice, escape* – shows there is a harmonious way out of difficulties, although it may involve giving up something.

So you can see that by studying the birth chart it is possible to get a good idea both of the character and potential of a person and of the kind of life which lies ahead of them. By looking at the birth chart an astrologer can also tell the likely timing of important events. We do this in two ways: by 'progressions', which is a process of moving the planets in the birth chart forward, and noting the aspects they then make to the planets in the original birth chart; and by

14

'transits', which are the aspects made to the planets in the birth chart by the current planets as they move, in their cycles, through the signs and houses of the birth chart.

As they do so, the planets once more reach the place where they were when we were born. The Moon does this in just over 28 days; the Sun in about a year; the slower planets in times which vary from 12 years or so for Jupiter to approximately 250 years for Pluto. When planets come back to their birth place, which is called a 'return', there is an intensification of that planet's influence. We get our first Saturn return, for instance, at the age of about 29, and for most people this is a critical time. The first reported marriage problems of the Princess of Wales, for example, coincided with her Saturn return. But the planets also affect us when they reach other specific points in their cycle and make aspects with their position in the birth chart. These show how easily the planetary energy will flow at the particular time when the aspect is made. The aspects start to come into effect when the planet is about a degree away, are at their most intense when they're exact, then tail off as the planets move away, although the repercussions from events which they set in motion may, of course, continue for some time afterwards – in fact, life may never be the same again.

The most sensitive times in the planetary cycle are when the planet makes its 'return' to its original place in the birth chart. This usually coincides with an intensification of the planet's influence and the ending of one cycle and the beginning of another in the matters and areas of life signified by that planet. The next really important developments, concerning the affairs symbolized by that planet, occur at the time when it makes a square aspect, 90 degrees or three signs away from its place in the birth chart. This usually indicates a time of challenge, when the plans and ventures started at the time of the conjunction may be tested and may need to be changed. Then, at the time of the opposition, when the planet reaches the point in the zodiac opposite its position in the birth chart, or 180 degrees away, it is as if we can view those matters signified by the planet from a distance, from the opposite point, and re-evaluate the situation. We may make changes as a result; this can, for example, be a time of separation. Then, as the planet continues round the circle, it makes another square aspect as it comes back to 90 degrees of its place in the birth chart, bringing the chance to make changes and adjustments before the planet again conjoins its own place in the birth chart, ending the cycle and beginning a new one.

If you think all this sounds rather challenging, I can only agree with you! But then, for the most part, life's like that. The planets *do* make other, harmonious aspects during the course of their cycle: there is the sextile aspect which comes after the conjunction, when the planets are two signs, or 60 degrees, apart, and indicates opportunity; and there is the trine, which follows the square, when the planets are four signs, or 120 degrees, apart, and shows stable, harmonious and expansive conditions. Generally, however, these harmonious aspects do not coincide with major events in our lives in the way in which the difficult ones do. So you will find it is mainly the difficult ones that I've concentrated on. We seem to need the inner conflict and friction which these aspects bring in order to draw out our potential and, as you will see in Part 2, difficult aspects by no means always mean negative events. A great deal depends on how we handle the circumstances we're confronted with at the time. As Gurdjieff said: 'If a man lives without inner struggle, if everything happens to him without opposition he will remain as he is.'

In Part 3 of this book you will find graphs of the movements of the planets and simple instructions for calculating the timing of the cycles. By being aware of these cycles and understanding how they shape our growth and development, we can work with them to achieve our fullest potential. In order to do that, we need first to look at each of the planets individually, at the life-principles for which it stands, and at its cycle.

PART ONE

The Planets
and
Their Cycles

THE SUN

The Sun is the most important single factor in a person's birth chart, although we need to take many other factors into consideration as well in order to get a full picture. Just as the Sun is the centre and life-giving force of our solar system, so in the birth chart the Sun symbolizes the life-force within us all, and our Sun sign shows our most essential personality. It's because the Sun influences our personality so strongly that most people find they can identify easily with the character descriptions of their Sun sign.

Because the Sun, and the sign in which it is placed, show our essential personality, we need a way of life which will allow us to express this as fully as we can. The more we can live in a way which is 'in tune' with our most essential personality, the happier and more fulfilled we are likely to be. When we are living in such a way, there is a feeling of 'rightness'; when we are not, we feel uncomfortable and may even become ill. Being healthy – physically, emotionally and psychologically – depends on being aware of this inner sense of 'rightness'. The more we become tuned in to our essential being, symbolized by the Sun, and learn to act on its promptings, the more we are able to express its radiance, vitality and creativity in our lives.

Sometimes, though, it is difficult for us to express our Sun sign fully. This is because all the planetary influences in the birth chart have to be expressed through our rising sign. This shows our outer personality, the side of us that we generally present to other people. If the sign in which the Sun is placed is very different in character from the one which is rising, it can be difficult for us to express our Sun sign. This usually occurs when incompatible elements are involved. As you may know, the signs of the zodiac are divided into four groups, fire, earth, air and water, according to their basic nature. The fire signs – Aries, Leo and Sagittarius – are outgoing, warm and enthusiastic. They're generally compatible with the air signs – Gemini,

Libra and Aquarius – which are also extrovert and detached with active minds. Earth signs – Taurus, Virgo and Capricorn – are careful, practical and introvert, and they combine harmoniously with the water signs – Cancer, Scorpio and Pisces – which are also rather withdrawn and cautious, as well as being easily swayed by their emotions. In general, a fire or air sign does not express itself easily when combined with an earth or water sign, and vice versa. When this is the case, there will be contradictions in the nature, and it's important that the lifestyle feels as comfortable as possible for them both, although the Sun sign should always have priority. If the Sun sign is stifled or repressed, the essential personality, the spark and spirit of the individual, will be deadened.

My own chart is a good example of this contradictory effect. The Sun is in home-loving, sensitive, traditional and introvert Cancer, but independent, detached, unconventional and friendly Aquarius is rising. I need space, and to be able to 'do my own thing', but if this cuts me off from my family life, I am not truly happy: I lose that inner sense of 'rightness' if my Sun sign cannot be expressed properly. The Princess of Wales's horoscope is rather similar, in that she, too, has the Sun in Cancer and an outgoing sign, Sagittarius, rising. So the Sagittarian part of her needs freedom, exercise, a good social life and challenges, while the Cancer part is firmly rooted in her home and family. The opposite can occur when the Sun is in a bold, outgoing sign such as Aries and there is a very controlled and cautious sign rising, like Capricorn or Virgo. In these cases there can be a build-up of inner pressure as the person feels that they really want to branch out, be more daring, take a risk, but their rising sign holds them back. On the other hand, if they do this, their careful, security-loving rising sign will be in a state of anxiety. It's a no-win situation in some respects but, in all these cases, a little astrological knowledge can be helpful in understanding why they feel and act as they do, and in pointing the way to finding a compromise, a way of life in which *both* aspects of the personality can be expressed.

The Sun shows our creativity; children, the theatre and our ability to play and enjoy life, to be 'alive' and full of vitality, to have fun, to take a risk. In the physical body, it symbolizes the heart and vitality. As well as signifying aspects of our character and areas of our physical body, each of the planets (and the signs, too) symbolizes particular types of people and things. The accuracy of these associations has been tested by astrologers over many hundreds of years. They are given in great detail in one of the classic astrological books which many modern astrologers still find valuable, *Christian Astrology* by William Lilly, first published in 1647; and in the introductory part of his book Lilly acknowledges the work of Ptolemy, who lived in the second century AD. Although the details of the planetary associations may have changed with the centuries, the basic principles have not. In Ptolemy's and Lilly's day the Sun, centre of our solar system, symbolized the heart in the physical body and people in positions of power in the world. To Lilly these were, among others, 'Kings, Princes, Emperours, &c. Dukes, Marquesses, Earles, Barons'; today they are more likely to be the supervisor at work or the head of a company. The Sun also symbolizes men in general and the father in particular; also, in a woman's chart, the husband. We always look at the sign and house-position of the Sun, and the aspects it makes, in order to see what kind of a father a person had, and, in the case of women, the type of husband they are likely to have. To give an example, in my own birth chart, the Sun makes a close square aspect to the planet Neptune, which, among other things, stands for spiritual matters. My father spent most of his life working for a New Age religious organization called the White Eagle Lodge, and my husband also worked there for a time and has always been deeply interested in religious matters. I was once shown the horoscope and life history of a woman who was virtually my astrological twin, born a few hours after me. In her case, the Sun square Neptune had been expressed in her life, and in particular in her relationships with men, by something else symbolized by Neptune: alcohol. Her father, husband and sub-sequent boyfriend were alcoholics.

By looking carefully at the birth chart we can glean much information, for things inevitably work out in accordance with the symbolism of the planets. The difficult part lies in knowing which of the different things that the planet stands for will prove to be correct in an individual case. I think this is where an element of free will and choice comes in; I have to accept that the important men in my life are always likely to be Neptunian, but I might have been equally drawn to a musician, say, or an actor – these are also ruled by Neptune – as to a religious man.

The Sun also symbolizes a person who is noble, honourable and trustworthy, with a liking for luxury; if it is not badly aspected or weak in the birth chart because it is in a sign or house with which it is not wholly compatible, it may show someone who is arrogant, snobbish, domineering and extravagant. It signifies gold and anything connected with it, such as goldsmiths and minters of money; rubies; the colours yellow, gold, red and purple; palaces and grand buildings, and aromatic plants such as bay and marigold.

The Cycle of the Sun

The Sun, as it moves through all the signs in its yearly cycle (365.25 days, to be precise), affects us all, although not, from an astrological point of view, as powerfully as do the cycles of the slower-moving planets, as we shall see. In keeping with its life-giving and vitalizing principle, the Sun tends to bring to our attention day-to-day matters concerned with the house of our horoscope through which it is passing each month. As the Sun's cycle is regular – it always enters Aries in March, Taurus in April and so on, as you can discover from the star page of any newspaper or magazine – it will pass through the various houses of your birth chart at the same time each year. This may explain why certain moods and events tend to repeat themselves for you year after year. For instance, I have noticed that late June and the first half of July, when the Sun is in my sixth house of work, are usually exceptionally busy. I have also noticed that the period from late October until Christmas inevitably brings more than the usual number of long journeys and activities concerned with my career as the Sun moves through the ninth and tenth houses, which have to do with these matters. However, in contrast to its importance in the birth chart, the effect of the transiting Sun through the houses, like all the faster-moving planets, is a minor one, as I have mentioned. There is, though, an important exception: when the Sun is involved with an eclipse, either solar or lunar. This can highlight affairs concerned with the house in which the eclipse falls; and if the eclipse happens to be close to one of the planets in the birth chart, the effects can be dramatic.

My first experience of the power of an eclipse was in 1984. I was working on the chart of the comedian Eric Morecambe, and wrote a piece about him for the May issue of *Here's Health*. It was well known that he had been ill with heart trouble, but when I looked at his chart I could not see any imminent problems. I had failed to notice the solar eclipse on 30 May, which fell in his eighth house of death. If I had spotted this, I should have been a little wary about the effect, but as the eclipse was 11 degrees of Gemini, and his Moon 15 degrees away at 27 degrees, I should not have considered it close enough for very profound effects. I have learnt from experience, because no sooner had my article been published than Eric Morecambe died suddenly. Uranus, the planet of sudden events, was in a close square aspect to his Moon, and the eclipse triggered this aspect into action, bringing a sudden event. The fact that Uranus was in the fifth house, which shows both entertainment and the heart, supplies additional information: Eric Morecambe collapsed on stage with a massive heart attack.

Eclipses do not always portend death and disaster, although they do usually bring change, or the need for a change of outlook and plans. On 22 October 1969 there was a solar eclipse at 29° 30' Virgo, the exact degree of my brother-in-law's ascendant, a clear indication, according to astrological tradition, of personal change (because the ascendant shows personal matters). Within the next six months he had met and married my sister, changed his job and moved to a different part of the country. In another case, a woman experienced a solar eclipse in the ninth house of her horoscope, the one associated with travel and foreign countries. Shortly afterwards she went to China, where she met and married her husband.

There are usually a couple of solar and lunar eclipses each year. Generally, the effect of lunar eclipses, which happen when the Sun and Moon are in opposition, is not as powerful as that of solar eclipses, when the Sun and Moon are in conjunction. After my experience with Eric Morecambe, and subsequent research, I now always note the degree and date of eclipses and they are one of the first things I look at when examining the future trends in a birth chart. For instance, as I write this, the Princess of Wales has been the focus of the world's media following the publication of revelations about her health and her marriage, which first hit the headlines on 8 June 1992. This was just before the lunar eclipse on 15 June, which occurred at 24° 20' of Sagittarius, quite close to the Princess's rising degree, 18° 25' of Sagittarius. However, the main impact came from the solar eclipse, which was at 8° 57' of Cancer, less than a degree away from the Princess's Sun at 9° 40' Cancer and in the seventh house of her horoscope. The seventh house signifies marriage, close one-to-one relationships, and also the general public. As I make final corrections to the manuscript of this book, the saga continues. On the day of the next lunar eclipse, 9 December 1992, it was announced from Buckingham Palace that the Prince and Princess of Wales were to separate. The eclipse occurred at 18° 10' of Gemini, in exact opposition to the Princess's rising degree, and in the house of her horoscope which shows marriage. The eclipses therefore brought to the fore both personal matters, shown by the eclipsed Moon in the Princess's rising sign, and her marriage, shown by the eclipsing Sun in her seventh house, along with enormous publicity.

Regarding the timing of events associated with eclipses, I have found that these usually occur *before* the eclipse – sometimes up to a month in advance – although the effects, and perhaps further changes which happen as a result, often continue for some months, even as much as a year, afterwards. A lunar eclipse, however, is not as powerful as a solar eclipse and the repercussions do not normally continue for more than a few weeks.

Before I leave the subject, I should like to mention a notable prediction, based on an eclipse, made by astrologer Dennis Elwell, who explains:

> In February [1987] I sent registered letters to two shipping carriers about the likely effects on their operations of the March eclipse. At the very least they were promised disrupted schedules, and at the worst a *Titanic*-like disaster. The tragic capsize of the *Herald of Free Enterprise* came [on 6 March] just nine days after P&O wrote to say their procedures could cope with the unexpected . . .

The eclipse on 30 March, at 8° 18' Aries, fell in a very close opposition to the ascendant in the United Kingdom chart, at 7° 10' Libra. And the eclipse was also in conjunction with the current Jupiter and square Neptune. So, as Dennis points out,

> Technically the eclipse was raising the temperature of a square of Jupiter and Neptune, planets which together suggest (among many

24

other things) both sea travel and big ships [see chapters on Jupiter and Neptune]. Eclipses bring the matters signified into high profile, and – perhaps because our attention is more surely grabbed when things are going wrong – they do tend to be associated with misfortunes, although positive outcomes are also possible.

THE MOON

In terms of what it can tell us about character, the Moon in the birth chart is second only to the Sun and the rising sign. In fact each tells us about a different part of the whole. While the rising sign describes our outer personality, and the Sun our essential nature, the Moon has a direct bearing on the feminine side of our nature, on our early childhood and our relationship with our parents, especially our mother, and on our feelings. The sign, house-position and aspects of the Moon show how we react emotionally and, indeed, how emotional we are; they show the conditions under which we feel most secure, and how sensitive we are to the needs and feelings of others. Our Moon sign shows our habitual responses, because these are the ones we learn at a very early age; and they are the ones we may revert to in later life at times of extreme pressure. When the going gets tough, for instance, someone with the Moon in Aries might react with anger; those with the Moon in Gemini would probably try and think – and talk – their way out of the situation; whereas those with the Moon in Taurus might dig in their heels and refuse to move.

In order to find out your Moon sign you need to calculate your birth chart, because the Moon moves so rapidly round the earth. Once you know your Moon sign, you will probably find that you can understand your emotional reactions much more clearly. If you have the Moon in one of the water signs – Cancer, Pisces or Scorpio – for example, it means you have strong emotions and respond easily to other people. The Moon in one of the fire signs – Aries, Leo or Sagittarius – indicates feelings which are quickly aroused; someone who is bright, enthusiastic and optimistic, but not always as sensitive as they might be to other people. Likewise, the Moon in one of the air signs – Gemini, Libra or Aquarius – gives rise to a quality of detachment which can mean that a person cuts themselves off from both their own true feelings and those of others. People with the

Moon in an air sign feel swamped when faced with emotion. The person with the Moon in an earth sign – Taurus, Virgo or Capricorn – brings a sense of practicality to their feelings and to emotional problems. They are also cautious: people with the Moon in earth signs are unlikely to let their feelings run away with them, being naturally aware of the practical aspects of any situation, and the probable outcome. Similarly, people with the Moon in an air sign tend to work out the various possibilities in their minds before rushing ahead. It's people with the Moon in a fire or water sign who are most likely to follow their feelings without thinking about the consequences. But these are generalizations; the aspects between the Moon and the other planets, as well as the Moon's house-position, and the signs and aspects of the Sun and rising sign, will also affect the situation.

There are basically two ways to react to emotion. One is to express feelings excessively; everything is either wonderful, or terrible, with the consequence that most of the energy of the emotion is dissipated and other people have to suffer from all the dramas. The other, because we associate feeling with pain, is to cut off and repress that part of our nature. People who adopt this cut-off, or 'split' approach to almost all emotion are not living fully, because they are denying themselves the energy which is inherent in our emotional life. This happens in both men and women, but is particularly noticeable in men who adopt the 'stiff upper lip' approach and are out of touch with much of the lunar side of their nature: their feelings, their imagination, their relationships with women. The ideal situation is to be able to feel emotion fully, and yet not be swamped, ignited or buffeted by it. So we experience the richness of our feelings without wasting the energy through outbursts of tears, anger and so on.

The Moon symbolizes the mother, family and home life, and its position in the birth chart influences both our early upbringing and the kind of family life we have. The kind of nurturing and the experiences we have in early childhood lay the foundations for our emotional responses in our adult lives. The Moon close or in an inharmonious aspect to Saturn, the planet which stands for coldness and hardship, for instance, shows the possibility of emotional deprivation, perhaps through early difficulties in the relationship with the mother, leading, later, to problems in expressing emotion and in nurturing others. The person with the Moon in such a position in their birth chart tends to freeze up when anyone gets close to them emotionally. So their adult relationships are effectively sabotaged, and they experience loneliness and, perhaps, bitterness, both Saturnine conditions.

An inharmonious aspect between the Moon and Saturn is one of the hardest to cope with, but most people have some painful early experiences which inhibit them. They are probably not aware of what is happening; but in a particular situation, when they are feeling stressed, they react automatically. This is very limiting; who wants to spend their life reacting like a two-year-old? We can, however, change our reactions in later life if we are prepared to look at ourselves honestly and face up to painful early experiences, acknowledging and accepting what occurred, and letting it go. It's important to realize that although we may have suffered in our childhood, we do not have to continue to be angry with those involved for what they did or did not do. We need to let the past go; to accept our parents for what they were; fallible human beings, trying to bring us up amid all the pressures of their lives. When we can forgive them for their failings and stop feeling angry and critical, then we are free to be ourselves. In attempting this process, it may be necessary to have some help from a good counsellor or therapist, either through personal counselling sessions or through taking part in a workshop.

The birth chart of the Princess of Wales demonstrates how the sign and aspects of the Moon reflect both our emotional responses and our early life. The Princess has her Moon in Aquarius, which gives her the ability to detach herself emotionally and to be quite cool and reasoned when it comes to her feelings, although her essential personality – shown by the Sun in Cancer – is sensitive, emotional and deeply caring, while Sagittarius rising makes her come across as warm-hearted, impulsive and optimistic. The Moon is also in opposition with Uranus, the planet which shows breaks, separation, independence. This combination reflects the Princess's separation from her mother at an early age, and suggests that the Princess probably finds it difficult to balance the Moon and Uranus factors in her own personality. She may be over-emotional and possessive if she is responding in a 'Moon' way, or she may be equally detached, independent and unpredictable if she is going the 'Uranus' way. In a close emotional situation she will tend to protect herself from hurt by putting up her Uranian defences of detachment and independence. She may suddenly feel the need to break away in situations where she feels herself becoming too vulnerable emotionally.

The Moon also symbolizes change and fluctuation, for example the tides of the sea; the general public; the mother, and women in general; the home, and family life; the sea and maritime matters; water and other liquids; food and drink; the digestive system, stomach and breasts; body fluids; and the sympathetic nervous system. Fleshy, watery plants like cucumbers and melons are also ruled by the Moon, as are lettuces and cabbages. Its metals and gems include silver, mother-of-pearl and stones with a reflective quality such as moonstone and crystal.

The Cycle of the Moon

It takes just 27.25 days for the Moon to orbit the Earth and thus move through all twelve signs of the zodiac, spending on average about 2.25 days in each sign and making thirteen cycles during the year. The effect of these Moon cycles is usually fairly slight, showing, at most, small day-to-day events and changes of mood. The new Moon can show a development in a matter to do with the house of the horoscope in which it falls, particularly if it is close to a planet in the birth chart, but, again, it is usually something fairly minor. It *can*, however, trigger an important event, so astrologers always note the dates and degrees of new Moons, but they are really significant only if they activate a more major trend, such as a progressed aspect (as described on page 14). Since they tend to fall around the same degree for several months, they can make a series of aspects to one particular planet, bringing matters to do with that planet to the fore. Astrological lore has it that the time after the new Moon is good for beginning a new project and that the full Moon shows matters coming to fruition, with the waning Moon being a good time to wind things up. This all seems logical, although I certainly do not rule my life by it. The exceptions to this are when the new or full Moons also happen to be eclipses of the Sun or Moon. These, particularly eclipses of the

Sun, can be very important, as I have already explained. I would not choose to start an important enterprise at the time of an eclipse. Once I allowed one of my books to be published the day before an eclipse, and it was a very strange experience. It's the only time I've had absolutely no publicity for a book after publication, almost as if the book, like the Sun in the eclipse, was blacked out.

MERCURY

Mercury, appropriately named after the god who in Roman mythology was the winged messenger, is the planet of communication. The sign in which Mercury is placed in our birth chart shows what kind of mind we have, how we like to communicate, learn and work; where our interests may lie. For example, people with Mercury in the fire signs – Aries, Leo and Sagittarius – generally pick up ideas quickly and become very enthusiastic about them. They make good teachers and salespeople, but they don't like too much detail. People with Mercury in one of the earth signs – Taurus, Virgo and Capricorn – are the opposite and like to work with facts, relating their knowledge to practical matters. They're careful and businesslike. People with Mercury in an air sign – Gemini, Libra or Aquarius – are the most natural communicators; they are full of ideas, very chatty and interested in many subjects, but not always practical. Those with Mercury in one of the water signs – Cancer, Scorpio or Pisces – tend, like the Princess of Wales, who has Mercury in Cancer, to be imaginative, sensitive and interested in the arts and social matters. They are also liable to be swayed in their judgement by their feelings, or those of other people.

It's quite easy to dismiss Mercury as 'the planet of the mind and of communication', without realizing its importance in determining the quality of our life. We experience the conditions around us and interpret what happens to us through our mind and our mental attitude. To quote *Emmanuel's Book* (a most helpful collection of the teachings of a spiritual being called Emmanuel, given through the mediumship of Pat Rodegast): 'You experience what you believe. The very world in which you exist, the positive and negative alike, is a product of what you hold to be true.' We are responsible for the light in which we view our life – and we can change it. As Patric Walker has said, 'Let things be exactly as they are; I can be hurt by

31

nothing but my thoughts.' Or, as the great Indian teacher Sri Ramana Maharshi says: 'Peace is your natural state. It is the mind that obstructs the natural state.'

Our thoughts can therefore colour the moment and determine whether we are going to be happy or unhappy. They can also hold us back or encourage us to make the most of our potential; as Henry Ford said: 'Those people who think they can do something, and those people who think they can't, are both right.' In addition, according to the writer and healer Louise Hay and many others, our thoughts are powerful in creating our future. Many books have been written on the power of positive thought. Techniques for this include visualization, where you keep picturing the conditions you want to create, and the use of affirmations, or positive statements such as 'I can do it' which you keep repeating. I have no doubt that these techniques work and that they bring change. It's important to remember, however, that every action has its consequences, so choose your affirmations, and what you visualize, with great care. Perhaps you have heard the story of the man who put a great deal of effort into visualizing a Rolls-Royce. Then one day he was awakened by a loud noise, and he found that a Rolls-Royce had crashed through the wall of his house, into his living-room. Another danger with using positive thought techniques is that they can reinforce the power of our ego. What you are doing is simply replacing an old, negative belief about yourself with a new, positive one. Actually, neither of these is the real 'you', or your essential being, which in fact lies outside or beyond beliefs. Eventually we have to let the ego go; and the stronger it gets, the more difficult this becomes, as we'll see in the second half of this book.

Mercury, like all the planets, also symbolizes practical and everyday things. For instance, it rules all messages and messengers, as well as the equipment used to convey them. Its position in the birth chart shows all forms of communication throughout life. For example, in the human body, it shows the brain and the coordination of the nervous system; in the personality, it rules the thought processes and our ability to learn and to express ourselves through speech, writing and other media, such as art and movement. In the world, Mercury symbolizes people involved with the process of communication: writers, journalists, secretaries, accountants, teachers, lecturers, messengers and so on. It also rules stationery, typewriters, documents and contracts and, in combination with Uranus (planet of electronic equipment), telephones, fax machines and word-processors, cars, short journeys and minor changes. Quicksilver and multi-coloured stones are ruled by Mercury, and its plants include carrots, celery, fennel, dill, parsley, lavender and hazelnuts.

The Cycle of Mercury

Mercury completes its circuit of the Sun in just 88 days, so it moves quite rapidly through the houses of the horoscope, sometimes changing sign twice in a month. Mercury's aspects to its own place last a matter of hours, a day at the most, and the conjunction, square and opposition of Mercury to its own place are likely to bring a particularly busy time with communication or journeys. If one has noted it, the day when Mercury returns to its own place is a propitious time to start a project or begin a journey, but the effect is minor.

Mercury passing through a house in your horoscope indicates a time when there could be more than the customary amount of correspondence, meetings or phone calls in connection with the affairs shown by that house. Because of the rapidity with which it passes through, however, the effect of Mercury in the houses is not usually particularly noticeable, and is not something I normally consider. There is, however, one exception to this, and that is when Mercury is retrograde, or apparently going backwards. Retrograde motion is a phenomenon which happens to all the planets except the Sun and the Moon. The motions of the planets round the Sun are fairly regular, but because we are seeing them from the Earth, and the Earth is also revolving around the Sun, the other planets do not always appear to move in the same direction. Imagine you're looking at a child on a roundabout in a playground, and that around the playground there are various landmarks: a gate, a tree, a church, a school. As the roundabout revolves, you will see the child move first left to right and then right to left against the background. This is very similar to the path that Mercury and Venus seem to trace from the Earth's point of view. In addition, if you imagine that you are

33

yourself walking slowly around the roundabout, the background against which you are seeing the child will vary also. So although the planets progress regularly round the Sun, from our point of view they may appear to wobble slightly backwards and forwards against the zodiac at times. When they appear to go backwards it is called retrograde motion, and if you look at the graphs at the back of this book you'll see how it affects the pattern that the paths of the planets make. Mercury generally goes retrograde about three times a year for periods of about 3 weeks. At these times it can bring muddles, misunderstandings and even downright mischief to do with communication. Letters (probably concerning matters to do with the house through which Mercury is passing) may go astray or be misconstrued; a conversation may be completely misunderstood; you may have trouble with your typewriter or bicycle. Sometimes I've found, especially if Mercury is retrograde in my sixth house of work, that I've had to go back over some matter which I thought I'd finished. As I've said, I do not consider myself astrologically superstitious, but I have to say that there are two things which I do not like doing: one is making plans for anything important around the time of a solar eclipse, and the other is signing important documents, such as contracts, during the three weeks or so when Mercury is retrograde. I had an example of Mercury's mischievous effect recently, when the terms of a verbal agreement which I had made when Mercury was retrograde were questioned. The agreement had been witnessed by two other people and I was able therefore to sort matters out quite easily, but this is the kind of thing which can happen under a retrograde Mercury, so it's a time to be extra careful about facts and details.

VENUS

Along with the Moon, Venus represents the gentle, feminine, feeling part of our nature, both in men and women. The position of Venus in our birth chart indicates the level of our responsiveness to beauty and pleasure; our capacity to give and receive love; how we relate to other people. When Venus is in one of the fire signs – Aries, Leo or Sagittarius – it means that our way of loving and relating to others is essentially warm, open, trusting and ardent, but only as long as the flames are burning – sometimes they can die down almost as quickly as they were kindled. People with Venus in one of the earth signs – Taurus, Virgo and Capricorn – have a practical, realistic approach to love. They can be romantic, but they believe that it is by deeds rather than words that we show our true feelings. If you have Venus in one of the air signs – Gemini, Libra or Aquarius – you can express your loving feelings well and can be charming, but you may try to rationalize your relationships too much. When Venus is in one of the water signs – Cancer, Scorpio or Pisces – the basic response to love is always emotional, sensitive and full of feeling, but there is a fear of rejection, so feelings are often concealed.

Venus also symbolizes money and possessions, and indicates our attitude towards these. But more than this, Venus shows what we value in our life; our sense of values generally and, especially, how much we love and value ourselves. This, as psychologists tell us, is closely linked with our capacity to love others and to make satisfactory relationships. Just as the Moon indicates both the kind of nurturing we received as a child and the kind we ourselves give, so Venus shows both the love and value felt as a child, and what we both give and receive later in our relationships. Again, the two things – what we got and what we give – are shown by the same factor in the horoscope, underlining the link between them. If, through being criticized, abused or neglected as a child, we have developed various defensive forms of behaviour, these can undermine our ability to make close and loving relationships later. For instance, in order to have a truly satisfying and fulfilling personal relationship, we might first have to give up certain destructive tendencies. For example, the need to be always right; the need to be first in everything and constantly in control; the need to change and 'improve' other people.

Many people come to astrologers because they have problems in their love-life; perhaps they are in an unsatisfactory relationship and they want guidance on how to handle it or to know when it is likely to end; others come because they are on their own and want to know how and when they are likely to meet someone to love. The possibility of difficulties in relationships is shown in the birth chart. In the birth chart of the Princess of Wales, for example, Venus, which is in the loyal and affectionate sign of Taurus, is in square aspect. This, as I've explained on page 13, links in harmoniously with both the Moon in Aquarius and Uranus in Leo. I've already described in the chapter on the Moon how the Moon–Uranus link works out, in terms of a constant swing from dependency to independence. Venus, which influences the Princess's ability to make relationships, is caught up in this. Venus in Taurus shows that she is someone who needs a stable, loving relationship; also that she's someone who is tactile and sensual. But her life and her personality do not allow easy expression of this; the Moon pulls her towards overdependence, and Uranus towards independence and separation. The ideal for her would be a relationship which offered plenty of love and support, but also a healthy respect for each partner's independence and individual interests.

The Princess of Wales has a particularly difficult combination of influences, but nearly every horoscope has some element of difficulty shown in this area. This is not surprising, because it's through relationships that most people experience both their greatest joy and deepest pain, so, for most of us, they are a superb way of learning and growing. A knowledge of our birth chart can help us to understand the reason for particular problems, and why we tend to repeat experiences: we get out of one difficult relationship only to find ourselves in another very similar one. If we want to break this pattern, what has to change is *us*: the way in which we handle things, come to terms with our needs and expectations, and cope with the stresses shown in our horoscope. A very important first step is to stop blaming others and to look within oneself for the answer. 'Why did I draw this situation into my life?' 'What is this teaching me about myself; my needs, my qualities, my strengths and weaknesses?'

This is not to say that you should take a whole load of blame upon yourself. That is just as negative and destructive in its way as blaming other people. What is needed is a loving and dispassionate view – and this, again, is where a knowledge of your birth chart can be very valuable, because it's easier when you can see the strengths and weaknesses spelt out in symbolic form. Knowing the birth chart of the other person concerned, and the way the two charts interact, can also be illuminating. Again, it's somehow easier to accept the difficulties when you can see clearly the stresses which you were under, and the way these were activated by the two charts. And change – either in ourselves or in others – begins when we can accept ourselves and others just as we or they are, and love them just the same. As Louise L. Hay says: 'When we really love ourselves, everything in our life works. We must be willing to begin to learn to love ourselves. Self-approval and self-acceptance in the now are the key to positive changes.'

It's when we dislike ourselves or do not believe that we're lovable that we feel possessive or jealous of others, or doubt our ability to make another relationship. When we feel content and at peace within we know that the companionship of another is simply a bonus, but that our happiness does not depend on it. We all have Venus within our charts; we can all be responsible for our own happiness. Then we can take that joy into a relationship with another, free from negative, self-destroying emotions. Louise Hay says that 'the bottom line for everyone is "I'm not good enough"; everyone suffers from self-hatred and guilt' – something we all pick up through the vulnerability and learning-experience of childhood. Sondra Ray, in her book *Loving Relationships*, also has some helpful things to say about self-hate/self-love: 'People hate themselves for a million different things. People who hate themselves often get fat and they hate themselves even more. Or they conjure up some other way to hate themselves. Self-hate makes one ugly. Every person I have seen who has given up their self-hate and who forgave everything became more and more beautiful right before my eyes.'

Sondra Ray says that we heal ourselves and our relationships by acknowledging and praising ourselves verbally; loving our body and admiring our beauty; turning negative thoughts about ourselves into affirmations; approving of our actions, and learning from them; rewarding, never punishing ourselves; having confidence in our ability; giving ourselves pleasure without feeling guilty; following our intuition, our inner feelings and hunches, and trusting ourselves; letting ourselves win, and be rich; and allowing others to love us, and letting ourselves enjoy sex and affection.

Shakti Gawain makes some similar observations in her book *Living in the Light*. She describes how, when she was out of a relationship and feeling rather lonely and sorry for herself, she began to think more lovingly about herself and her needs; to care for herself as a kind and considerate lover might; to spoil herself with little treats, to behave as if she was in love with herself. All this is encouraging love; and as you feel better and more loving towards yourself, you radiate a love and harmony which others sense and are attracted to. Your happiness spreads.

As you become more tolerant of yourself, loving and accepting yourself for what you are rather than what you think you should be, in a strange way you also become more able to accept other people as they are and to begin to love them unconditionally. Unconditional love is freeing and healing; when it is present in a relationship, whether it be between husband and wife, or lovers, or parent and child, the people feel that they can truly be themselves; they do not have to hide anything, because all will be understood and accepted.

As well as love and our ability to relate to others, Venus also shows pleasure and luxury; artistic expression, clothes, fashion and beauty; food, wine and love-making; finance; young women. Its colours are pastels like sky blue and rose pink, and the metals and gems associated with it are copper, lapis lazuli, blue sapphires, coral, alabaster and cornelian. Plants which come under Venus are many of the fruiting ones, such as apples, peaches, apricots, roses and elderflowers, as well as violets and mint. And in the body Venus rules the throat, kidneys and parathyroid, as well as the lumbar region.

The Cycle of Venus

It takes 225 days, or just under 9 months, for Venus to complete an orbit of the Sun and thus move through all the signs. The day of our Venus return each year – when Venus gets back to the same place it was when we were born – should be a happy one, like a birthday; and the days when Venus is in square or opposition to its place may bring a relationship or financial matter to the fore, but, as with the influence of Mercury, the effect is relatively minor, because Venus is so fast-moving. Similarly, as Venus moves through the houses of the birth chart, taking perhaps 3 weeks in each, it can have a mildly stabilizing influence on matters concerned with the house in question, maintaining the status quo rather than bringing change or important developments. It can also bring some mildly pleasant events. I have found that the day when Venus is in conjunction with my Sun is often a happy one: only recently, I was handsomely wined and dined and ended up with a huge bouquet of flowers. That's Venus at her best!

MARS

Mars is the planet of energy, the planet which enables us to take the inspiration of the Sun, the feelings of the Moon, the ideas of Mercury and the love of Venus and act on them. The Mars energy can manifest itself in various ways: as passion, enthusiasm, sex-drive and anger; heat and even fever in the body. Traditionally, Mars was known as 'the lesser malefic' planet, Saturn being the 'greater malefic'. This was before the discovery of the planets Uranus, Neptune and Pluto; just what the ancient astrologers would have called those, had they known about them, I cannot imagine, as their effect can be far more disruptive and apparently negative than that of either Saturn or Mars. In common with most modern astrologers, however, I prefer to think of the energies of the planets as neutral. It is the way in which we allow ourselves to be influenced by them that determines whether the effect is constructive or destructive.

The Mars energy is therefore the fire which can drive people forward to perform both feats of amazing courage and selflessness, and acts of violence or destruction. It can give the initiative needed to develop a gift shown in the horoscope, or it can allow dissipation of opportunity through unnecessary rebellion, irritability and other non-productive uses of energy. The most talented chart in the world will not amount to anything unless there is enough Mars energy shown to give the 'get-up-and-go' necessary to make use of it. I've found, for instance, that there's always a strong Mars present in the charts of successful musicians: a strong Venus, which indicates artistic talent, simply isn't enough on its own.

The sign in which Mars is placed at the moment of birth gives a good idea of the amount of drive, energy and initiative we have, how assertive we are, the manner in which we set about getting things done and how we respond when under attack. And the house in which Mars is placed shows the area of life in which it is natural for

40

us to take the initiative and expend effort and energy. As well as these factors, an astrologer assessing a horoscope takes into account how well Mars fits in with the other planets, and how easily it can operate alongside the signs of the Sun, Moon and ascendant. For example, Mars might be very dynamic placed, say, in Aries or Leo, but if the Sun, Moon and ascendant are gentle, non-aggressive signs such as Pisces, Cancer and Libra, the Mars energy will be muted and probably directed more towards creativity and social contacts, than go-getting. Equally, a strong Mars, which could perhaps be rather wild and impulsive, would be held in check and used more productively if the Sun, Moon and rising sign were of the practical, cautious type, such as Capricorn, Taurus or Virgo – as long as they didn't thwart it so much that it couldn't act. This is important to consider, because a thwarted Mars can have as negative an effect as an over-active one. If they are stifled, the Mars anger and energy can turn inwards, resulting in them being expressed as bitterness, depression or psycho-somatic illness, as this passage from *The Dance of Anger*, by Harriet Goldbor Lerner, explains:

> Anger is a signal, and one worth listening to. Our anger may be a message that we are being hurt, that our rights are being violated, that our needs or wants are not being adequately met, or simply that something is not right. Our anger may tell us that we are not addressing an important emotional issue in our lives, or that too much of our self – our beliefs, values, desires or ambitions – is being compromised in a relationship. Our anger may be a signal that we are doing more and giving more than we can comfortably do or give. Our anger may warn us that others are doing too much for us, at the expense of our own competence and growth. Just as physical pain tells us to take our hand off the hot stove, the pain of our anger can motivate us to say 'no' to the ways in which we are defined by others and 'yes' to the dictates of our inner self.

Knowing where Mars is in your horoscope, and the aspects it makes to other planets, enables you to understand more about your inner energy or anger. It tells you about your assertiveness and your energy flow, and how to make the most of them. It can also show the most productive area for you to express them; the manner which is natural for you, and the difficulties you might experience in doing

41

so. If Mars is in one of the fire signs – Aries, Leo or Sagittarius – you have plenty of energy and enthusiasm which need to be well controlled and directed to get the best results. Mars in an earth sign – Taurus, Virgo or Capricorn – gives the ability to use energy in a very practical way to good effect. When it's in an air sign – Gemini, Libra or Aquarius – much energy gets expended in ideas and talking, sometimes instead of doing. And in a water sign – Cancer, Scorpio or Pisces – there's a great deal of emotional energy and lively feelings which, again, can get in the way of actual achievement of aims and goals. These qualities can be reinforced or balanced by other signs which are prominent in the horoscope (the rising sign, and the signs of the Sun and Moon) and also by any aspects which Mars makes with other planets. For example, a harmonious link between Mars and Saturn is very helpful in making the most of Mars energy, whatever sign it's in.

It is interesting to note that in Buddhism there is a saying that 'the passions are the Buddha nature, and the Buddha nature is the passions'. In other words, only when the energy is channelled through the ego does it manifest as anger and passion. When the primitive fires of Martian energy are tamed, the energy is seen to be identical with our essential being.

As well as symbolizing energy, initiative, physical exercise, effort, rebellion and courage, Mars shows pain, quarrels, fires, accidents, cuts and burns; sharp instruments, war and weapons; young men, firemen, soldiers, surgeons; quarrelsome and aggressive people; the muscular and urinogenital system; the gonads and kidneys. Its colours are those of fire: yellow, red and orange; its metals and gems are iron and jasper and its plants tend to be hot, for example garlic, onions, radishes and mustard.

The Cycle of Mars

It takes on average 687 days, or just 43 days short of 2 years, for Mars to get through all the signs of the zodiac and complete its circuit of the houses of the birth chart. As it does so, it brings energy, extra activity, and sometimes challenges and aggravation to each in turn, and its presence in the houses of the horoscope is quite noticeable. So the couple of months or so when Mars is in the first house of our birth chart, for instance, is usually a good time for asserting ourselves and getting ahead with personal plans – it can also make us more argumentative than usual. When Mars is in the second house it's a good time for taking the initiative over money matters, but it can also bring arguments – and extravagance – where these are concerned.

Mars in the third house brings action where correspondence and communication are concerned; this is usually a particularly busy period, with many demands on one's attention. I usually find it's one of those times when I seem to live in my car, making the 'short journeys' which are typical of the third house! There can also be action – and sometimes arguments – where brothers, sisters and neighbours are concerned. When Mars went into the third house of a friend of mine recently her sister was taken seriously ill and she found herself making many more short journeys than usual, visiting her sister in hospital and taking care of her elderly brother-in-law. The third house also rules the close environment, and sometimes Mars in this house can show disruption here: someone I know had the pavement around their house pulled up for cable-laying during the time Mars was passing through their third house.

Disruption actually inside the home can be one result of Mars passing through the fourth house of the home and family. I had my kitchen pulled out and re-done when Mars was in my fourth house (not *my* timing: that's how it worked out). Sometimes Mars here can show a particularly demanding time with family commitments, or arguments in the family. Mars passing through the fifth house can bring fun and social activities; it often brings quite an active time with children and young people, and can also stimulate creativity. Mars was in my fifth house this summer when I had a particularly good holiday. It was also a busy time for me creatively, because I was getting up early each morning and working on this book before breakfast in order to meet my deadline!

Mars in the sixth house of health and work *can* show a demanding time, but it can also be a good time to carry out the Martian activities of sport and exercise for the sake of fitness and health. I experienced this for several weeks in the autumn of 1992. From the moment Mars entered this house, in October, I had a particularly busy period, with the publication of two books and a publicity tour which involved my giving cookery demonstrations in bookshops all over the country, as well as many other commitments. I also managed to get a good exercise routine going.

Mars in the seventh house puts the focus on marriage, partnership and close one-to-one relationships, and it can bring passion in the form of arguments or love. Perhaps they're opposite sides of the same coin in any case. During the summer of 1992, when the speculation about her marriage was at its height, the Princess of Wales had Mars passing through this house, and it stayed there until the end of April 1993. Mars moved more slowly than usual during this period, owing to retrograde motion: it does this periodically, and instead of moving through a house in about 6 to 8 weeks, takes several months.

Mars in the eighth house generally brings financial matters to the fore, particularly those shared with other people, or with a legal element, such as contracts and insurance matters. It can also put the focus on other matters ruled by this house, such as sex, birth, healing and death.

In the ninth house, Mars can bring long-distance travel, dealings – perhaps arguments – with foreigners, publishers, religious organizations or the law. Mars passing through the tenth house can show arguments or difficulties with people in positions of authority, as well as activity, hard work and enterprise in career matters. The eleventh house rules hopes, wishes and dreams, and when Mars is here it's often a good time for taking the plunge over something you've been wanting to do for a long time. You may find you're extra busy with friends, groups and societies during the time that Mars is passing through this house.

The time when Mars is in the twelfth house can be a difficult one. Actions taken at this point have a way of back-firing on you and it's a period when, as the ancient astrologers used to note, 'secret enemies may be active'. In other words, it's a time to be careful in whom you confide, and for conserving your energies and planning for the future, rather than going all out towards your goals. A few years ago, because of the retrograde action I've described, Mars was in the twelfth house of my horoscope for 6 months. As well as the things I've mentioned, it represents the unconscious and, during that period, I was putting a great deal of time and energy into a course of self-awareness. This was most appropriate, although I have to say that I did not consciously plan things this way; I was in the middle of the course when I realized the significance of the timing.

If you have two or more planets in a particular house in your horoscope you'll be particularly aware of Mars's passage through that house, because not only will it bring to the fore matters to do with that house, but it will also activate each of the planets, bringing developments to do with the matters ruled by these planets, on the 2 days or so during which it shares the same degree.

It's both interesting and helpful to know when a new Mars cycle begins, and the times during that cycle when it squares, opposes and squares again its own place in the birth chart. At the start of a Mars cycle there's the opportunity to start afresh in a project or relationship, or in the way you use your time and energy. Roughly 6 months later, when Mars is 90 degrees away from its starting-point, or in square aspect, progress will be tested by some kind of a crisis or opportunity for change. You'll have the chance to adjust your plans if they're not working as you'd hoped. Then, approximately a year later, when Mars is 180 degrees, or in opposition to its original place, you will be able to review the situation, seeing it, as it were, from the opposite point of view. You will know whether you are achieving your aim, or whether you've been wasting your time and energy. Actually, though, if you believe, as I do, that life is about experience and growth, there are no mistakes and nothing is wasted. Six months later, when Mars makes its final square aspect, 90 degrees away from its position in the birth chart, you'll have a chance to sort matters out and clear the decks ready to make the most of the next Mars cycle. What you begin then could be important for the next 2 years, so it's worth giving it some careful thought. Going with your Mars cycle like this, bearing it in mind when you make your plans and being aware of the times in the cycle when you could make changes, and when you need to guard against over-hasty or self-destructive action, can be very worthwhile.

Once every 2 years or so, during the fortnight in which Mars ends one cycle and begins another, you will have the opportunity to reappraise the way you use your energy in your life to create the conditions which you want, whether it is in your career, your relationships, or your personal plans and home life. Life is about growth and about change; it's about making the most positive use of the conditions in which you find yourself, and using your own resources to improve them. I had an interesting case of a woman who was in a destructive relationship with a married man. She kept trying to end the relationship and would break with her lover and stay out of contact with him for some months, but would then find herself getting pulled back into it again. Eventually she managed to make a final, complete break by choosing the time when she was ending a Mars cycle.

Another example of the effect of the Mars cycle can be seen in the events which occurred in Margaret Thatcher's life in 1982. This is, I think, particularly interesting because it involves aspects of life which Mars symbolizes: young men, competition, soldiers and war. At the time of her Mars return in January 1982, Margaret Thatcher's son, Mark, went missing in the Sahara desert during the Paris–Dakar rally. Because of retrograde motion, she had another Mars return that April, when the Argentines invaded the Falklands and Britain went to war. Mars then went forward again, giving her a third Mars return in June, which coincided with Britain winning the war.

Because Mars brings action, it can trigger other planetary forces into operation, and the day when Mars crosses a sensitive part of the horoscope, or conjoins one of the planets, is often the time when the event happens. It's as if the planets are like a time-bomb which is set off when Mars crosses it. If a horoscope has a set-up which shows the possibility of accidents, it's always a good idea to be particularly careful on those days when Mars is crossing the sensitive points. I have noticed in my own case that, fired by the energy of Mars, I'm inclined to be impatient, impulsive or extra hasty on those days, and less careful and more accident-prone than usual. When accidents do occur, Mars is often involved. Mars also shows challenges to be overcome; when it's much in evidence it shows a demanding, hard-working, busy time which can be tiring but productive. It's a period when, through tests and pressures, we can find our own power and become stronger people as a result.

2

JUPITER

Jupiter is the planet in the birth chart which shows expansion, opportunities and the ability to go beyond our present limits. It's the planet which gives us the inspiration – or good fortune – to go forward, guides us into the future and helps us to develop and expand. In the personality, Jupiter brings the qualities of hope, justice, nobility, optimism, joviality and faith. It gives a breadth of view which can see beyond small problems and the present time into the future; it gives an openness to ideas and possibilities which uplifts and inspires. It is the planet which shows religion, but it is not limited by petty dogma. Religion, in the Jupiterian sense, is man's faith, or need to believe, in a power greater than himself, or in some universal law which makes sense of life.

Whereas the position of Mercury in the birth chart indicates a person's mental attitude and outlook, moment-by-moment communication and learning skills, the position of Jupiter shows the power to go beyond these limits, bringing faith and trust in a power greater than that of the individual, broadening the mind through new interests, higher learning, and communication on a larger scale, through publishing and publicity.

The sign and house in which Jupiter is placed in our birth chart show the way, and the sphere, in which we can operate at our best; also, where we're most likely to experience good fortune, and the area from which success is likely to come. It shows how and where we can expand and improve ourselves and widen our experience. Of course, like every other influence in the birth chart, Jupiter has to be considered as part of the whole. For example, has its expansive influence the scope it needs, or is it hindered by too much caution, practicality and evidence of blocks? Alternatively, does the chart show so much enthusiasm and impracticality that the presence of Jupiter will tip it over the edge into extravagant excess? Jupiter certainly

47

magnifies the characteristics of any planet which is close to it in our birth chart. It may be because of its tendency to exaggerate that Jupiter has been described as 'evil, most odious to God because it leades to such vices as insolence, arrogance, hubris, haughtiness, disobedience, boasting, ambition, vainglory, ostentation, obstinacy, vanity... Its opposite is humility or meekness...' Jupiter always brings expansion – and this applies to both the positive and negative characteristics.

In the physical body, Jupiter rules the largest organ, the liver, and also the pituitary gland. The joyful exuberance of Jupiter can lead to excesses in someone's lifestyle – with consequent liver problems. However, Jupiter can also add to a person's general vitality and bring a faith and optimism which can greatly contribute to good health.

As Jupiter stays around a year in a sign, its influence in the birth chart is common to many people, but it shows how expansive we are; how we respond to philosophical and cultural ideas, and education. To the fire signs – Aries, Leo and Sagittarius – Jupiter brings warmth, confidence, added vitality, faith and optimism. To the earth signs – Taurus, Virgo and Capricorn – Jupiter gives a natural appreciation of the practical aspects of life and the ability to handle them successfully. Philosophical ideas and theories are tested with plenty of down-to-earth commonsense; they have to work in everyday life to be of interest to people with Jupiter in these signs. When Jupiter is in the air signs – Gemini, Libra and Aquarius – the principles of expansion and aspiration are expressed in mental interests, thought and communication with other people. People with Jupiter in one of the water signs – Cancer, Scorpio or Pisces – have expansive emotions, an innate understanding of other people and sensitivity towards them.

People and organizations represented by Jupiter in the horoscope are all those to do with the Church and religion, higher education and universities, the law and judges, publishers and publishing. It symbolizes long journeys – widening the horizons physically as well as metaphorically – and foreign countries and foreigners. Also under Jupiter's domain come all forms of sport; the Olympic Games are typical of the idealism of Jupiter, the bringing together of people from many countries to celebrate the highest achievement in athletic ability. As well as judges, lawyers, clergymen and publishers, Jupiter also rules foreigners and middle-aged men. In the plant kingdom,

Jupiter rules the sweet chestnut and maple trees, dandelions, asparagus, bilberries and sage; its metals and gems are tin, amethyst, topaz, emerald and marble. The colours of Jupiter are deep blues verging on indigo and purple; Jupiterian places are universities, churches, courts of justice and buildings which have to do with foreign countries.

The Cycle of Jupiter

The Jupiter cycle takes about 11.86 years. As Jupiter moves through each sign and house of our birth chart it brings the possibility of opportunities and expansion to that area of life, and its return to its own place can coincide with an extra dose of the Jupiter influence, again, perhaps bringing good luck or the chance to realize an ambition, in accordance with the sign and house in which Jupiter is placed.

Jupiter in the first house shows expansion in personal matters and interests and can bring good fortune. The astrologer the late Ingrid Lind once said to me that she found she gained a pound or two when Jupiter was in her first house: personal expansion at its most literal! But Jupiter in that part of the horoscope can bring relaxation, a feeling of bonhomie, joviality, enjoyment of the good things in life. Jupiter's passage through the second house can bring an improvement in one's finances – perhaps some luck here – but it also brings the temptation to over-spend or to take on too large a financial commitment for the future. When Jupiter is in the third house it's usually a good time for relationships with brothers and sisters; for short journeys, for starting a course of education. Jupiter in the fourth house puts the focus on home and domestic matters; I bought my first home when Jupiter was in my fourth house. The fifth house represents children, creativity and pleasure, so the twelve months or thereabouts that it spends in this part of the birth chart can be enjoyable. I had two pregnancies, twelve years apart, when Jupiter was in my fifth house! Jupiter in the sixth house can be helpful and expansive for either health or work, or both, since these are the areas of life represented by this house. Again, there can be the tendency to over-extend oneself and to be careless. I was working hard on my first book, *Simply Delicious*, when Jupiter was in my sixth house. This is another of those neat demonstrations of astrological symbolism, for Jupiter is the planet of publishing.

When it's in the seventh house, Jupiter can bring marriage, or a flowering of a close relationship, or the formation of a business partnership. Jupiter in the eighth house can coincide with a legacy or the maturation of an insurance policy, or some other financial benefit; and in the ninth house it can bring a widening of one's horizons through long-distance travel, religious experiences, publishing or education. My sister inherited some money from her godmother when Jupiter was in her eighth house, enabling her to travel extensively the following year, which coincided with Jupiter's passage through her ninth house. Jupiter in the next house, the tenth, can bring success and publicity; a writer was offered her own column in a national magazine when Jupiter was in her tenth house. The publicity may not always be welcome, though; Jupiter passed through the Duchess of York's tenth house at the time of the photographs which were taken of her on holiday in the south of France and the press furore which followed.

When it's in the eleventh house, Jupiter often brings a widening of one's social circle; new societies to join, new friends to make. Since this is the house of hopes and wishes, Jupiter here can bring the realization of a cherished dream. Things may appear calm on the surface when Jupiter is in the twelfth house of retirement, contemplation and the unconscious, but it can be a time for the quiet development of ideas and plans prior to a blossoming when Jupiter moves back into the first house and the cycle begins again. Jupiter in the twelfth house can show good work with charities.

The 12-year Jupiter cycle as it conjoins, squares, opposes, squares and again conjoins its own place affects everyone, regardless of which sign or house the planet is placed in in their birth chart. Once every 12 years there is the chance to begin a new cycle of expansion and to take advantage of opportunities. This is often a time when we take a risk or start a new venture. At the time of the Jupiter return, Anita Roddick started her first Body Shop, and Tina Turner finally managed to leave her violent marriage. Both these cases demonstrate the influence of Jupiter. The reason Anita Roddick started the Body Shop was that her husband wanted to expand his horizons by travel; and for Tina Turner, the Jupiter return brought freedom, another Jupiterian quality. Three years after the return, Jupiter squares its original position, and there is a further development or turning-point. After 6 years, at the half-way point in the cycle, Jupiter is opposite its own place, so there is the chance to review progress and perhaps reach out in a different way. Three years after that there's a further development, as Jupiter again squares its own place on its return journey. These Jupiter cycles repeat themselves throughout our lives and the aspects which Jupiter makes to itself are relevant to everyone.

Taking a variance of 7 months either way, we experience the first Jupiter square at the age of 3, followed by the opposition when we are 6, another square at the age of 9 and our first Jupiter return at 12. The square occurs again at 15, which often seems to bring foreign travel; the opposition at 17 to 18, which for many coincides with freedom from school and the beginning of a period of further education, both freedom and further education being symbolized by Jupiter; the return at around the age of 24, the square at around 26 years 9 months and the opposition at around 29 years 9 months. At the age of 32 to 33 we experience the first square of the next Jupiter cycle and for many this seems to be a time when we become aware of our inner power, culminating in important changes – and sometimes a bid for freedom – at 35 years 8 months when we experience the next Jupiter return. Then there's a Jupiter square when we're about 38 years 8 months, an opposition at 41 years 7 months, another square at 44 years 7 months, a return at 47 years 6 months, a square at 50 years 6 months, an opposition at 53 years 5 months, a square at 56 years 5 months and return at 59 years 5 months. The Jupiter square at around the age of 62 years 4 months often seems to be a time of success or fruition, as does the opposition at 65 years 4 months. There's another square when we're around 68 years 3 months and a return at around 71 years 3 months which, again, seems to be a time of potential success and fulfilment. Squares and oppositions then follow at the ages of about 74, 77 and 80, with a return at around 84. Any of these aspects can show success, fulfilment, or a breakthrough to freedom leading to expansion of the life and interests.

SATURN

Saturn is the last of the traditional planets, encircling them in its orbit just as it is itself encircled by its rings. Appropriately, one of the main principles of Saturn is that of setting limits and creating boundaries; even in the body Saturn rules the skin. It is also the planet of form, structure and building and, again, this is shown clearly in Saturn's rulership of the skeleton and the teeth. Saturn is the planet which symbolizes the process of creating form and structure; it is also the planet of crystallization, contraction and rigidity: Saturn solidifies, brings us down to earth, controls, disciplines, separates, clarifies. In the character Saturn stands for patience, perseverance, prudence, a sense of duty and responsibility, and hard work. Its position in the birth chart and aspects with other planets show the areas of life in which we will have to apply these qualities, and how easy we will find it to do so. If we try to dodge the issue, Saturn crops up again in the form of difficulties and blocks to our progress: not for nothing has it been called 'the planet of karma', or 'the grim reaper', since it ensures that we get back exactly what we give out.

Because of this, Saturn has something of a reputation for being a difficult planet. The image given it by ancient astrologers as 'the greater malefic' has stuck to some extent. Modern astrologers, however, view Saturn in a very different way and believe that, like the rest of the planets, it stands for principles of life which are neither 'good' nor 'bad' but neutral. Saturn brings challenges, and it is the way in which we respond to them that determines the outcome. Indeed, without the Saturn principle of discipline, structure, planning, organization and practicality, it would be difficult to achieve much. I discovered this in a graphic way quite early on in my astrological career when a client came to me with career problems. He was highly qualified, with first-class honours degrees in both arts and sciences, and also a BSc in engineering, but had never been able to hold down a job for more than six months. At first glance I could see no obvious reason for this in his birth chart, which did indeed show excellent mental faculties. Then I noticed that Saturn was placed in a sign through which it could not function easily, and that the only aspect which it made with other planets was a very weak one (semi-sextile). In other words, although the talent was there, Saturn's lack of strength meant that he could not relate it to practical life.

As I've already mentioned, one of the principles of Saturn is discipline. Its position in the birth chart determines the discipline which we receive, both from people and from events and circumstances. This principle applies throughout our life, but the way in which we are corrected and moulded in earliest childhood is particularly relevant because it lays the foundation (another Saturnine principle!) for the way in which we then correct and discipline ourselves. It's the voice inside our head which says 'You *should* do this' or 'You *shouldn't* do that', 'You mustn't cry', 'You must work hard', and so on. Mixed up with these injunctions, and also part of our lifescript, are beliefs we have picked up about ourselves and fears which we have absorbed from those around us as we were growing up: 'You never do anything right', 'You're stupid', 'You can't handle money', 'It's wrong to be angry', 'It's better to play safe than to take a risk.' These have the effect on us of one of Saturn's other principles, limitation. They were limiting when we were children, and can limit us even more as adults, particularly as, for the most part, they are probably old scripts which no longer apply to us, but which have become so impressed upon us that we do not even question them. Indeed, we may be hardly aware of these limiting conversations going on inside our head, holding us back, pushing us into action (or inaction) which is not really in keeping with our true self.

Life is about growth, and if, or when, the structures and attitudes which we have built around ourselves begin to prevent this – by becoming too tight or too constraining – then we will begin to burst out, like a plant pushing its way through the floorboards or a tarmac road. The natural reaction is to batten down the boards tighter, but this increases the tension. This process of breaking out is discussed further under the planets Uranus and Pluto, as well as in Part 2 of this book, which describes how the cycles of the planets mean that these changes are most likely to happen at certain ages which are critical for everyone.

In order to hide the fears which we all pick up from babyhood – or, in some cases, pre-babyhood, when we absorbed fears from our mother while we were still in the womb – we build a defence around ourselves, another Saturn principle. So we have a face we show the world which protects the vulnerable creature we are inside. This has sometimes been described as a 'shield'. Once we have found that a certain way of reacting works for us, the temptation is to keep on using it. The shield can then become a prison – an automatic reaction which may have worked previously, but which may not now be applicable to us in our present stage in life. If it is impeding our growth – the expression of the real creative, 'alive', fun-loving person that is within us – or if it is inhibiting the expression of something in our personality which our higher self wants to bring out, then it has to crack.

Once they begin to notice the negative thoughts which hold them back, which come from the part of our psyche which is known as the super-ego, also known as 'the parrot on the shoulder', most people are amazed at the extent of them. It's illuminating to write down all the beliefs you can think of and see how you have been allowing them to limit your life. Once you're aware of your limiting beliefs, try to stop using the word 'should'; instead, do as Louise Hay suggests in her book *You Can Heal Your Life*, and say: 'If I really wanted to, I could . . .' You may be surprised to realize that you do not really *want* to do the things you feel you should be doing; that you may be following old programming given to you in your childhood and which you need no longer follow. For instance, I have known people who, on doing this exercise, suddenly realized that the reason they were working in their particular career, which they did not really like, was because it was the one which their parents felt they 'ought' to do. They had initially got into it in order to please their parents, although they did not realize their motive at the time. I know someone else who, when reflecting on her unsatisfactory marriage, realized that she had gone into it in order to please her mother, who had a high opinion of her husband. Then there was the woman who was exhausted trying to do a part-time job as well as look after two young children with little support from her husband.

When she did this exercise, she realized that she was going out to work not because they were desperate for the money, or because she really wanted to work, but because she felt she 'should' be contributing to the family income. Once she realized this, she was able to allow herself to be a full-time mother. She felt happier, her health improved, the children were easier to deal with and the atmosphere in the home completely changed, to the benefit of the whole family. When you free yourself from the negative constraints of Saturn and do what you really want to do, it is surprising how things tend to fall into place to help you: 'Act boldly, and unseen forces will come to your aid', as the old saying goes.

Cutting away the Saturnine beliefs, criticisms and fears which no longer apply can free you to express yourself without limitation. Those criticisms which *do* apply can be turned into positive statements or affirmations which, when repeated frequently, can help you to become what you would like to be. For example, instead of thinking, 'I don't like being fat', say to yourself, 'I am slim and lithe' or words to that effect. But remember that acceptance, and love of yourself exactly as you are, is the most freeing attitude of all.

To illustrate the effect of limiting beliefs, I'd like to share with you the following words, written by 85-year-old Nadine Stair, from Louisville, Kentucky:

If I had my life to live over . . .

I'd like to make more mistakes next time. I'd relax. I would limber up. I would be sillier than I have been this trip. I would take fewer things seriously. I would take more chances, I would climb more mountains and swim more rivers. I would eat more ice cream and less beans. I would perhaps have more actual troubles, but I'd have fewer imaginary ones.

You see, I'm one of those people who live sensibly and sanely hour after hour, day after day. Oh, I've had my moments, and if I had to do it over again, I'd have more of them. In fact, I'd try to have nothing else. Just moments, one after another, instead of living so many years ahead of each day. I've been one of those persons who never goes anywhere without a thermometer, a hot water bottle, a raincoat, and a parachute. If I had to do it again, I would travel lighter than I have.

If I had my life to live over, I would start barefoot earlier in the spring and stay that way later in the fall. I would go to more dances. I would ride more merry-go-rounds. I would pick more daisies.

The reason why many of us travel with such caution is that we have plenty of that praiseworthy Saturn virtue, prudence. Or is it? Is it instead another of Saturn's principles, fear, which prevents us from travelling light? While prudence may enable us to make our plans work successfully, fear cramps our style and prevents us from doing what our essential being would really like to do. Fear starts very early in life, often in babyhood when we realize that we are separate from our mother but totally dependent on her for our survival. Similarly, when a certain experience has given us pain, we register it either consciously or unconsciously and try to avoid it happening again. For instance, if our mother has rejected us as a baby we may fear that if we open ourselves to another, or make ourselves emotionally vulnerable (like a baby) we will experience again the great pain of rejection. As a result, we may have closed up our heart very young and always find it difficult to trust others enough to form loving, trusting, satisfactory emotional relationships.

Some of our automatic reactions to old fears are less obvious and we need to be both quite perceptive with ourselves and very honest in order to understand them. This is because, in order to compensate for a quality which we feel we lack, we behave in the opposite way. For example, if we lack confidence and are afraid of failure, in order to cover this up we behave in an over-confident manner, perhaps being rather critical of other people. We can recognize that we do this if we find that we are ourselves particularly irritated by people who are bossy or over-confident. The person who says, 'I'm not going to let anyone get the better of me, I always give as good as I get' is in fact clearly saying, 'I'm terrified of being dominated and put down by other people and I have an inferiority complex.'

Obviously, when we know from experience that a certain situation brings us pain or holds problems for us, we try to avoid it. Apart from, once again, limiting ourselves as a result, when we try to avoid something we set in motion a strange law. There is a saying: 'What you resist is what you get.' It is as if the fear of something generates that very thing and the more we try to avoid it, the more we have to face it. That is the principle of Saturn at work, both restricting us and assisting our growth in trying to make us face up to our fears. The funny thing is, when we begin to analyse what we are really afraid of, and why, it begins to lose its power over us.

Fear can be unlearned and, curiously enough, the way to tackle this Saturnine emotion is to use Saturnine techniques of practicality, realism and planning. The Buddhist principle of giving your whole attention to the present moment is also extremely helpful in over-coming fear. Being completely aware of how you are feeling *now* prevents worry about the future.

The sign and house in which Saturn is placed, and the aspects which it makes with other planets, indicate the areas of life where we are most prone to fear, most vulnerable or feel the strongest sense of duty and responsibility, and possibly the most frustration too. It also shows where we put in the most effort, and the quality which, as a result, we have an opportunity to develop.

Saturn spends about 2.5 years in each sign, so its sign-position shows an aspect of our personality which we share with everyone else born during that time. Those who have Saturn in a fire sign – Aries, Leo and Sagittarius – may be lacking in confidence, spontaneity and sense of purpose, which can lead to self-centredness and pride. For those with Saturn in the earth signs – Taurus, Virgo and Capricorn – Saturn's fears, limitation and sense of duty affect their approach to material matters, including money, comfort, security, health and well-being, and also the way in which they value themselves, both generally and through their work and success in the world. The air signs – Gemini, Libra and Aquarius – are concerned with the mind and thought-processes, so Saturn in these signs shows that there is the chance to put in hard work and effort here. At the same time, there may be a fear of inadequacy with respect to them, and loneliness because of a sense of being unable to communicate deeper thoughts with others. Saturn in the water signs – Cancer, Scorpio or Pisces – means that a person's emotions are affected by their fears and sense of vulnerability, one affecting the other, and are difficult to disentangle.

Other matters that Saturn symbolizes in the birth chart are hard work, organization and practicality; sound long-term plans, delays, patience, perseverance and the inevitable; old people; bones, skin and teeth; the spleen, the gall bladder and the vagus nerve, also the crystallization of acid in the joints; cold and colds; low vitality and depression. Places associated with Saturn are, among others, deserts and churchyards; its plants include barley and comfrey, its colour is black and its metals and stones are lead, diamonds and all hard, black stones.

Saturn, our Shadow and Projection

Saturn, the outermost of the personal planets, symbolizes, as we've already seen, the boundary of the personality and the shield or mask which we use to hide from others our vulnerability and fears. We do not want others to know about these things, but we may not even want to know about them ourselves. So we concentrate on the parts of our personality which are acceptable to us, pushing the other parts – the fears, the negative emotions, or those feelings which we were told as children we should not have – out of our mind. But they do not go away; they remain in our unconscious as a part of our psyche which psychologists call the shadow.

The natural urge of our being is towards wholeness, and if we continue to refuse to acknowledge this shadow part of ourselves, it simply becomes stronger. We have already seen how by resisting things we simply make ourselves more likely to have to face them; that is the way in which the shadow rattles on the floorboards as we desperately try to keep them battened down. Our psyche is trying to become whole by getting us to acknowledge and accept the dark part of ourselves, and to realize that neither the part of ourselves which we find acceptable, such as, for instance, the view we may have of ourselves as attractive, kind, caring parents, successful in our career, and so on, nor the dark shadow, is the real us, just images of ourselves which we have created. Also, for every positive trait that we acknowledge, there is the negative side – the fear of being ugly, cruel, a bad parent, a failure, for instance, stored in our unconscious.

When our shadow begins to rattle the floorboards, it is, as I describe in Part 2 of this book, an excellent sign and an opportunity for growth which recurs throughout our life. Even before the rattling starts, or when it's just a gentle tapping, we can get an idea of what we are resisting by the way in which we view the world and other people. One of the ways in which our shadow reveals itself to us is through a process called projection. Projection occurs because we cannot face looking at the negative qualities in ourselves, and instead see them in other people. So when we describe and criticize others, we are in fact revealing aspects of ourselves, some of which we would probably prefer to keep hidden. The more we can be aware of, and accept, our shadow, the stronger we become, like a plant putting its roots down into the deep and fertile soil. We realize that our fears are not the dragons and demons we once thought; that what we thought were our failings and weaknesses alone we share with all human beings.

I'd like to end this section with some words of Liz Greene, from her book *Saturn*:

> The main impact of Saturn to the three outer planets lies in the fact that Saturn is the last outpost or shell of the personality and is, for the majority of people, occupied in fortifying his city walls so that no one else can get in. Before a man has come to terms with and integrated his darker half, it is rare that he can experience any feeling of a common bond with the rest of humanity because the shadow stands between him and others; he uses it to reaffirm his differences and assures himself that he is better, wiser, more rational, and more right than they because the more inferior or immature qualities are conveniently tucked away into the shadow. Consequently everyone else looks darker, and the man looks lighter to himself. To this kind of man the energies of the outer planets are like the intoxicating air of the mountain peaks; but he is afraid of heights. They threaten his illusions because they carry the reality of common or collective experience where there are no differences, no barriers, and no bases for judgement.

The Cycle of Saturn

Saturn takes 29.46 years to complete its orbit of the Sun, but because of retrograde motion there is a variation of plus or minus 8 months in the time it takes to get back to its original place in the birth chart.

As it does so, Saturn moves through each house of the birth chart, spending an average of 2.5 years in each. When Saturn is in a certain house, its presence is noticeable; it is as if our attention is directed to the area of our lives connected with that house. The effect of Saturn in the houses is especially pronounced if it also makes important aspects with planets in our birth chart. Yes, there can be difficulties, delays and restrictions of some kind or another; choices may have to be made. But I have also found that one thing which Saturn does do, if you let it, is allow us to see things as they really are. It takes off the blinkers and brings us face to face with reality. It brings things into sharp focus, which can be quite a relief if you have been going through a period of Neptunian confusion and indecision! Saturn is the planet both of clarity and of acceptance. Once you accept the reality of Saturn, it loses its power to scare and frustrate.

I have recently experienced Saturn passing through my first house and I found that the moment it crossed my ascendant into this house a period of muddle and indecision came to a close; suddenly, I was able to make practical plans. In keeping with Saturn, these demanded some constraints, but they felt right and are certainly proving worthwhile. Saturn in the first house can bring personal problems and worries, too: the Queen, during her '*annus horribilis*', had Saturn here. When it's in the second house, Saturn demands some cut-back or careful planning in connection with personal finances or possessions; this is an excellent time for having a clear-out and organizing your life. It is interesting that the issue of the Queen paying income tax and generally streamlining the royal purse came to the fore at this time, with Saturn approaching her second house. (Saturn enters the Queen's second house in April 1995.)

When Saturn is in the third house we may find our mobility or ability to communicate restricted to some extent, or there could be a difficulty to be overcome, or a responsibility to be undertaken, in connection with a sister, brother or neighbour, or with our immediate environment. Or we may decide to put disciplined effort into a course of study. Family or domestic responsibilities are often shown during the time when Saturn is in the fourth house; a move to a smaller house is one way in which this influence can work out. Alternatively, true to Saturn's tendency to bring extra responsibility, it could mean a move to a house with a granny-annexe in order to accommodate a parent.

Saturn passing through the fifth house can bring worries, responsibilities or restrictions through children; a curtailment of pleasure activities for one reason or another, or a need to combine work with pleasure. Work is generally a key issue when Saturn is passing through the sixth house, which represents both work and health. Work may be onerous and demanding, with additional responsibilities; it may be restricting; there may be difficulties at work. Perhaps there may be hardship through *loss* of work; whichever way it works out, Saturn in this house will bring lessons through work, and these may take many forms. The same applies to health matters, though you won't necessarily have problems with both of these areas of your life. Also, the key may be opportunity and success achieved through having to work hard, discipline yourself, and so on: Saturn's influence is by no means wholly negative.

Saturn in the seventh house puts the focus on partnership, marriage, rivalry or other close one-to-one relationships. Sometimes people get married at this time – the Queen did – or they may separate, get divorced or be widowed: all conditions which teach us more about the way in which we relate closely to another and, ultimately, about ourselves and how we respond to and cope with different situations. Some people who know a little about astrology worry when Saturn enters their eighth house, knowing that this is the house of death. Well, that's true, but death is only one of the things represented by this house. It also signifies sex, birth and shared finances and resources.

Saturn in the next house, the ninth, can coincide with a period of hard work through study, or of intensive travel overseas, forcing one to restrict other areas of one's life. Saturn in the tenth house of the career and parents frequently seems to bring extra responsibilities: Margaret Thatcher had Saturn in her tenth house when she became Prime Minister. When it's in the eleventh house, Saturn can help us to make our dreams come true through hard work and practicality; or we may feel that we are burdened by taking too much responsibility for a friend, or for a group to which we belong, since both of these are signified by this house too. Astrologers working in the seventeenth century and earlier believed that Saturn in the twelfth house was generally rather unfortunate, since this was known as 'the house of self-undoing' and of secret enemies. Having recently experienced Saturn's passage through this area of the horoscope for myself, I have to admit reluctantly that I believe there is a grain of truth in this. My main feeling at the time was of confusion; even with the advantage of astrology, I found it impossible to make plans!

By the time Saturn has completed its cycle we have had to focus on all the houses, to a greater or lesser degree, according to the emphasis of our individual chart. Then we start on the next circuit. On the second time around, we get another chance to handle the lessons, which may have some similarities to our experiences the first time. It can be quite helpful to look back and compare what was happening then with what is happening now, and see how we can make better use of our opportunities for growth this time.

When Saturn has completed its cycle and got back to its original place in the birth chart, astrologers call it a 'Saturn return'. This is, for most people, a particularly significant time. During our first Saturn cycle, we find out who we are and we build a life for ourselves. Then, at our first Saturn return, we find ourselves reviewing our life and our situation, and if these don't truly express who we are, we feel uncomfortable. (I think that the Princess of Wales allegedly wanting the truth about her marriage and her illness to be known to the public at the time of her Saturn return is an excellent example of this process.) So, as a result, many people make changes in their lives at this time. Then they start the process of building again, until they reach the next Saturn return, another crucial time, when they're around 59. At this point, something brings them up short and they begin to think about what they've done with their lives, and what they still want to do. They may feel the years are flying by, and be conscious of their mortality. For those who live until their nineties, this process happens again, at the time of the third Saturn return!

In between the time of the Saturn returns, Saturn squares and opposes its birth position at 7-year intervals, and at these times we feel an influx of the Saturn energy in our life. The approximate ages at which we experience the major aspects in the Saturn cycle start when we're about 7, when we get the first square; at 14 to 15 we experience the opposition and, at 21, the waning square as Saturn makes its way back to where it was when we were born – the

Saturn return, which occurs when we're around 29½. The first square of this cycle happens when we're about 37, followed by the opposition at about 44, the waning square at 51 to 52 and the second return at around 59. Then we experience a square at around the age of 66 and the opposition at 73 to 74. I haven't generally considered trines in this book, because their effect is less noticeable, but there is a Saturn trine at the age of 78 to 79 which often seems to coincide with some kind of success or period of fruition, as I've explained in the chapter on the seventies. The waning Saturn square occurs when we're about 81 and the third Saturn return at 88 to 89, with a square at 95 and the final opposition at 103!

At these periods in our life we may be forced to look at our responsibilities; to reconsider our goals, and, most important of all, to look critically at ourselves, which may necessitate making changes. Because of Saturn's retrograde motion, these times of change and re-evaluation last for about a year, although the results may be more far-reaching. These are times when we get the chance to shed a skin and to grow, if we can make the most of the opportunities with which we're presented. They may not be the opportunities we'd like; indeed, they may not even appear to be opportunities at all. But if we look at them from the point of view of our growth, ask ourselves what they are telling us, what chance they mask, they can be extremely constructive. As Liz Greene says in *Saturn*:

> Man creates his world all the time, according to the thought patterns he generates, and he brings about a reality which is the outward expression of these patterns. The experiences which an individual encounters are in some mysterious way attracted into his life by the creative power of his own psyche, and although we do not fully understand the synchronous fashion in which the inner and the outer reflect each other, we know that it happens in every person's life. One has only to observe an individual undergoing a process of self-development to see that the outer circumstances of his life always follow in an immediate fashion the inner psychic changes which he undergoes. He does not consciously create these circum-stances; it is the larger self, the total psyche, which is the dynamic energy behind the individual's unfoldment and if the individual makes no effort to expand his conscious so that he can understand the nature of his total unfoldment and can begin to cooperate with

it, then it will seem that he is the pawn of fate and has no control over his life. He can only earn his freedom by learning about himself so that he can understand what value a particular experience has for the development of his whole self. And nothing stimulates a man into this kind of exploration faster than frustration, which is the gift of Saturn.

Or, put another way, this time by Richard Bach in *Illusions*: 'There is no such thing as a problem without a gift for you in its hands. You seek problems because you need their gifts.' Each time Saturn makes a contact with its own position, we are challenged in some way, the shadow or unconscious may rattle the floorboards, circumstances may force us to look at ourselves and our lives with total honesty, cracking open the rigid shell which we have formed around ourselves.

URANUS

Ancient astrologers were aware of just seven planets, including the Sun and the Moon, ending with Saturn, and found that these explained character and events in a perfectly satisfactory way. Then, in 1781, as if to herald the French Revolution, the American War of Independence and the great changes of the agricultural and industrial revolutions, Herschel discovered Uranus. From Uranus's irregular path the presence of another planet, Neptune, was deduced and then discovered in 1846, with Pluto being spotted in 1930.

Since their discovery, astrologers have noted the characteristics shown on the birth chart by Uranus, Neptune and Pluto and have been able to link them with certain signs of the zodiac, in the same way that the ancient astrologers linked the original seven planets, which were each said to rule two signs, except for the Sun and the Moon, which each ruled one, Leo and Cancer respectively. These traditional rulerships still apply, but now three signs, Aquarius, Pisces and Scorpio, have each been allotted another planetary ruler – Uranus, Neptune and Pluto, respectively (see page 223 for a full list of these). The new co-rulers do not replace the traditional rulers of the signs, sometimes known as the personal planets, which remain highly important and relevant; rather, they add an extra dimension. As far as our development is concerned, Saturn marks the boundary, the crystallization, the ultimate formation of the personality, while the planets outside its orbit stand for powerful principles of change, dissolution, elimination and regeneration which help to crack the Saturn shell, to prevent stultification and stagnation and allow for growth and contact with higher transpersonal aspects of our being.

Uranus is, above all, the planet of change. It symbolizes internal change, such as a change of attitude, but also external change, of circumstances and events. The changes of Uranus are often sudden and unexpected; they seem to come from nowhere and can disappear just as quickly. You cannot rely on Uranus, except to do the unexpected.

Uranus is also the planet of individuality, independence and unconventionality, qualities expressed in its physical nature in that it spins in the opposite direction from the other planets around an axis which is horizontal to the ecliptic, whereas all the others are perpendicular. Similarly Jupiter, whose principle is abundance and expansion, is by far the largest of the planets; and Saturn, whose influence has to do with limits and boundaries, is itself encased in rings.

People who have Uranus strong in their horoscopes often seem to be going in a different direction from other people. Sometimes they may appear to act in a certain way simply to rebel. But the truth is that generally they have such a strong inner drive that they cannot help but follow it, even if it forces them to take a totally different route from everyone else. In the process they may refuse to behave in ways which conform to the accepted norm; they may show no respect for rules and conventions, and they may appear to ignore the wishes and rights of other people. This disregard for others may seem to contradict their views about the rights of the individual, but an overdose of Uranus can lead to very selfish behaviour. On the other hand, when properly integrated and used, the Uranian influence, which we all have in our charts to a greater or lesser degree, gives an urge to be honest and true to ourselves which is both powerful and inspiring. It gives an openness to new ideas and inspiration which can lead to major progress, both in an individual life and also in a way which affects many people. Uranus symbolizes the flash of genius behind inventions and great creative works. Mozart, for example, had Uranus strong in his chart and was obviously responding to its principle, even though the planet had not been discovered when he was born; the same applies to Lord Byron, Richard Wagner and Picasso. Taken to extremes, however, a strong Uranus can give so much originality and deviance from the norm that it becomes lunacy. And it's not always easy to tell, just from the chart, whether it belongs to a genius or a madman. Much depends on the balance of the chart as a whole and, above all, on the essential being of the person who is using it during this incarnation.

Since both the Sun and Uranus stand for the principle of individuality, you may wonder how these differ. The 'individuality' which the Sun stands for is our innermost core, our creative centre, our vital identity, the part of us closest to our essential being, which is not shown in the birth chart. Uranus shows our originality and our attunement to truth – which may well be the ability to understand what our essential being and the Sun part of ourselves want for our growth and development. Uranus, lying outside the planet of boundaries, Saturn, is the planet of freedom; of breaking down and of breaking out. It is the planet which cracks the shell of Saturn's routine, so that we can grow and thus express our essential being more fully, like a snake shedding its skin.

There are numerous ways in which Uranus cracks Saturn's shell; some of these are described in the next section, on the cycles of Uranus, and in Part 2 of this book under the various ages when these cycles come into play. No matter how the shell is cracked, our Saturn principle tries to patch up the holes and keep us safely inside. So if Uranus brings unexpected change, Saturn counteracts with fear of the future and efforts to keep things as they are. If Uranus brings us the insight to see that we are not fulfilling ourselves through our way of life, and with it the desire to change, Saturn may find any number of ways to try and keep us stuck: feelings of guilt and fear among them.

As I've said, the principle of Uranus can be selfish or self-centred; and people with this planet strong in their horoscope can show a breathtaking lack of consideration for others. The most supremely self-centred person I've ever met had Uranus extremely strong in her chart and seemed totally unaware of the feelings of other people, although she did not realize this and in fact often described herself as 'sensitive'. She was certainly 'sensitive' to her own needs and wishes. On the other hand, I knew another person, with a rather similar chart, in which Uranus was equally strong, and this man was remarkably thoughtful towards everyone he met, with the utter lack of awareness of barriers of class, colour or creed that you'd expect from a 'good' Uranus. In this man the Uranian 'hard-heartedness' was expressed as cool detachment, so that you never felt that his kind deeds had strings attached; indeed, he gave them in an almost casual, matter-of-fact way. But only as and when he chose; you could never get help from him by exerting any kind of pressure on him. And that's true of all people who have Uranus strong in their birth chart: the more you push them, the more determined they become *not* to do what you want them to. If you're dealing with one of these people, it's best to state your needs directly and unemotionally, then give them time to think about the situation before you mention it again.

For most of us, when prompted by Uranus to do something which we know will certainly not go down well with others, there's a dilemma. Do we go ahead and risk upsetting them and feeling guilty, or do we give in to their wishes, give up our plans and feel resentful and frustrated? Either action, you will notice, may bring a Saturnian result: guilt, or resentment and frustration. The answer lies in using the positive qualities of both Uranus and Saturn: the gift of Uranus to cut through all the trappings and see the truth and to respond to our innermost need for growth, and the ability of Saturn to be practical, patient and responsible in the way in which we go about putting it into action and making sound plans which help to allay fears. While Saturn helps us to control our feelings (sometimes to the point of bottling them up too much), Uranus gives us the ability to detach ourselves from them, and that is vital. If you look again at the original question: 'Do we go ahead and *risk upsetting them and feeling guilty*, or do we give in to their wishes, give up our plans and *feel resentful and frustrated?*' you will notice that in both instances it is feelings and emotions – either our own or those of other people – which are complicating the decision. Uranus helps us to cut through emotion, feeling and sentiment to see truth; or to take action regardless of it. As I said earlier, people with a strong Uranus in their chart may appear heartless, or, as I have also shown, they may be truly detached; open-hearted and loving, yet unswayed by passing emotion. That does not mean to say they do not feel anything; indeed, to be totally cut off from feeling does not lead to growth and development, but to the reverse. The secret lies in feeling the emotions and realizing that they, and your life, are your responsibility. No one can make you feel a particular emotion, just as you are in no way responsible for how *they* feel. This truth frees us from the guilt of 'upsetting' others – it also means we cannot blame them for our own feelings. This was expressed by Gita Bellin, co-founder of Self-Transformation, who taught self-awareness in Australia, New Zealand and the UK in the 1980s: 'The fastest way to freedom is to feel and choose your feelings.' Taken further, once you accept full responsibility for your life, realizing that you are the creative source, then you stop blaming circumstances and events, too. That's when you suddenly experience true independence and freedom: and when growth really accelerates.

Uranus stands for the new, the original and the revolutionary in life. It is a planet which can give a craving for excitement, change and variety. People often experience considerable change in the affairs of the house of the horoscope in which Uranus is placed, or they may be of a nature which expresses the characteristics of this planet.

There's much that is contradictory about the Uranian principle, one of whose qualities is contradictoriness. For example, Uranus is the planet of groups and friendship but also of independence. People with Uranus strong in their horoscope, or in the relationship houses of their chart, do not find it easy to make long-lasting, stable relationships; and their relationships may not be the conventional monogamous heterosexual ones. Uranus influencing one relationship area of the horoscope (that is, the seventh house of marriage, partnership and so on) does not always work out in obvious ways, however. In the case of one woman, for instance, Uranus in this house did not result in numerous relationships, but in a stable and long-lasting marriage to a partner with a strongly Uranian horoscope (five planets in Aquarius, the sign of the zodiac which is ruled by Uranus, and the Sun also close to Uranus). It seems that this gave an unpredictable and unconventional enough personality to satisfy the need for change and excitement in close relationships which Uranus in that house of the horoscope gives. And he, being so strongly Uranian, was, as you might guess, highly independent, allowing her the space she required. Close relationships and independence do not always fit together so well. Often when people have Uranus in one of the houses which show these, or in a close aspect with the planet of relationships, Venus, they have problems in reconciling these two principles: their desire to be close to someone and their need for independence, not to mention change and excitement. Elizabeth Taylor's many marriages may be attributable to the close conjunction of Uranus with Venus in her chart.

As it takes Uranus about 7 years to pass through a sign of the zodiac, everyone born in that period will have Uranus in the same sign in their birth chart. So when you're looking at a birth chart in order to know more about someone's personality, the sign-position of Uranus will not tell you precise characteristics, individual to that person, in the way in which those of the faster-moving planets, particularly the Sun, Moon, Mercury, Venus and Mars, will. But the fact that whole groups of people – almost a generation – are born with Uranus in the same sign means that they share certain general qualities and gives their generation a particular flavour. The impact of this upon the world is not felt until around 20 or more years later, as that generation impresses its personality upon the world. Tracing the effect of these astrological groups on social trends would make for interesting research; it is the subject for a book in its own right.

Although the sign-position of Uranus in a birth chart only shows general characteristics, the house-position, which changes on average every 2 hours of the day, and also the aspects which Uranus makes to the faster-moving planets (especially the Sun, Moon, Mercury, Venus and Mars), are important. The principles of Uranus – independence, change, desire for variety and excitement – apply to the area of life shown by the house in which Uranus is placed. In the chart of one man I know, for example, Uranus is in the second house of money; after getting a degree in science and spending a year working in the well-paid job which followed, this man then left to practise astrology, which he had been studying in his spare time. His income – which has been erratic, true to the nature of Uranus – has come from astrology, a subject symbolized by Uranus, ever since.

As well as astrology, matters symbolized by Uranus are: sudden and/or unexpected change and moves, which break up old conditions and make way for new opportunities; separation and disruption; the new and surprising; modern science; electronic instruments; computers; the circulatory system; cramp and paralysis; sexual deviation. Its colours are usually said to be psychedelic or unusually striking, for example electric blue or shocking pink, and its metal is uranium.

The Cycle of Uranus

It takes Uranus 84.02 years to orbit the Sun, which means that it spends about 7 years in each sign. (I say 'about' because, as I've already explained, timing varies as a result of retrograde motion.) As it is a slow-moving planet, its effect is noticeable. As it moves through the houses Uranus brings to each its principle of change, breaking up old conditions and bringing the chance for growth. The change may not necessarily apply to material conditions, although it often does. It can show a change of mind and outlook towards the affairs shown by the house in which it is placed; often it signifies both inner and outer change. Sometimes the affairs of the house through which Uranus is moving suddenly become more Uranian in quality.

When Uranus passes over our rising sign and into our first house these changes affect us at a personal level and, indeed, we may find that we become more highly-strung, unpredictable and 'Uranian' in nature. We may wonder what new experience is going to hit us next, demanding that we re-think our views and way of life. The Queen had Uranus (and also Neptune) hovering around her ascendant during the whole of 1992, a year which saw the break-up of the marriages of two of her sons, the serious fire at Windsor Castle, and discussion in the country about the role of the royal family in the late twentieth century. I think that with Uranus moving through the Queen's first house her attitude to many things is likely to change a good deal, and the monarchy with it. When Uranus moves into the next house in her horoscope, the second, which has to do with finance and possessions, the Queen, like anyone else, will almost certainly experience changes connected with her finances and personal possessions and in her values.

Uranus in the third house may bring changes in your environment or to do with the affairs of your brothers and sisters; it can be a good time for studying something which comes under the rulership of Uranus, such as astrology or electronics. A move or disruption in the family is likely when Uranus is in the fourth house, and changes concerning children, creative projects, spare-time enterprises when it is in the fifth house. Uranus in the sixth house may bring unexpected

71

developments concerning health, work and the daily routine; in the seventh house, these will affect close personal relationships such as marriage. My mother was widowed as Uranus approached her seventh house, and as Uranus has passed through this house she has had to learn the Uranian lesson of independence in connection with close relationships.

Uranus in the eighth house may bring the chance to look at and transform our beliefs concerning shared finances and resources, life, birth and death; when it is in the ninth things may happen in our life which make us re-think our fundamental beliefs, or new experiences may come through travel and contact with foreign countries. Uranus in the tenth house brings changes of, or within, our career – I started producing horoscopes on a computer when Uranus was in my tenth house. When it is in the eleventh house we may learn a great deal and perhaps change our outlook as the result of a friendship or contact with a group or society; and when it is in the twelfth house there may be a great deal going on at inner levels of our being: this can be an excellent time to have some counselling or take a course in psychotherapy or a workshop in self-awareness or assertiveness.

Whenever I know that Uranus is active in my chart I try to keep my plans flexible to allow for the changes of plan which Uranus often brings. On one occasion, having made an appointment to see a magazine editor about a cookery article, I noticed that there was a strong Uranian influence in my chart that day affecting meetings, so I wondered whether the date would be cancelled. Sure enough, early on the day we were due to meet, the editor telephoned me to say that she was ill and couldn't make it. I think she was rather taken aback when I replied that I'd been expecting it because of Uranus, and she promptly offered me the job of writing the star page for the magazine!

Everyone is subject to the cycle of Uranian aspects to its own position in the birth chart. So, roughly every 7 years, as the current Uranus reaches the same degree as that of Uranus in our birth chart, the transformational energy of Uranus is triggered in our life to help us to move on to the next stage of development. The actual timing varies a bit depending on the year you were born and on whether or not Uranus was retrograde. The Uranus aspect of a semi-sextile, which occurs when we are about 7 years old, shows our growing independence and awareness of our individuality; the next one, a sextile, which occurs when we are about 14, coincides with adolescence. Then Uranus squares its position in our birth chart when we are about 21, making this a time of major change and readjustment. The next Uranus aspect, a trine, often happens at around the same time as the first Saturn return, when we are about 28, underlining the importance of this age for our growth and development. Then, when we are around the age of 42, Uranus reaches the halfway point in its cycle and is in opposition to its position when we were born. So this is a time when it is natural for us to review and re-evaluate our life and possibly make, or experience, significant changes as a result. This is a particularly important time because the major Uranus aspect often happens at the same time as a number of other strong aspects, including the squares of Neptune and Pluto and the opposition of Saturn to their place in the birth chart. The trine, which happens when we're about 56, may coincide with success and harmonious change; the square, which occurs when we're around the age of 63, may coincide with retirement, although in some charts it shows late success and a change in career. There's a sextile aspect when we're about 70, a semi-sextile, which is a minor aspect, when we're 77, and Uranus completes its cycle, returning to its original position in our birth chart, when we are about 84, after which the cycle begins again.

NEPTUNE

Neptune, the second of the planets which lie outside the orbit of Saturn, stands for the principles of nebulousness, impressionability, imagination, dissolution, self-sacrifice and escape. While Uranus breaks through the Saturnine shell with the unexpected event, Neptune dissolves, undermines and dismantles it. The way in which the Berlin Wall seemed almost to disappear before our eyes in December 1990 was typically Neptunian. It's interesting that this event, and the subsequent relaxation of barriers in the Eastern Bloc, should follow the conjunction of Neptune, planet of dissolution, with Saturn, planet of boundaries and walls, in the sign of Capricorn, which, among other things, symbolizes established orders, traditions and governments.

The position of Neptune in our birth chart shows the area or areas of our life where we are most likely to be confused or yearning for something which is nebulous, or out of reach: the impossible dream. Because Neptune cannot be contained or confined, there is always a feeling of dissatisfaction, of wanting something more than we've got. One client who has Neptune in the house of partnership in her horoscope recently described this feeling perfectly: 'I seem to be living most of my life in a fantasy world. I have had relationships with men my own age and offers of marriage, but for me there is always something missing. I simply crave, and fantasize over older men . . .' The phrases 'living most of my life in a fantasy world', 'for me there is always something missing', and 'I simply crave, and fantasize over' all describe the quality of Neptune. Another client, who also has Neptune in the house of partnership, experienced a number of disappointing relationships. Eventually she met a man with whom she felt an immediate bond and she hardly dared believe that her happiness would last. Interestingly, the man also had Neptune in his house of partnership and he, too, had experienced difficulties and sorrow in this area of his life. The couple wanted to get married and legalize their union but they were advised by an astrologer (not me) that it would be better to go with the principle of Neptune and keep things fluid rather than create a bond or boundary which Neptune might then try and dissolve. So my client simply started using the man's name. This certainly made sense astrologically and the couple are still happily together today after nine years. In this context, I think that the position of Venus, planet of love, close to Neptune in Prince Charles's birth chart is interesting in view of the revelations about his unfulfilled relationship with his ex-girlfriend, Camilla Parker-Bowles, and his unhappy marriage. When Venus is close to Neptune it *is* difficult to find happiness in a close relationship, because of Neptune's tendency always to want more than you can have; and if you then get what you thought you wanted, you want more, or something a bit different. This is because you cannot pin Neptune down; it's limitless, like the ocean, with no boundaries. You just need to accept that whichever house in your chart Neptune happens to be in, this is an area of your life about which you'll probably feel dissatisfied and, to some extent, unfulfilled. You may also deceive or delude yourself or other people about the matters shown by that house (since Neptune also symbolizes illusion, delusion and deception), finding it difficult to face up to the true situation.

It's easy to see how the Neptunian desire to dissolve barriers makes this the planet of escapism. For a long time, though, I pondered on how it could also be the planet of prisons and imprisonment, which seems to be a complete contradiction of its principle. Then I realized that for many criminals prison is in fact an escape from life; and it's their action of trying to dissolve or overlook (another Neptunian characteristic) the restrictions imposed by the law which has brought them there. Asylums, monasteries and hospitals also come under Neptune.

As we've already seen, all the planets have a positive and a negative side, and this is as true of Neptune as of any of the others. But the dividing line between the two states can be particularly tenuous and difficult to define in Neptune's case. Well, being the planet which dissolves barriers, it would be, wouldn't it? It is extraordinary how astrological symbolism works, even down to small details. At what point does an imaginative or even a spiritual nature become a deluded one? When does the enjoyment of a relaxing drink slide into that other

Neptunian state, alcoholism? Or the use of drugs turn to addiction? Neptune shows states of altered consciousness, no matter by what means these are achieved. Just as Uranus needs the practicality of Saturn to bring the best out of its qualities, so Neptune needs Saturn's common sense and discipline. When a strong Neptune in a horoscope is balanced by an equally powerful Saturn, there is the ability to bring the vision of Neptune into form; or to make the mundane magical and uplifting.

Neptune gives the desire to transcend the boundaries of the self and to merge with others. This can result in the ability to put one-self and one's desires aside and show true compassion and charity towards others; or to open oneself to receive inspiration, dreams and visions from higher spheres. Neptune is frequently prominent in the horoscopes of musicians, artists and writers, as well as those of mystics and seers.

Neptune spends about 14 years in each sign of the zodiac, so, like Uranus and Pluto, it is an influence which is common to a generation. The sign in which Neptune is placed therefore shows ideals, dreams and visions which are shared by all those born during that 14-year period. The generation with Neptune in Cancer, for instance, born between about 1902 and 1915, might be said to show the Cancerian qualities of patriotism and conservation of family life and values. The ideals of the next generation, with Neptune in Leo, born from around 1915 until late 1928, centre on matters symbolized by Leo: royalty, glamour and power; father-figures; children; leisure and pleasure. Those with Neptune in Virgo, born from the end of 1920 until around 1943, are idealistic about things ruled by Virgo: health, diet, work and working conditions; while the next generation, born between 1943 and the end of 1956, are idealistic, and perhaps disillusioned too, about partnership, marriage and personal relation-ships, which are ruled by Libra. Those born from late 1956 until around 1970 have idealistic, nebulous ideas about sex, birth and death.

Other matters which are symbolized by Neptune are the sea; muddle and confusion as well as inspiration and ecstasy; poetry, dreams and visions as well as sensitivity and self-sacrifice; also delusion, fraud, greed and deception of self and others; dashed hopes; drugs, poisons, gas and anaesthetics; institutions, prisons and hospitals; photography and the cinema; the mental and nervous processes and the spinal canal; the thalamus. Its colours are the sea shades, ranging from misty grey to deep purple.

The Cycle of Neptune

It takes 164.79 years for Neptune to move through all the signs of the zodiac and complete an orbit of the Sun, so its cycle is obviously longer than a normal life-span. We will therefore only experience the effect of Neptune's influence in certain houses of our horoscope, not all of them. Neptune tends to bring confusion to the affairs of the house through which it is passing, melting rigid views, sweeping away preconceived ideas, undermining structures or views which we had hitherto considered rock-solid.

When Neptune is in our first house, it will be our ideas about ourself and our personal plans which become blurred, and we may find we become more sensitive to the mood and thoughts around us, more artistic, more psychic. Neptune in the second house may bring confusion to our finances or, in an appropriate chart, it could show that Neptunian matters such as music become a source of income. In a third house Neptune can show that we have the opportunity to learn more about an artistic or creative subject or that we're drawn towards the sea. I know someone who suddenly began to spend a great deal of time on a Greek island during the years in which Neptune was passing through her third house, a house which shows our environment and short journeys. Neptune in the fourth house can bring uncertainty to our home and domestic arrangements. The wife of one man on my files left him while Neptune was in his fourth house, but they remained friends and she kept coming back home for short periods of time so that his domestic arrangements became very confused.

When Neptune is in the next house, the fifth, there may be muddle concerning children, or a yearning for them, since Neptune can show that, too; when it's in the sixth house, our work may bring us in touch with the sea or with other things ruled by Neptune – drugs, gases, alcohol, as well as confusion and uncertainty – or we may experience these things in connection with our health. Sometimes Neptune in the sixth house coincides with an illusive illness or allergy which no one can get to the bottom of. During the time that Neptune is in our seventh house we will probably experience some indecision and heart-searching over partnership or marriage. When Neptune was in her seventh house one woman known to me found that her husband was becoming increasingly alcoholic. He would not accept this and refused any kind of therapy. Eventually she left him and ended the marriage. So, for her, two of the principles of Neptune – alcohol and dissolution – were clearly evident in her marriage. She also experienced other aspects of Neptune, confusion and loss, as it continued through her eighth house of shared finances; her divorce went through but she got what seemed like a very unfair settlement.

As Neptune moves through the ninth house of religion and higher learning, it can slowly and inexorably erode our beliefs, making way for new ones – this is what happened to me; and as it moves through the tenth house of the career, it can do much the same. We may feel restless and vaguely dissatisfied; we may become involved with a career of a Neptunian nature. Someone I know made a success of fish-farming while Neptune was passing through his career house: Neptunian symbolism clearly at work here.

When it's in our eleventh house of friends, groups, hopes and wishes, we may find ourselves chasing after – and *perhaps* achieving – an impossible dream; we may find ourselves becoming involved with friends or a society of a Neptunian nature – psychic, musical, artistic, nautical, drug-taking, alcholic, deceptive. Neptune in the twelfth house, that of secret enemies, *can* show unscrupulous people working against our interests; but it can just as easily show our involvement with a charity, or with some study that looks at the working of our unconscious, such as psychotherapy, or understanding the meaning of dreams and their relevance in daily life, since these matters also come under the rulership of Neptune and the twelfth house.

Because, like Uranus and Pluto, Neptune is relatively long-lasting, most of the time we're likely to be aware of this Neptune influence only in the background. We may sense that there's a muddle in one particular area of our life, or that things are unsatisfactory or not quite what they seem, or that old barriers are dissolving, without having either the inclination or the opportunity to sort matters out.

From time to time the influence will become more focused as Neptune makes aspects with planets in our birth chart. Then there will be a sense of confusion, muddle, loss, deceit or, on the other side of the Neptune coin, vision and inspiration, to do with the matters which that planet stands for. Often there will be a mixture of both: a period of confusion leading to wider understanding, an expansion of consciousness, and a greater awareness of our oneness with the rest of mankind. During the period of confusion, our confidence may be greatly undermined; we may doubt ourselves, our values, the very structure on which we feel our life is built. As one client said to me: 'It's as if everything is slipping away from me. Everything that I thought was certain in my life just seems to dissolve in my hand as I reach out to grasp it. I feel I should be making decisions about the future, yet I feel so confused and unsure of myself, I simply don't know what to do for the best.' In my opinion the best thing to do in this situation is to accept that there *is* confusion, but equally that it *will* clear; and to postpone major decisions until it does so – which will be when Neptune has moved away from whatever sensitive point it is aspecting in your chart. There is, however, one thing you need to watch, and that is that in putting off decisions you do not allow a difficult situation to slide into something even more serious. It may be that there simply is no action you can take, and that you have no other option but to allow things to take their course. But the influence of Neptune is undermining and invasive, like the sea washing away at sand, and sometimes by taking action you can prevent total collapse. Also, there may be elements to the situation of which you are unaware, or which you prefer to overlook, to deceive yourself about, or to allow others to do so. So these possibilities need to be considered in order to avoid having an even worse, or more confused, situation to deal with later. However, if that's what your inner being or core self requires for your growth, then no amount of shoring up will stop it from happening. Neptune's influence is dissolving the hard shell of your ego, washing away your shield, allowing your unconscious to flood in and put you in touch with parts of your own being, and of the universal consciousness, which you never knew existed. Often, part of this process can involve incidents which force us to realize the impermanence of material things. Something which we value may become lost or taken away from us: this is graphically shown in the case of the Queen, who had Neptune close to her rising sign throughout 1992, during which she suffered the destruction of a large part of her home, Windsor Castle.

We all experience the Neptune influence to a greater or lesser degree during the course of our lives, as Neptune makes aspects to its own place in our birth chart. At these times there is an intensification of the Neptune influence and we may feel some of the emotions which I have described. At each stage, Neptune brings the need for letting go. As we accept that we will not attain our youthful fantasies, hopes, dreams and goals, we need to allow ourselves to acknowledge the loss and to grieve. Letting go of an illusion can be painful, whether the illusion is of a person, of ourselves, of our capabilities, or of our hopes which have not been realized. We really just need to surrender the illusion; accept that that was what we thought before the veils were lifted from our eyes, and that we are now wiser as a result. We need not add to our pain by punishing ourselves for having had the illusion. Life would be duller without its hopes and dreams.

The first of Neptune's aspects to its own place occurs when we are around 14 years old, coinciding with our need to redefine our borders as we leave childhood behind and enter adolescence. It also reinforces the idealism of this age, and our ability to be stirred by images and 'impossible dreams' outside ourselves. The next Neptune aspect happens when we are about 28, and joins with the aspects from Saturn and Uranus in making this one of the major turning-points in life. The most testing Neptune aspect is, however, the one which occurs when we are about 41. As with all the aspects mentioned, the exact age at which this happens can vary by some months – see the tables and graphs. Here Neptune's aspect coincides with those of Uranus, Saturn and, possibly, Pluto, adding confusion, inner misgivings and perhaps a sense of 'what might have been' and the lure of an impossible dream to the mixture. No wonder people talk about the mid-life crisis! For more about this, and the other cycles which we all share, see Part 2.

The other Neptune crisis points occur when we are around the ages 55, 69 and 82 to 83. On each occasion Neptune will encourage us to dissolve rigid views and habits, and overdependence on material things or outgrown beliefs, so that we can grow spiritual and perhaps get a glimpse of who we really are beneath all the layers of veneer.

Throughout our life, Neptune can help us, through our experiences, to dissolve the barriers which get between us and other people and appreciate our common humanity. It is a joyful and releasing feeling which floods us with love.

PLUTO

Pluto is the last of the extra-Saturnian planets, and the outermost planet in our solar system. After Uranus has loosened Saturn's boundaries with restlessness and change, and Neptune has dissolved and softened them, Pluto opens up the cracks and brings release. At a human level, Pluto rules birth, death, sex, power, elimination and transformation. It brings experiences which can reveal to us the richness of our unconscious and, through that, the collective unconscious. It takes us beyond our limits and, in doing so, puts us in touch with the stream of consciousness which is common to everyone. Cleansed of our egotistical boundaries, we are, paradoxically, open and free to be ourselves, in touch with our own source of power, 'plugged in' without any of the wires crossed. The person who has been through the experiences of Pluto and truly allowed the transformation to take place is indeed a remarkable human being, and a 'transformer' for others. One such person was described by Marion Woodman in an interview with Barbara Goodrich-Dunn in the March/April 1989 issue of the US magazine *Common Boundary*:

> I knew an old man ... who saved my life. Dr E. A. Bennet, whom I write about in my books, was an 80-year-old analyst. He could put me in touch with my feelings when I, who was so smart and rational, couldn't feel anything. He would just sit there and wait and feel for me until I got the message. Tears would start to run down my face, not because I was sad, but because I recognized myself. I was picking up my own feelings from him. Then I realized what I really do value. He could perceive the feeling values I had lost touch with. I think such people will be incredibly important in the future. It's unbelievable how wise old people are treated in our culture, how people who have been honoured all their lives are thrown out into the dust pile. In so many tiny ways, feeling is just

tossed aside. How to recapture it without being with someone who can feel, I don't know. A heart attack, a kidney breakdown, perhaps.

In our birth chart, Pluto represents deep, intense feelings; feelings which are so strong that they can be compulsive, obsessive, all-engulfing. These feelings are often aroused in us through experiencing aspects of life which are symbolized by Pluto: through finding ourselves in a position of power; through death and birth; through the ending and beginning of significant chapters in our life. By their searing intensity these feelings put us in touch with that other great aspect of life which Pluto symbolizes, our unconscious, with all its fears and hidden depths as well as its riches and potential transforming power as it brings us to our core, to reunion with our essential being.

Pluto gives us the opportunity and the experiences which enable us to get in touch with our own inner power and intensity, but it often does so through forcing us to experience its opposite – powerlessness, and intense feelings from others. We experience these through circumstances to do with the house in which Pluto is placed. So if, for instance, Pluto is in the seventh house, we will experience power and intensity through marriage and partnership. We may do this by becoming attracted to someone who stirs in us extremely intense feelings which can be acute to the point of obsession, another Pluto characteristic. We may experience power through actually feeling power*less* in the face of this extreme emotion; and we may associate the emotion with the other person, believing that we need them because they make us feel alive and full of energy and power. And so we may become overdependent on the person concerned, feeling that on our own we are weak, helpless and unable to cope, thus becoming jealous, demanding and manipulative, losing touch with our own centre and sense of self-worth. Or we may find that we are attracted to powerful people who may also be demanding, dominating, judgemental and jealous, or who have an otherwise destructive effect on us. In all these cases what we are experiencing is power outside ourselves; and what we need to do, what Pluto teaches us to do, is to find power *within* ourselves. We have to build up our self-worth in the ways which I have described earlier in the book; through activities independent of our partner which we find invigorating and which bring us that feeling of intensity and 'aliveness' which Pluto makes us seek; through constantly letting go if we feel the need to hold and possess.

It's easy to see how we experience the power and intensity of Pluto when this planet is in the houses of the horoscope which show our relationships, whether these are partnerships, as I've described, or those with our children, friends, parents or people in authority. But we will also experience intense feelings and power (and its opposite side, powerlessness) when Pluto is in the other houses of the horoscope in connection with such things as money, possessions, ideas and studies, work or hobbies. When we feel the fury of anger or jealousy we need to get right into this burning, inner fire and realize that what we are feeling is our own power. It's no good stifling it, feeling we 'shouldn't' be experiencing it and hoping it will go away. Neither is it productive to take it out on other people. What we need to do is allow ourselves to feel it fully, knowing at the same time that it isn't the true us, so that we are experiencing it and yet at the same time watching it, like a storm sweeping across the sky. If we really flow with this fire, let it burn through us, we will almost certainly have to face losing our most cherished dreams and ideas about ourselves, our beliefs, relationships, achievements, security. The pain may be intense, and the more we try and hang on to things, to keep them the way they were, the worse it gets. We may feel as if we are being torn up by our roots, as if everything that we thought was secure in our life is being moved from under our feet. We may feel as if we are going to die. And, if we let this process take its course, owning the feelings, accepting that we, in common with every human being, have these dark and primal passions, a part of us is surely dying. That part is our ego, the part which keeps us separate from others, our 'shield', our shell. As we have the courage to let go and face the loss or the possibility of loss which Pluto brings, we find that an old part of us – and possibly quite a few aspects of our outer life – has gone; we have been broken down, cleansed and transformed. As a result, we are more in touch with that source of power within us, more alive, vital and full of energy, because there are no blocks in the way; we are regenerated.

Those who have had the courage to experience fully the Pluto process are never the same again. They have known what it is to face up to loss; to be swept through the seemingly never-ending depths;

to face and acknowledge that they have passions such as greed, jealousy, hate, anger, desire. As a result they have found their source of power, so they no longer feel powerless nor the need to dominate, which is part of the same thing; they have become comfortable with themselves and thus with other people, for they no longer need to project their own dark emotions on to them, nor to blame them. Having been transformed by the fires of suffering, they have a healing quality which is balm to others.

To sum up, matters ruled by Pluto include beginnings and endings of phases of life; breaking down, recycling, elimination and transformation; power and obsession; big business; underworld crime and gang warfare; the power of public opinion; the creative and regenerative processes of the body; the unconscious and modern depth psychology. In the body, it rules the gonads; its metal is plutonium.

The Cycle of Pluto

It takes Pluto 248.4 years to make a complete circuit of the Sun. If its orbit and speed were regular, Pluto would spend about 20 years in each sign. However, variations in its speed mean that at its slowest Pluto remains about 30 years in each sign, while at its fastest it spends about 15 years, roughly the same as Neptune. This means, of course, that even when Pluto is moving at its quickest, it will be in the same sign for a whole generation. It can, however, be in any of the twelve houses, depending on the rising sign, which changes approximately every 2 hours, so Pluto's house has more significance in an individual chart. Astrologer and counsellor Melanie Rheinhart says, 'Where Pluto moves, transformation follows', and Pluto's house shows the area of our life in which we are likely to experience the searing emotions which lead the way to transformation. And the stronger the influence of Pluto in the chart as a whole – if Pluto is rising, in the mid-heaven or making strong aspects to important planets, for instance – the more pressing the urge towards transformation will be.

However, Pluto's movement means that everyone experiences its influence in one way or another during their life. The house through

TABLE 1   Ages at which Pluto makes aspects for people born in the
twentieth century

Pluto aspect	Year of birth										
	1900 y-m	1910 y-m	1920 y-m	1930 y-m	1940 y-m	1950 y-m	1960 y-m	1970 y-m	1980 y-m	1990 y-m	2000 y-m
semi-sextile	28–3	26–6	24	21–3	18–6	16	13–6	12–6	12–3	13–3	13–9
sextile	49–6	46	41–3	37–3	33	29–3	25–6	24–6	22–3	27–3	27–9
square	65–6	61	55–3	50–6	45	41–6	37–3	36–6	38–6	44–9	51–6
trine	78–9	73	67	62–9	56–9	51–6	50–6	51–9	55–6	65–3	77–3
1st quincunx	90–9	84–9	79	72–9	69–6	67–9	66–6	70–3	78–9	92	–
opposition	100–9	97	92–3	89	85–3	84–9	86–9	93–9	106	–	–
2nd quincunx	116–2	112	108–3	106	103–3	107–9	111–6	121–9	–	–	–

The table shows the ages in years and months at which people born in
different decades in the twentieth century will get the various Pluto aspects.
So someone born in 1920 will get the sextile aged about 41 years 3 months,
while another born in 1960 would be aged about 25 years 6 months. The
dates have an uncertainty of plus or minus about 1 year because of the
effects of retrograde motion as the earth orbits the sun. In the next century
the uncertainty will increase to plus or minus 2 years.

The ages are accurate for the years shown, but should be interpolated for
dates of birth between the decades. So someone born in 1925 will have the
Pluto square aged about 52 years 10 months plus or minus 1 year.

---

which it is moving at any time indicates the area of life where transformation is currently taking place, slowly, inexorably. So Pluto brings
these fundamental changes, over a long period, in the first house, to
our personal life and outlook; in the second, to our values and
finances; in the third, to our education and views; in the fourth, to
our home and our attitude towards our roots. When it's passing
through the fifth house Pluto will affect our attitude towards children,
creativity and pleasure; in the sixth, to health and work; and in the
seventh, to partnership. In the eighth house, Pluto may transform

our attitude towards death, sex or shared finances; and, in the ninth, towards any religious beliefs we may hold. Pluto in the tenth house can bring great success, or the reverse and, possibly, a slow but significant change in our career. Lessons will come through friendship, groups and societies when Pluto is in the eleventh house, and, through our unconscious, the actions of secret enemies or charity work when it is in the twelfth house.

We are most aware of Pluto's influence when it reaches a degree which forms an aspect with one of the planets in our birth chart, or with its own position in the birth chart. Of course the aspects of Pluto to its own position are common to us all. We may not all experience Pluto in aspect to our Sun or Moon, but during the late twentieth and first half of the twenty-first centuries everyone of a certain age will have Pluto in a sextile and then a square to its own place.

The age at which we experience these Pluto aspects varies considerably depending on which decade we were born in. For instance, people who were born in 1900–10 experienced their Pluto sextile when they were around 49, while those born in the 1980s will get it when they are around 22. The approximate ages at which the Pluto aspects are most likely to occur are given in Table 1 (p. 86). I've explained the variations, and what they mean in terms of our development and the events in our lives, in detail in Part 2 of this book.

PART TWO

The Cycles through Life

CHILDHOOD

The first planetary cycles we experience are the return of the Moon to its birth position when we're 4 weeks old, followed by the returns of Mercury and Venus within the first year, and of the Sun on our first birthday. Later in life the effect of these cycles is very minor, and is usually lost among the other more powerful influences which come into operation. But in the case of a baby, experiencing them for the first time, they are relevant, and it's interesting to note that their timing coincides with certain aspects of development. It is significant, for example, that the first 4 weeks, or the first lunar cycle, is the period of time during which, in cultures such as the Vietnamese, a nursing mother remains in seclusion with her baby. This allows the mother to concentrate on getting to know and bond with her new baby, establishing the feeding process and building up her own emotional and physical resources. Such a period of peace and closeness to its mother, so well symbolized by the first lunar cycle, must, I think, be a perfect start for a baby as it makes the huge adjustment which birth demands.

Sometimes, when the planets are in retrograde motion at, or shortly after, our birth, they may go over their birth position, giving us a return of these planets at a very early age. This may show in some difficulties in our early months. In one case I know, in which Pluto made a return during the first year, the child experienced several operations in his early months, and in another, when Saturn, Uranus, Neptune and Pluto all made returns, there was a good deal of tension between the parents and domestic stress. Usually, however, the returns which follow that of the Moon are those of Mercury and Venus and occur at around 3 and 9 months respectively – times when communication, a Mercurial principle, and the early making of relationships, a Venusian one, are beginning.

The Sun completes its cycle on the first birthday as the child is

TABLE 2   Aspects made by slow planets during years 0 to 10

Age y-m	Period months	Planet	Cycle	Aspect	Strength 1 to 7
2–1	±7	Jupiter	1	1st sextile	**
3–1	±7	Jupiter	1	**1st square**	****
3–12	±7	Jupiter	1	1st trine	***
4–12	±7	Jupiter	1	1st quincunx	*
4–12	±8	Saturn	1	1st sextile	***
5–12	±7	Jupiter	1	**opposition**	****
6–12	±7	Jupiter	1	2nd quincunx	*
7–5	±8	Saturn	1	**1st square**	*****
7–12	±7	Jupiter	1	2nd trine	***
8–12	±7	Jupiter	1	**2nd square**	****
9–11	±8	Saturn	1	1st trine	****
9–12	±7	Jupiter	1	2nd sextile	**

The aspects printed in **bold** are those described in the text.
The aspects may apply up to three times during the periods shown.
The number of stars shows the approximate strength and importance of the
    aspect, on a scale of 1 to 7.
There are no Pluto aspects.

becoming much more of a character in its own right. From this time, mobility and independence are increasing rapidly; the weight gain is slowing down, so that by the time the first Mars cycle is completed, at around the second birthday, babyhood is over. Children of this age certainly express the characteristics of Mars with their fervent passions and boundless energy. It is at this stage that the child becomes aware of his will and tries it out in the temper tantrums for which the 'terrible twos' stage is noted. The stronger the Mars influence in the birth chart, the more forceful the child is likely to be at this stage, and the more he needs the opportunity to express his energy safely and constructively. The way in which a parent handles the situation can affect the child's attitude to his own power and anger in later life. When a 2- or 3-year-old is thwarted in what he wants to do, the

surge of Martian energy, or anger, which he feels may be overpower-
ing and sometimes even frightening to him. Once he gets caught up
in it, he does not know how to stop; all he is aware of is the power
which has overwhelmed him.

If a child is made to feel that it is wrong to experience anger, or
indeed any emotions, he may repress them and remain cut off from
his feelings in later life. A parent who takes their child's tantrums in
their stride, neither scolding the child for having one, nor giving in to
him because of it, simply making sure that the child is safe from
damaging himself or others and maybe holding him (if he likes that)
until the rage has passed, is helping him to grow up with a positive
attitude towards his own anger and feelings, so he is able to use them
constructively. Even in adults, the effect of Mars is to make us want
things immediately, to be pushing and 'me-first'. So, in a toddler
experiencing his first Mars return, with little experience of handling
his passions, these responses are only to be expected. They are normal.
Neither does a toddler's memory extend for more than a few minutes;
life has all the immediacy of Mars. So he is both easily diverted, and
unable to hold instructions and danger warnings in his head. It's no
good expecting a child of this age to make decisions about what he
wants to do, or to make bargains and promises. He simply cannot
remember for long enough. What he can do is to respond to a Mars
challenge such as 'Let's see if we can pick up all your bricks before
Daddy gets back', or 'I bet you can't put your books away before I've
laid the table.'

Mars is the planet of independence, and the first Mars return
coincides with the child's increasing awareness of himself as a separate
person. He naturally wants to do things for himself, to be less dependent and to take control of his life. It can be a frustrating time,
though, when he comes up against the limitations imposed by his
size, his competence, and the world around him. He needs to be
shown how to do things for himself, and to be given plenty of time
to do so; a child who is rushed and pressurized will feel even more
frustrated, and may express the Mars energy in a temper tantrum.
Patience, on the part of parents or carers, is the best antidote to
an overdose of Mars independence and frustration. A child whose
environment allows him the chance to explore and do things safely,
who has comfortable, unrestricting clothing which he can get as dirty

93

as he likes, and who knows that his mother or carer is near by, will get through this stage with the maximum benefit and the minimum disruption. It may be a testing and tiring time, but it is one which swiftly passes.

By a child's third birthday the influence of Mars is giving way to that of Jupiter, making the first square of its first cycle, expanding his horizons and his consciousness. He is beginning to discover the exciting world outside his home, to develop his ability to communicate and, increasingly, to reach out to other children and make his first friends. The Jupiter influence shows in the way in which the child begins to be able to grasp abstract ideas, to use his imagination and to develop his speech, which can all be encouraged through 'pretending' games. Plenty of play materials such as sand, water, dough or modelling clay, containers, bricks, large sheets of paper, crayons and books will all help a child's development at this stage. Listening patiently to what he has to say, giving him time to express himself without rushing him, and respecting what he does and says, all help a child to grow up confident and with a sense of self-worth, as he moves through this expansive Jupiter phase and into the next, the first Jupiter opposition, which occurs around 5 to 6 years. For most children this coincides with the beginning of school life, expanding the boundaries still further and stimulating the mind, both so typical of Jupiter. An opposition aspect always gives us the chance to reflect and compare. So the widening of our horizons which our first Jupiter opposition brings gives us the chance to look back at ourselves; for the first time we begin to evaluate and compare ourselves, our home and our parents with those of our peers. And we reach out to others, learning to make friends, widening our social sphere.

We do not experience any major aspects in the Saturn cycle until we are 6 to 7 years old. Astrologically, this means that our boundaries, a principle of Saturn, are unformed; we haven't yet got a very strong protective shell around ourselves. So until this point we are extremely open to what is going on around us; our experiences and the beliefs about life and about ourselves which we pick up during this early period of our life before the first Saturn square make a lasting impression on us. They will be with us for the rest of our life. We pick up beliefs and memories from the way in which we are treated. For instance, the experience of simply being a small child leaves most of us with the feeling that we're not very clever and we mustn't make a fuss. How many people do you know who begin nearly every sentence with 'I hope you won't mind me saying so, but . . .', or 'I'm sorry to bother you, but . . .'? If our parents have been too busy to listen to what we have to say, or have dismissed our views as silly or unimportant, we may also pick up the belief that our view doesn't count and we have nothing relevant to say. If we have been frequently told not to make a fuss, or 'Don't cry, it will upset your mother', or 'Big boys don't cry', we may have picked up the belief that such emotions are 'wrong', and learnt to suppress them. Parents who listen attentively and non-critically while their children tell them how they *really* feel, and allow them to pour out their fears and worries, are few and far between. We quickly learn, too, the kind of behaviour which is likely to bring the best response from our parents or carers, and get us what we want. This may be to be good, kind and polite, to look pretty, to smile and do what we're told; or it may be to kick and shout and scream, or in other words to rebel. Many of us are still responding to these beliefs long after our childhood days have passed. Many of us grow up constantly apologizing for what we say and feel, simply because of such childhood beliefs; we may feel that we have to look attractive and to hide our feelings behind a smile, in order to be acceptable to others. If as a child we found we got our goodies by being the well-behaved or 'well-adapted' child, we feel that we want to fit in, that we mustn't make a fuss, rock the boat. If we found that rebel behaviour brought the best results, we may continue to react in that way. I certainly know 30-, 40- and 50-year-olds who are still so hooked into the rebel reaction that 'Why should I?' is their immediate response to any request or order. We cannot avoid picking up these childhood beliefs, but as adults we can learn to be aware of them and how they are limiting us.

As well as what we're told, and the things which happen to us during these first 6 to 7 years, we are also acutely aware of what is going on in our environment at an unconscious level. Having not yet experienced a major aspect in the cycle of Saturn, the planet of barriers, it's as if there's no clear line between our own unconscious and that of the people around us. So we're highly impressionable and open to the feelings and unexpressed thoughts surrounding us. We can be deeply affected by the fears and repressed feelings which our parents have buried in their unconscious. It's almost as if there is a merging of the unconscious of the child and that of parent or parents. It's no good parents trying to cover something up, or saying one thing and doing another; the child will instinctively know the truth. This has been shown many times by therapists working with disturbed children who, through their own dreams, express the fears and feelings which their parents have repressed. There is a most interesting chapter on this subject in *The Inner World of Childhood*, by Frances G. Wickes, who says:

> We are all at times at the mercy of unknown forces within ourselves. We must therefore look carefully at the nature of the underlying motives if we feel any dislike or resentment toward a child. It is possible that this child stands between us and something which we desire or which arouses things in our subconscious which we fear to face. Instead of trying to forget the antagonistic feeling we must examine it with the greatest care and remain conscious of its existence when we are dealing with the child. Our whole attitude toward childish traits and individual children must be highly conscious and lovingly understanding.
>
> The whole mechanism of projection is repeatedly employed in cases where the parents have resentments toward each other. The things which they repress in their conscious relations are vented upon the children. Often one child who in some physical aspect or mental characteristic resembles the hated parent will receive the full brunt of this projected hatred while the others go scotfree. The parent reacts toward the child as though he actually were the other parent. Since the love situation is repressed, the unconscious assumes control, and the emotions so displayed are of a primitive emotional type. Such a child, to whom normal love is denied, will often become deceitful, cheating and stealing to obtain praise and approval.

Being honest about how we feel, looking within ourselves for the cause, rather than blaming other people or circumstances, and facing the dark parts of ourselves, acknowledging and accepting them, helps us to recognize when we are projecting our own feelings on our child or, indeed, on anyone else in our journey through life, as I've explained on pages 58–59.

One of the main principles which Saturn stands for is discipline and authority, and often with this first Saturn square come our first experiences of receiving these from people other than our parents. Frequently it is not an altogether happy experience – 'shades of the prison-house begin to close', as Wordsworth put it. Since I have been working on this book I have come across many cases where this Saturn square coincided with early difficulties at school, and often the child felt unable to talk about them at the time. Perhaps it would be helpful if parents were aware of the timing of the Saturn square so that they could be sensitive to possible problems that the child is going through at this time.

At around the time of the Saturn square the child is also learning the process of what M. Scott Peck, in *The Road Less Travelled*, calls 'delaying gratification', whereby he disciplines himself to get the tiresome tasks over first before enjoying himself, to let other children have their turn first, or to eat the cake before the icing. This is valuable self-control which provides a vital foundation for later, but it is much influenced by what the child sees and experiences around him, and the way in which he is treated. As Scott Peck says:

> For children to develop the capacity to delay gratification, it is necessary for them to have self-disciplined role models, a sense of self-worth, and a degree of trust in the safety of their existence. These 'possessions' are ideally acquired through the self-discipline and consistent, genuine caring of their parents; they are the most precious gifts of themselves that mothers and fathers can bequeath. When these gifts have not been proffered by one's parents, it is possible to acquire them from other sources, but in that case the process of their acquisition is invariably an uphill struggle, often of lifelong duration and often unsuccessful.

The Saturn square can arrive at the same time as the first Jupiter opposition, and when this happens, since these influences are so contradictory, it can be a particularly confusing time for a child. The Jupiterian urge to reach outwards will be tempered by fear, or by restrictions which may be imposed on the child by his parents, or by circumstances. So there will be a mixture of expansion and contraction, optimism and fear. Parents who are sensitive to this can help their child to expand his boundaries at a pace which he can cope with, aiming to achieve that delicate balance of giving the child the support he needs without being over-protective and holding him back.

The final Jupiter square occurs when we are about 8 or 9, once again urging us to move outwards and upwards, stimulating our brain, giving us new boundaries to exceed, new goals to attain. This is a time of mental and physical stimulation, with increasing opportunities for friendship, sport and activities outside the home. Children may take up interests and hobbies such as Cub Scouts and Brownies, ballet, riding or gymnastics. Jupiter is widening their horizons by the day, and there is the need for freedom, adventure and independence.

When we are between 11 and 12 years old, Jupiter completes its first cycle and we experience our first Jupiter return. This coincides with the completion of the first phase of childhood and the growth-spurt which shows the beginning of puberty and our passage into the teen years and adulthood. As Jupiter arrives back at its birth position, our bodies expand and begin to change; we have to re-evaluate ourselves and our place in society. We are no longer children, but we still have to make that transition into adulthood. It's a time when we have to adjust our view of ourselves. We are not quite sure where we fit into society, because we are no longer children, yet we are not accepted as adult. The puberty rites of other cultures are helpful in defining the point at which we become adult, making this transition easier. In Britain, many children make the change from primary school to secondary school at around the time of their first Jupiter return, often moving from a relatively small school to one which is much larger. Now, instead of being the oldest and biggest children, they find themselves the youngest and smallest. Again, social adjustments have to be made. This is also the age of hero-worship – another Jupiterian principle. We find someone whom we admire so that we can model ourselves on them and have some sense of direction in a time of change and confusion. Our relationships with our peers are also tremendously important at this time; we measure ourselves against them and have a desperate need to be admired, approved of, respected, liked, accepted and loved. Our dress, behaviour, the kind of music we listen to, and so on, have to conform, so that we feel we fit in with our group.

As childhood draws to a close and the teenage years beckon, I'd like to end with another thoughtful passage from Frances G. Wickes:

> If a child has not the experience and development, the sense of security and trust that are the outgrowth of the proper parent–child relation, he will be unable to cope with the greater demands of adult relationships. But he should not remain in these relationships too long, any more than he should repeat grades. The relationship of the parent and child should be continuously progressive. Its aim should be the liberation of the child as an individual, so that he may follow his own path whether or not that path is the one that we would have chosen for him. He should be united to us only by the bonds of comradeship and understanding. In the larger sense we can choose nothing for our children. We can try to choose our own path clearly and then use our clearness of vision to help the child upon his own way.

TEENS

In our early teens we experience a group of aspects, all at very much the same time, the like of which we'll not experience again until we reach the age of 40. Between 13 and 14 we experience aspects from Uranus, Neptune, Jupiter, Saturn and sometimes Pluto too. Uranus brings the urge for change and possibly change itself, while Neptune unsettles us with vague longings and confusion; Jupiter gives us the desire to expand and reach out, while Saturn holds us back. And Pluto, if it's also part of the cocktail, puts us in touch with deep, dark feelings, passion and power. Quite a lot of different influences to handle, especially when it's your first experience of some of them, and a clear astrological reason for the turmoil which many people feel in their teens.

As I've explained before, the exact timing of the aspects varies from person to person, since the planetary motions are not completely regular. This fact was brought home to me only recently when my youngest daughter had just turned 14, we were looking up the dates of these cycles for her and her close friends. To our surprise we found that although she is 6 months younger than the rest of her group, she in fact gets all these aspects a month or more ahead of the others, since Saturn, Uranus, Neptune and Pluto all began a period of retrograde movement in the spring or summer of 1978, so, when Claire was born in mid-July, they were all earlier in their signs than in December 1977 and January 1978 when her friends were born.

Usually one of the first of these aspects which we experience is the Uranus sextile, and this, as you might expect, generally coincides with a time of change. A sextile aspect is harmonious, and it's one of opportunity. This influence, then, often brings change which may lead to opportunity. Actually, I believe that every change, indeed every event in our lives, for that matter, is also an opportunity, although it can be extremely painful too. However, because of the nature of the aspect, this particular time of change is easier than some, since the harmonious aspect means that it's easier for us to adapt. It is in fact natural for us to want to make changes at this time, since these are part of the process of becoming independent of our parents. This is also a time when we get an overwhelming desire to be ourselves; to find out who *we* are as distinct from our parents and family and to begin the process of breaking way. It's both natural and right for us to take steps in this process; indeed, the problems come if we have over-protective parents who try to shield us too much, or other circumstances in our life which hold us back from taking the strides which our inner being is crying out to take. If this happens, the next Uranus aspect, when we are in our late teens, will be harder; and if we cannot experience *that* one fully, we'll have to handle a great deal of Uranian energy in our early forties at the time of the Uranus opposition, and that's a much tougher time to deal with it.

For many people the changes which Uranus brings at around 13 or 14 are natural and inevitable. For me, they coincided with a disruptive time when the grammar school which I attended was threatened with closure. I did not find this too difficult to handle; what really unsettled me was that my parents initiated a public campaign to fight the proposed closure, issuing leaflets outside the school gates, giving interviews to the local press and sending a large petition to the Minister of Education. This fits in with the fact that in my birth chart Uranus is in the fourth house, which shows the home and family. In the end the school did have to close, in spite of a brilliant campaign, and I had to change schools in the middle of my 'O' level course. By then, though, the Uranus aspect was behind me and, inwardly, I did not feel nearly as unsettled by the change of school as I had by the publicity of my parents' save-the-school campaign. During the campaign I can remember wanting to disown my parents, to have nothing to do with them, because of the embarrassment their public activities were causing me. My eldest daughter, Katy, also experienced a period of considerable change and upheaval at the time of her Uranus sextile when her father changed his job. We moved from the house in which she'd been born, and where she had been extremely happy, and her youngest sister, Claire, was born. For both Katy and me the Uranus sextile was quite stressful. Some-

TABLE 3A   Aspects made by slow planets during years 10 to 20

Age y-m	Period months	Planet	Cycle	Aspect	Strength 1 to 7
11–11	±7	Jupiter	1	**return**	****
12–4	±8	Saturn	1	1st quincunx	***
13–10	±9	Neptune	1	**1st semi-sextile**	***
13–11	±7	Jupiter	2	1st sextile	**
14–1	±9	Uranus	1	**1st sextile**	****
14–10	±8	Saturn	1	**opposition**	******
14–11	±7	Jupiter	2	**1st square**	****
15–11	±7	Jupiter	2	1st trine	***
16–11	±7	Jupiter	2	1st quincunx	*
17–3	±8	Saturn	1	2nd quincunx	***
17–10	±7	Jupiter	2	**opposition**	****
18–10	±7	Jupiter	2	2nd quincunx	*
19–9	±8	Saturn	1	2nd trine	****
19–10	±7	Jupiter	2	2nd trine	***

The aspects printed in **bold** are those described in the text.

The aspects may apply up to three times during the periods shown.

The number of stars shows the approximate strength and importance of the aspect, on a scale of 1 to 7.

The ages in years and months at which Pluto is likely to aspect its natal position for people in this age group are shown for various birth dates in the table below. As usual there will be some variation due to retrograde motion.

TABLE 3B   Aspects made by Pluto during years 10 to 20

Pluto aspect	Year of birth										
	1900 y-m	1910 y-m	1920 y-m	1930 y-m	1940 y-m	1950 y-m	1960 y-m	1970 y-m	1980 y-m	1990 y-m	2000 y-m
semi-sextile					18–6	16–0	13–6	12–6	12–3	13–3	13–9

102

times it's less so; much depends on where it is placed in the birth chart, and the general planetary set-up. For instance, in the case of one of Claire's friends, Anna, Uranus made the sextile aspect to its own place three times, and each time coincided with a holiday abroad without her parents. As she had not been away on her own for any length of time before, these times of separation made quite an impact on her; she felt the need to be self-reliant, and became more independent as a result.

Children need to begin the process of separation at this time and as parents we can help them by being sensitive to their needs; by giving them the information and, if necessary, the opportunities they need. Some children, if they are clingy and unsure of themselves, need a gentle push, and perhaps to be allowed to become independent in small steps, rather than in leaps. On the other hand, outgoing, adventurous children may need guidance and practical advice to prevent them from making sweeping changes and taking on more than they can handle, although it is not always possible to do so. In his book *The Road Less Travelled*, M. Scott Peck describes his experience of following his own inner guidance when he was 14, which was the time of his Uranus sextile. Deeply unhappy at his school, having tried to adapt to it for $2\frac{1}{2}$ years, he returned home for the Easter holidays and informed his parents that he was not returning. His parents told him that he must be crazy and immediately took him to a psychiatrist who stated that he was depressed and recommended a month's stay in a psychiatric hospital, giving him a day to decide whether or not that was what he wanted. He began to doubt his own sanity. As he says:

> I was terrified. But then, at the moment of my greatest despair, from my unconscious there came a sequence of words, like a strange disembodied oracle from a voice that was not mine: 'The only real security in life lies in relishing life's insecurity.' Even if it meant being crazy and out of step with all that seemed holy, I had decided to be me. I rested. In the morning I went to see the psychiatrist again and told him that I would never return to Exeter [the school] but that I was ready to enter his hospital. I had taken the leap into the unknown. I had taken my destiny into my own hands.

The writer and poet Herman Hesse was certainly acting under

the influence of *his* Uranus sextile when, at the end of 1889, at the age of 12½, he began to rebel against formal education, finally deciding to leave school and educate himself. Of course it's worth remembering that for many people in the past in England (my father's generation, for instance) the Uranus sextile coincided with leaving school: a clear break with childhood.

At around the same time as the Uranus sextile, when we're about 14, Neptune also makes its first aspect. It's only a semi-sextile, so is fairly weak, but Neptune moves so slowly and, as this is our first experience of this planet's cycle, I think it's worth mentioning. Neptune is the planet of glamour, illusion, aspiration and longing, tying in with the idealism and uncertainty which we feel at this time and the susceptibility of this age group to fashions and fads, role models and advertisements. If we do in fact experience the Neptune sextile at exactly the same time as the Uranus sextile, this can be a strange period when we may be open to all kinds of influences and find it difficult to keep in touch with reality. Neptune is the planet concerned with drugs, alcohol and altered states of consciousness and this influence, together with the Uranian urge to rebel and be unconventional, shows, astrologically, why this age group is particularly vulnerable.

Another powerful influence which I should mention here is the first aspect of the Pluto cycle. Again, it's only a semi-sextile aspect, but because, like Neptune, Pluto moves so slowly, its effect is noticeable. It's interesting that, because of Pluto's changing speed, the age at which different generations experience it varies by some years. My generation, for example, experienced the Pluto semi-sextile at around the age of 16, but my daughter Claire and her friends had it when they were around 12 years old, as will those children born in the 1980s and 1990s. This ties in with the speed with which Claire's generation seem to be growing up – the 'age 12-going-on-16' syndrome – and their early introduction to the Pluto issues of violence, sex, power and pain through the media. This contact of Pluto with its own place may put us in touch with intense emotions; we may become acutely aware of the suffering of humanity or of the animal kingdom for the first time; we may feel the strength of our own sexuality, or the stirring of the deep, dark feelings which we all have hidden in our unconscious, perhaps through strange dreams or the heavy moods which hit us inexplicably. My mother's generation did not experience this Pluto aspect until their mid twenties: no wonder they say today's children lose their innocence early!

At around 14 to 15 we experience the first square of our second Jupiter cycle. Jupiter gives us the urge, and frequently the opportunity too, to widen our horizons, but at the same time the square aspect indicates that there is effort involved. That is why, as I explained earlier, a square aspect, which is technically one of conflict, brings more obvious events than a trine, which is more harmonious. It's the stress of the square which causes us to take action and make things happen. So at the time of the Jupiter square we experience pressure to expand which stretches us beyond our limits and helps us develop educationally, physically and socially. For many teenagers, the Jupiter square coincides with increasing opportunities for matters ruled by Jupiter: education, sport and travel. For Claire's friend Anna, for instance, it coincided with her last Uranus sextile and a school trip to Germany; for my daughter Katy, with a particularly memorable holiday in France; for me, with learning astrology and taking part in Girl Guiding with great enthusiasm. Along with the opportunities and expansion comes some stress as we try to adapt our image to fit in with those of our contemporaries and also of our role-models. We need to come to terms with an increasingly mature body, to make tentative moves towards members of the opposite sex. At the same time we probably experience some conflict with our parents or author-ity figures as they find it difficult to allow us the freedom we require. Indeed, parental opposition to this may be reinforced by other cir-cumstances in our lives at this time which seem to hold us back and go against our Jupiterian urge to expand and move forward. These are explained by the opposition of Saturn to its own place, which may happen at exactly the same time as the Jupiter square or may be separated by some months.

The Saturn opposition is a powerful and important aspect. It marks the half-way point in Saturn's first cycle, during which we form our ego – that protective shield of concepts and beliefs about ourselves that makes up a great deal of our personality. Being an opposition, this aspect of Saturn gives us the chance to look back at what we've already achieved and to evaluate ourselves against the Saturnine aspects of life: authority figures and the disciplined structure of our lives. We chafe against authority – or feel insecure (another Saturnine quality) if it isn't present in our lives – and in the process we discover our own inner discipline. By pitting ourselves against the Saturn factor in our outer life, we become aware of our inner Saturn and become more adult and responsible as a result. We are most likely not aware of what is happening at the time, however. What we notice are the testing and frustrating conditions and situations which confront us during this period. These, being of the nature of Saturn, feel as if they are limiting us, preventing us from doing what we would really like, cramping our style. They may be imposed by parents or authority figures forcing us to work for examinations, get home by a certain time at night, obey rules and regulations. Or the Saturn restriction in our life may come from circumstances totally beyond our control; we may be acutely aware, perhaps for the first time, of our parents' lack of money which prevents us from having the same clothes or lifestyle as our friends; we may have an unexpected burden of responsibility placed on our shoulders; we may experience a period of ill-health.

For a friend of mine the Saturn opposition coincided with a sad time when, because he did well at school, he was pushed up into a higher class where he had no friends and felt very lonely. The interesting thing was that he'd had exactly the same experience some 6 or 7 years earlier at his first Saturn square. It's often the case that we get a series of similar experiences throughout a planet's cycle, each aspect bringing a variation on what becomes a familiar theme. Whatever the exact situation, whenever we experience an aspect in the Saturn cycle in our lives we have to come to terms with ourselves and our life as they are at this point. You simply cannot get round Saturn; if you manage to get over one set of barriers, another set just comes along to replace them. The way to handle Saturn is to accept the restrictions and look for the possibilities they offer. This, of course, is difficult at any age and particularly so at 14. This Saturnine period does not last for ever, however – perhaps a year or 18 months, as Saturn approaches its position, passes by, then perhaps retrogrades past it and then forwards again.

What happens at this time, and how we handle it, can affect us for the rest of our lives. Most children are working for the examinations which provide the foundation for further education or for getting a job. Work put in at this time makes all the difference to their future prospects, material security and chances of success in the world – all Saturnine qualities. Although work can be re-done and examinations re-taken, it is much harder the second time around. Far better to knuckle down now when Saturn asks us to, rather than waste energy trying to avoid it. This, I think, is where a knowledge of astrology can help young teenagers; an understanding of what is happening and the timing involved can make Saturn's restrictions easier to bear. They are also easier to handle if a child has been given a basic framework of discipline, which, as I mentioned when describing the first Saturn square, may have been restricting at the time but makes subsequent Saturn aspects, like this one, easier to handle, because the tools to do so are already there and in use.

The exact way in which this opposition works out depends on our birth chart and, in particular, on the sign and house in which Saturn is placed and the aspects which Saturn receives from other planets. The influence of all these will be activated by the opposition of Saturn to its own place. In my own case, Saturn is in the sixth house of work. So, guess what, the Saturn opposition forced me to work extremely hard. The reason, as I've mentioned earlier, was that the school I was attending closed down and I had to change schools half-way through my two-year 'O' level course. At my new school the courses were not identical: the subjects were being taught in a different order, so I found I had missed important chunks of the syllabus, and I realized that in some subjects I had been badly taught because the standard of teaching at my old school had deteriorated as staff had left because of the possibility of the school closing. So I knew I had to work very hard indeed to catch up. This was a difficult and lonely time, but one in which I developed work-skills, as well as basic educational qualifications, which have been useful ever since.

For Jane Fonda, when Saturn, which in her birth chart is in the second house of money, reached the half-way mark in its cycle and opposed its place from the eighth house which signifies, amongst other things, death, her mother committed suicide and Jane and her brother were the chief beneficiaries of her wealth. You can see how precisely the house-position of Saturn worked out in her case. But what is also very interesting is how her mother's death affected her subsequent achievements. Years later, when she was interviewed about the success of her Workout Program and the movement which followed it, Jane revealed how much her mother's suicide, at a time when she feared the effects of getting older, had affected her own attitude towards age and her body and, hence, the Workout. This, in turn, brought her a great deal of wealth, absolutely in keeping with the position of Saturn in the financial sector of her birth chart.

Teenagers who fight against the hard work and rules of Saturn find that in the end this only leads to *more* Saturn: greater restriction through disciplinary action; or lack of money because they haven't gained the qualifications necessary to earn more; and lack of self-worth. I believe that children need certain rules and regulations at this time; and if they have a role-model of parents or authority figures who are disciplined and hard-working, this helps them to acquire these qualities themselves. They will undoubtedly kick against them but, psychologically, they require them for their development. They need to be able to confront Saturn both within themselves and outside, and to test the structure thoroughly. They feel, instinctively, that if their parents care, they will set boundaries.

Although, as I've shown in other sections, all the planets and the signs of the zodiac rule specific parts of the body and its functions, Saturn rules the physical body in general. At the time of Saturn opposition we are acutely aware of our body and, as a result, we appraise, judge and evaluate it. We may feel worried about spots or puppy-fat, or the fact that we do not have the shape and features of our favourite celebrity. We are also coming to terms with a rapidly maturing adult body and the responsibilities and restrictions which this brings with it. I believe that we pick up our basic attitude to sex and, indeed, to our bodies in general, from a very early age; perhaps even before we are born, through the legacy of the unconscious which our parents pass on to us, along with our genes and physical characteristics. Certainly as young children we pick up our parents' ease or lack of ease with sex and the physical body, and this colours, perhaps unconsciously, our own attitude towards our sexuality. Parents who see sex as a natural and joyful aspect of life, albeit one which calls for a sense of responsibility plus practical information, make this transition natural and easy – but in order to do this the parents need to have been very honest with themselves and to have worked through their own guilt and hang-ups about it. It's then possible to talk naturally and openly with their teenage children; to discuss their fears and worries about sex in a way which enables them to feel comfortable. I do feel that there is a great deal of pressure on young teenagers to get sexually involved before they really want to, because they feel it's the thing to do. This is encouraged by what they see on films and television and also read in teenage magazines and books, which can be sexually explicit but often do not discuss emotional or practical issues, or say, 'Hey, it's perfectly OK not to get sexually involved until you're ready.' Teenagers need to be able to talk to open, sensible and non-judgemental adults at this time when they are trying to work out their own morals and approach. They certainly need to feel able to speak to someone – and to know that they will be listened to and helped if they are worried about abuse or unwelcome sexual advances, whether from a stranger or from someone they know well. If this has occurred the teenager takes on a great burden of guilt, feeling that it has happened because of something 'wrong' with them. They need to be able to talk about it and to be reassured that there is no blame whatsoever attached to them. On the other hand, young teenagers may not be aware of their sexual attractiveness, which can lead to situations which they do not want and cannot handle; so they need wise, practical guidance on this, too. I feel that one of the greatest gifts that parents or carers can give to teenagers experiencing this Saturn contact is a sense of their value as individuals; an awareness of their own special qualities, appearance and uniqueness. A good sense of self-worth at this age can help so much in their relationships and their emotional and educational development and help them to reach their highest potential.

The next major aspect we experience is the opposition of Jupiter to its own place when we are 17 to 18. As we have seen, Jupiter is the planet which brings expansion into our lives and helps us to reach upwards and outwards. Because it's an opposition aspect we again get a period of evaluation, measuring ourselves against others academically and also socially. As I explained in the chapter on Jupiter, the planet also stands for higher education and foreign travel. I find it interesting that we experience this opposition at a time when our life is opening out, with, for many teenagers, the opportunity to travel, to go to university, or to widen our horizons by starting work.

Perhaps we'll never be so free in our lives, or have so many options to choose from, as at this point.

At very much the same time as the Jupiter opposition, around 17 to 18, we may also experience our first really testing aspect of the Uranus cycle, the square – though it may not happen until we are in our early twenties. Uranus stands for, among other things, the principles of change, independence and individuality. It often brings the desire to tear up roots and make a fresh start; there is a strong 'gotta be me' feeling about it. All emotions which any 18- to 22-year-old will recognize. Very often this first Uranus square coincides with big changes: leaving school and making the major transition to work, university or training college; in some cases, getting married; living away from home for the first time and being responsible for ourselves. Although this may be exactly what we want, and, indeed, we may have been longing for this moment, it probably still comes as something of a wrench for most people. Sometimes when we make the break with our family and roots, it is so traumatic that we have a 'rebound' period when we return home. It is interesting to note that this often happens if, through retrograde motion, Uranus makes the square aspect three times – once on its normal route, again as it retraces its steps, and then a third and final time as it gets going again. Each time the Uranus square becomes exact, it coincides with a big change.

There was no to-ing and fro-ing, however (and no retrograde motion of Uranus) in the case of my eldest daughter, Katy, who made a major change at the time of her Uranus square. Our family life was happy, and as a local college offered the course she wanted to do she had enrolled there and had been accepted for their degree course in art and drama. She was intending to live at home. With all the details fixed, she went abroad on holiday with a girlfriend – her first foreign holiday on her own. While away, she had a holiday romance and fell deeply in love. She returned home wondering whether she would ever see the man (who lived in Belfast) again, but a couple of weeks before she was due to start her course, he and a friend invited her and her girlfriend to go and stay with them for a few days. While she was there, she knew that, whatever happened, she wanted to live near him. So, acting with a decisiveness and courage, not to say recklessness, typical of Uranus, she took her destiny in her own hands. By several lucky coincidences, she managed to obtain one of the coveted places in the English and drama course at Ulster Poly (now part of Ulster University) and arranged for accommodation at the Poly. Then all she had to do was return home, just days before she was due to begin her original course, and face her irate parents. This was absolutely typical of her birth chart, with Uranus placed in the house which shows authority, parents and career. She said, 'I was absolutely determined. I *knew* it was right for me. I have never been so sure of anything. If I hadn't been able to go to university in Belfast, I'd have gone anyway and got a job there. This was also an important time for me because it was the first time I'd ever really stood up to my father. When I came back for Christmas, I knew I could never live at home again. I'd gained independence and confidence in myself as a person. I really grew up at that point.' As one of her parents, I found it a great shock when she returned from her few days in Belfast and announced her intentions. On the face of it, it seemed irrational to alter all her plans on the strength of a holiday romance, not to mention my fears about her living amid the dangers and violence of Belfast. I must say that this was an occasion in my life when I found astrology really helpful. When I looked at Katy's chart and saw that she was just approaching the beginning of her Uranus square, I knew that the break was inevitable. If she hadn't gone then, I have no doubt that she would have done so when the aspect became exact, although it's only recently that she told me that even if she hadn't been able to fix up her course she would have gone anyway. Such is the power of Uranus!

In fact it is not unusual for this combination of aspects from Jupiter and Uranus to bring, for a girl particularly, marriage or a serious relationship which affects her deeply; she did just that for me. In her book *Passages*, Gail Sheehy makes the point that girls who break away from their parents by getting married rather than experiencing some time on their own are not usually able to cut the ties with home and family fully, which can lead to difficulties later. It is actually very healthy and satisfactory to be able to make a big change at the time of the Uranus square. If we only half do it, or if it is stifled because of parental or other pressures, we tend to have to meet the situation again later, perhaps at the time of the Uranus opposition in our early forties, and then it isn't nearly so easy to handle. As Gail Sheehy goes on to say:

The tasks of this passage are to locate ourselves in a peer group role, a sex role, an anticipated occupation, an ideology or world view. As a result, we gather the impetus to leave home physically and the identity to *begin* leaving home emotionally. Even as one part of us seeks to be an individual, another part longs to restore the safety and comfort of merging with another. Thus one of the most popular myths of this passage is: we can piggyback our development by attaching to a Stronger One. But people who marry during this time often prolong financial and emotional ties to the family and relatives that impede them from becoming self-sufficient.

A stormy passage through the Pulling Up Roots years will probably facilitate the normal progression of the adult life cycle. If one doesn't have an identity crisis at this point, it will erupt during a later transition, when the penalties may be harder to bear.

So, even if we follow the Uranian urge to break away, and it doesn't work out as well as in the case I've described, who is to say that we've made a mistake? The experience was no doubt exactly what we needed for our growth and development. It might well have been far more damaging to us had we gone against all that we believed, stifled the promptings of Uranus, and done something which felt boring and 'wrong', perhaps to please our parents or others in authority.

TWENTIES

As we enter this decade, some of us may be experiencing the Uranus square, or the repercussions of the changes which took place then, while for others these are still to come. Princess Margaret, for instance, experienced the square in 1952–3, when she was 22 to 23, and the aspect coincided with her love affair with Group-Captain Peter Townsend. During this time she experienced not only the emotions of falling in love, but also separation, another quality of the planet Uranus, when she and Townsend were parted. Unfortunately for her, it was considered that it would be disastrous for the Queen to give permission for her sister to marry a man who had been divorced, particularly in Coronation year. So Peter Townsend was sent to Belgium to take up a job as an air attaché, while Princess Margaret continued with her public duties in Britain, convinced that they would be able to get married in the summer of 1955, by which time she would be 25 and would no longer need the Queen's permission to do so. By then, however, the Uranus square had passed. Great pressure was put on Princess Margaret to try to persuade her not to marry Peter Townsend. She was told that if she married a divorced man she could not remain in line of succession, and would have to live in exile outside Britain. On 31 October 1955 she told the nation of her decision not to marry him. I wonder, however, had she had a thorough Uranian rebellion and ignored the pressure, whether she would have had an easier time in her early forties when she experienced a particularly bumpy period at the Uranus opposition, as we'll see later.

Once the Uranus square of our late teens or very early twenties is behind us, we experience a series of Jupiter and Saturn aspects; later there are two harmonious ones, from Neptune and Uranus, followed, just before we reach the age of 30, by one of the major turning-points in the planetary cycles, the Saturn return, when Saturn

TABLE 4A   Aspects made by slow planets during years 20 to 30

Age y-m	Period months	Planet	Cycle	Aspect	Strength 1 to 7
20–10	±7	Jupiter	2	**2nd square**	****
21–1	±9	Uranus	1	**1st square**	******
21–10	±7	Jupiter	2	2nd sextile	**
22–2	±8	Saturn	1	**2nd square**	*****
23–10	±7	Jupiter	2	**return**	****
24–8	±8	Saturn	1	2nd sextile	***
25–9	±7	Jupiter	3	1st sextile	**
26–9	±7	Jupiter	3	**1st square**	****
27–7	±9	Neptune	1	**1st sextile**	****
27–9	±7	Jupiter	3	1st trine	***
28–1	±9	Uranus	1	**1st trine**	*****
28–9	±7	Jupiter	3	1st quincunx	*
29–7	±8	Saturn	1	**return**	*******
29–9	±7	Jupiter	3	**opposition**	****

The aspects printed in **bold** are those described in the text.

The aspects may apply up to three times during the periods shown.

The number of stars shows the approximate strength and importance of the aspect, on a scale of 1 to 7.

The ages in years and months at which Pluto is likely to aspect its natal position for people in this age group are shown for various birth dates in the table below. As usual there will be some variation due to retrograde motion.

TABLE 4B   Aspects made by Pluto during years 20 to 30

Pluto aspect	Year of birth										
	1900 y-m	1910 y-m	1920 y-m	1930 y-m	1940 y-m	1950 y-m	1960 y-m	1970 y-m	1980 y-m	1990 y-m	2000 y-m
semi-sextile	28–3	26–6	24	21–3							
sextile						29–3	25–6	24–6	22–3	27–3	27–9

gets back to the position in our chart that it occupied at our birth. So, in general, from an astrological point of view, this is a decade of stabilization and expansion, often beginning and ending with major change and turbulence.

Our twenties are an exhilarating and challenging time, for there is much to be done. We have to create a picture of ourselves and our life's work which will fill us with energy and optimism, inspire us and motivate us towards our goals. We have to find a role-model or mentor if possible; and we have to learn how to make close relationships with others while at the same time retaining the sense of ourselves and our values which we have already discovered. So, tentatively, we begin to build the structure of our lives.

The first influences we experience in our early twenties are those of that contradictory pair, Saturn and Jupiter, each making the final square of their respective cycle. So we have from Saturn an acute awareness of our responsibilities; the need for stability and security. From Jupiter comes the urge and opportunity to expand our life, gain new experiences and widen our sphere of influence. Gail Sheehy could be describing these two squares when she says of this period:

> Two impulses, as always, are at work. One is to build a firm, safe structure for the future by making strong commitments, to 'be set'. Yet people who slip into ready-made form without much self-examination are likely to find themselves *locked in*. The other urge is to explore and experiment, keeping any structure tentative and therefore easily reversible. Taken to the extreme, these are people who skip from one trial job and one limited personal encounter to another, spending their twenties in a *transient* state.

The Jupiter square, which occurs when we are 20 to 21, brings a sense of freedom. In Britain it used to coincide with 'coming of age', until this was lowered to 18. In any case, there is the sense of being free and of wanting to move forward, to push out the boundaries again. We may be leaving university; we may be experiencing the pleasure of a wide and full social life; we may be becoming deeply involved in a committed relationship or getting married. Jupiter may give us the feeling that life is opening up ahead of us, with many opportunities. Or we may feel restless – another Jupiter characteristic – not knowing what direction we want to go in, unsure of our bearings. We may feel the conflicting pulls of Jupiter, wanting to broaden our lives, and Saturn, bringing constraint and the desire for stability, especially if we experience these two aspects very close together.

We experience the Saturn square slightly later, when we are 21 to 22. This is a time when we feel we are standing on our own; we are much engaged in the Saturnine activities of establishing ourselves in the world, becoming self-reliant, building – another good Saturn term – our own independent life. As always with a square aspect, there is a struggle involved. Life may be hard; there may be little money available. If we have been to university, we may be trying to get established in a career, experiencing the tough world of the job-market for the first time; or, with Saturn's desire for stability and for taking on responsibility, we may marry or enter into a serious and committed relationship. If this is the case, or if we have married early, money may be short; we may be working hard, with young children to care for. The Princess of Wales experienced this Saturn square from November 1982 and throughout 1983 when, having fallen in love and got married under the Jupiter trine and struggled to learn how to fulfil her new role, she felt the impact of the desolation and loneliness of her life. In the Princess's case, Saturn is in the first house of her horoscope, so this planet always affects her at an intensely personal level, chipping away at her self-confidence and self-worth and bringing limitation in a very personal way. Whatever the exact circumstances of our life, one thing is certain: our inner resources, self-discipline, ability to work hard and to endure, are again tested and, we hope, strengthened by the events we experience during this Saturn square. In fact, a great deal of growing up is done at this time.

The period between the ages of about 22 and 27 is strongly under the influence of Jupiter. With the Saturn square behind us, and the structure of our life and of our ego more firmly established as a result, we now move on to the Jupiter return, which occurs when we are 23 to 24, and the first square of the new Jupiter cycle, when we are about 27. With Jupiter so prominent, the urge to expand is strong and for many people operates at a social and emotional level, although there is also the drive to get on with our career and to be successful. So we are pushing upwards and outwards, as is typical of

Jupiter. This can be a time of great freedom and opportunity, although Jupiter often brings restlessness, too, as its principle of expansion gives us the urge to push out our boundaries. If we are married and perhaps have a young family we feel the expansion through experiences which are different from the career ones, but none the less enriching. According to her biographies, the Princess of Wales felt great happiness and satisfaction through her children during this Jupiterian period; and Prince Harry was born in September 1984 as she approached her Jupiter return the following March. For a woman, this Jupiter return frequently brings marriage or the birth of a child.

The main Jupiter square, which happens when we are around 27, coincides with another thrust of achievement or of pushing out the boundaries of our life. It was at the time of this aspect that the Princess of Wales found greater confidence. As it says in Nicholas Davies's biography, *Diana: A Princess and Her Troubled Marriage*:

> By 1987 [when her Jupiter square was exact] Diana had become the undisputed mistress of Kensington Palace. The staff, the secretaries, the officials, and the servants realized that Diana had taken over the reins of power and that she was to be obeyed. Diana found that being the mother of the two young princes gave her far greater authority than ever before, and people began to ask her all the questions of the household that had previously been deferred to Charles. She was in charge, and she liked the power.

If we haven't found our direction in life by the time of our second Jupiter return, when we are 23 to 24, the strong influence of Jupiter may mean that we have a restless and unsettled time during our mid-twenties. We may try one thing and then another, or perhaps travel a bit, in keeping with the nature of Jupiter, because there is no strong cyclical Saturn influence during this time to anchor us. In fact, as Gail Sheehy says in *Passages*, decision-making is frightening during our twenties because we're afraid of making irrevocable decisions which chain us later. The strong Jupiter influence makes it difficult for us to commit ourselves for the future. Marriage and child-bearing are exceptions, because these come about as a result of Jupiter's expansive effect on our feelings rather than our logic and our fears. So the Jupiter return at the age of 23 to 24 often brings a turning-point in our attitude towards relationships and the beginning of a 12-year period, the third Jupiter cycle, in which relationships will expand and develop. For many this will mean marriage or commitment to a relationship and starting a family (the average age for both men and women is between 21 and 24). For others, of course, decisions and opportunities taken up at the beginning of this third Jupiter cycle will be more concerned with career-building. The start of a Jupiter cycle, or indeed of a Saturn or Mars cycle, is almost always a good time to begin something new; if you miss that, then try to do it on a trine aspect. This is the aspect which follows the square – the planets are four signs apart and of the same element, fire, earth, air or water. I have not discussed these aspects very much in this part of the book so far because, as I've already pointed out, being harmonious, they do not bring the stress and tension of growth and development. They do not push us into taking action because of pain and discomfort; they may therefore pass by without notice. They are not part of the general growth-structure, but they occur at times when things go smoothly.

As we move towards our late twenties, however, things begin to change as we are hit by a number of important influences, culminating in the Saturn return. First there is the trine of Uranus to its own place, which occurs when we are about 26 to 27. Being a harmonious aspect, this does not usually bring with it highly disruptive, unsettling change. It is easier than the Uranus square, for example, which we experience at the end of our teens. It usually brings some kind of change in our attitude and possibly in our lifestyle, too. Sarah Ferguson married Prince Andrew at the time of her Uranus trine. At around the same age, 26 to 27, we get the first sextile of the Neptune cycle and the first square of the second Jupiter cycle. As always with the first square of a cycle, this is a time when the decisions and plans we made at the beginning of the cycle are tested by events or by our own feelings of 'This isn't quite right' or 'This isn't working', and adjustments can be made.

At a psychological level during our first 30 years, or our first Saturn cycle, we are building and strengthening our ego, or the shield around ourselves which tells us who we are, as a result of our job, what we've achieved and where we live; and which protects us by beliefs we've built up as to our value, and limits us by our inner

118

judgements – all the 'shoulds' and 'should nots' which we have gathered to ourselves since our birth, and probably from long before, through the rich pool of the collective unconscious which I believe we inherit along with our genes. Now, as we approach 30, with our life established in a certain pattern and everything apparently set and in place, Saturn completes its cycle and returns to where it was when we were born, and as a result we begin to question the ego, or the structure we have built, the beliefs we have adopted and the life we have made. We begin to feel uncomfortable with, constrained by, the life-structures which we've spent our first 30 years working so hard to build up. As we approach the age of 30, the way of life which seemed perfectly right for us before – indeed, highly desirable, even – suddenly doesn't feel that way any more. On the contrary, it may feel exactly the opposite. Somehow it no longer seems to be a true expression of us as we truly are; our inner self feels as if it is at odds with our outer life. So we feel an increasing need to re-examine our choices and commitments; to make changes. As a result, we may feel a good deal of inner conflict and turmoil, perhaps bringing us near breaking-point. Yet, in spite of the disruption, something within us is urging us to go on; we simply cannot accept the limitations any longer.

As a consequence of this inner pressure, many people make important and far-reaching changes between the ages of about 28 and 32, at the time of, or as a result of, their Saturn return. Almost everyone who has been in a marriage or partnership for several years at this point feels the need for change; for some this can mean divorce, for others, a serious review of the relationship and a willingness to make the required adjustments within it. Those who have remained single, on the other hand, may feel the urge to get married or make a long-term commitment. A woman who has previously been content to concentrate on her career feels the urge to have a child, while the woman who has been at home caring for children decides it's time to get out into the world again. For some, it can mean tearing up roots and moving to another country; for others, having the courage to make a complete change of career, perhaps going back to college or university in order to do so.

It was at the time of her Saturn return, in January 1962, that Elizabeth Taylor fell in love with Richard Burton on the set of *Antony and Cleopatra.* As Alexander Walker says in his biography, *Elizabeth*: 'Walter Wanger, watching from the edge of the set, wrote in the diary he was keeping: "There comes a time during a movie when the actors become the characters they play. That happened today . . . you could almost feel the electricity between Liz and Burton." ' Elizabeth Taylor's marriage to Eddie Fisher ended that March, and she married Richard Burton in March 1964, 9 days after her divorce became final.

Another interesting public example of the effect of the Saturn return is again provided by the Princess of Wales. I do not think that it was any coincidence that Andrew Morton's biography, *Diana, Her True Story*, was published at around the time of her Saturn return. As we've already seen, Saturn in the Princess's birth chart is in the first house of intensely personal matters with the seventh house of marriage as its opposite. At her first Saturn square, when she was 7 (April/May 1969), her parents divorced; at the Saturn opposition, when she was 14 (August/September 1975), she was experiencing the pain of her father's impending remarriage; at the final square (November 1982) she was herself newly married and experiencing her early difficulties. She continued to cope privately with these until the time of her Saturn return, which actually happened in late January 1991. At that point, the fit began to feel too tight and, it seems, she decided to allow the truth to be told. You will notice that at each point in her Saturn cycle the issues were of her deeply personal relationship to marriage: first that of her parents, then her father's new marriage, and then her own marriage and her feelings about it. Our Saturn testings and struggles are always about issues related to the house in which this planet is placed in our birth chart. In my own instance, with Saturn in the sixth house, they have been issues of work and health; in another chart which I have before me, with Saturn in the second house, the issues have been those of self-worth and financial security. Each time Saturn makes a major contact with its own place, there is another turn in the spiral, another aspect of the issue to be faced, another facet of the jewel to be cut and smoothed. This process continues throughout our life as we get into our second and third Saturn cycles, with, as we shall see in the later chapters of this book, always the same underlying theme, related to the house in which Saturn is placed in our birth chart.

At some time during their twenties, people born between the mid 1950s and the end of the 1990s (see Table 1, p. 86) experience Pluto making a sextile aspect to its own place. Again, because of Pluto's variable speed and orbit, those born in the 1940s and early 1950s did not experience this until they were around the age of 30, while those born in the earlier decades of the century experienced it even later: for Margaret Thatcher, born in 1925, it occurred when she was 39, and for my mother when she was approaching her mid forties. Whenever Pluto makes an aspect to its own place, things happen in our lives which put us in touch with deep feelings, and these lead us on to a new phase in our life. The sextile aspect, being harmonious, is usually easier to handle than the square, which comes next. When it occurs at the time of the Saturn return, as it did for those born in the 1940s and 1950s, it strengthens the tendency towards change which the Saturn return brings and probably intensifies the feelings experienced. For one man on my files, again experiencing the Pluto sextile at the same time as the Saturn return and also the Neptune sextile, it brought some traumatic love problems but also gave him the courage to come out as a homosexual and live openly with his lover. For the Princess of Wales, for whom the aspect was exact in February 1985, a few months after the birth of Prince Harry, I think it signified a pretty low point, but also, perhaps, helped her to get in touch with her own power – very much a Pluto quality – and begin the journey from despair and dependency to hope, strength and independence.

As our twenties draw to a close and we approach the age of 30, we can reflect on a decade which has brought great changes, both inwardly and outwardly. If we compare ourselves as we are now with the person who entered the decade so full of hope, enthusiasm and perhaps a touch of arrogance, we can see how much we've developed. In the process, we may have had to make courageous choices, perhaps in our career, relationships or lifestyle. Perhaps most of all, though, we will have learnt more about ourselves, our strengths and weaknesses, our likes and dislikes, as well as becoming more realistic about – and perhaps more able to accept – those of other people. We have gained a clearer idea of what feels right for us in our life, and have begun to take action based on this, rather than following the earlier patterns which were largely based on the ideas and priorities we learnt from others – our families, friends, schools and peers. We have achieved much but, for many, the period of change is not yet over and, as we shall see, continues as we cross the threshold into our thirties.

THIRTIES

Although the Saturn return takes place before we turn 30, most people are still feeling its effects after they enter their fourth decade. Indeed, it is often not until our early thirties that we express in our life the changes prompted by the profound effect which the Saturn return has had on our inner being. The tightness, the restriction, the feeling of 'this isn't it' which we get about our life at the time of the Saturn return is often expressed a year or so later as we seek to alter the outer experiences to fit our inner feelings, rather like the process of a snake shedding a skin as it grows.

By the time of our Saturn return we have established who we think we are; we have found some material security, probably discovered what we think we are going to do in our life and maybe who we think we are going to share it with. We have worked hard building a structure around ourselves, and yet suddenly it doesn't feel quite right; it doesn't express who we really *are* now; it feels restricting and unauthentic. We feel compelled to make changes, possibly drastic ones. Many people get married or divorced at this time; or they change their job. The crises in the marriages of both the Princess of Wales and the Duchess of York were, I am sure, public examples of the pain and transformation which happens at the time of the Saturn return. These are deep changes which are about growth; they are healthy and natural and they lead us forward along our life-path. But they are not easy, and they are not without pain.

For Jane Fonda, the Saturn return brought a change in her way of eating and exercising. In Michael Freedland's biography of her she is quoted as saying:

> My body was literally telling me things. Sleep more. Eat better. I found myself drinking a lot of milk – something I hadn't done before. I no longer wanted coffee or cigarettes. I bought my first books on nutrition. Every woman owes it to herself to keep fit. You

TABLE 5A Aspects made by slow planets during years 30 to 40

Age y-m	Period months	Planet	Cycle	Aspect	Strength 1 to 7
30–9	±7	Jupiter	3	2nd quincunx	*
31–9	±7	Jupiter	3	2nd trine	***
32–8	±7	Jupiter	3	**2nd square**	****
33–8	±7	Jupiter	3	2nd sextile	**
34–5	±8	Saturn	2	1st sextile	***
35–1	±9	Uranus	1	1st quincunx	****
35–8	±7	Jupiter	3	**return**	****
36–11	±8	Saturn	2	**1st square**	*****
37–8	±7	Jupiter	4	1st sextile	**
38–8	±7	Jupiter	4	**1st square**	****
39–4	±8	Saturn	2	1st trine	****
39–7	±7	Jupiter	4	1st trine	***

The aspects printed in **bold** are those described in the text.

The aspects may apply up to three times during the periods shown.

The number of stars shows the approximate strength and importance of the aspect, on a scale of 1 to 7.

The ages in years and months at which Pluto is likely to aspect its natal position for people in this age group are shown for various birth dates in the table below. As usual there will be some variation due to retrograde motion.

TABLE 5B Aspects made by Pluto during years 30 to 40

Pluto aspect	Year of birth										
	1900 y-m	1910 y-m	1920 y-m	1930 y-m	1940 y-m	1950 y-m	1960 y-m	1970 y-m	1980 y-m	1990 y-m	2000 y-m
sextile				37–3	33						
square							37–3	36–6	38–6		

can't be liberated when you remain a slave to bad physical and nutritional habits. Getting fit is a political act. You are taking charge of your life.

My own Saturn return was one of the most difficult periods of my life. Having spent my life up until then in a religious organization founded by my grandmother, and having been brought up to believe that when she died it was my mission to take over the leadership, rather like a royal succession, I was living and working at the centre of this organization and thought that my life was all mapped out. However, as I reached my Saturn return (which fell in the sixth house of work in my birth chart), I became filled with increasing misgivings. Did I really believe in every aspect of the religion? Was this what I wanted to express in my life? I had been told from babyhood what I *should* believe, but did I really believe this? What did *I* believe, if anything? My husband had given up his job to work in the organization with me; our home and tiny income were dependent upon working for it. I felt desperate. I knew that if I left the organization my departure would cause great disruption and I did not want to make life difficult for my family who were still working in it. Yet I knew that I just could not go on. I did a lot of praying at this time, although I did not know whether I believed in anything. But in a miraculous way things did work out. Out of the blue I was asked to do a series of lucrative cookery articles, which I was able to fit into my spare time; my husband, who had been experiencing a similar crisis, was able to return to the job which he had left nine years earlier, although at a much lower grade, and we moved to a house near his place of work. During the time of pain and upheaval leading to the move I heard about the workshops in Transpersonal Psychology run by Barbara Somers and Ian Gordon-Brown and received great help from them. Through these workshops I was able to understand something of the process of growth and development that was going on in my life, and to realize that it was natural and, indeed, to be welcomed. I learned for the first time of the power of the unconscious and the need we all have to own and integrate the shadow aspect of ourselves. What I learned at that time really changed my outlook on life in a most helpful way and has been invaluable ever since. Although I had felt inwardly the effects of the Saturn return at

125

the age of 28 to 29, the changes evoked by it did not take place until 4 to 5 years later, and I believe this timing is quite typical. Sometimes at the time of the Saturn return the feelings of pressure well up inside us seemingly of their own accord. What has previously seemed perfectly acceptable and harmonious in our life begins to feel uncomfortable, not right any more. For other people the Saturn return may coincide with a change imposed on them by circumstances or by others. Both produce the same results: the need for us to make changes to allow for further growth. It does not matter whether the push comes apparently from within or without; if change is necessary for our growth, it will be brought to us in some way; and if we stifle our inner promptings, or our unconscious, then it will externalize and come to us in the form of an event or a circumstance which will force us to change. Trying to hold back the unconscious is as impossible as trying to hold back the tides of the sea.

I like the way in which Gail Sheehy likens our process of growth to that of the lobster, which forms a hard shell, then casts it off as it grows and the shell becomes too tight. Each time it discards its shell, the lobster is left vulnerable and unprotected until it has formed a new one. And so it is with us. Every time our way of life becomes too confining and stultifying, it has to be broken down and discarded, to allow us to grow and expand. So we feel an increasing urge for change, or we reach a crisis-point when change is inevitable, or we experience an event which brings disruption to our way of life and forces us to change and thus to grow. Change is not without its pain: it brings the need to let go of something valuable and precious, it brings with it fear of the future, and it tests our strength of character. It leaves us, like the lobster, feeling vulnerable and exposed. In the process, however, we grow, we find new avenues of expression, we become more tolerant, more accepting of ourselves and others. In adapting to fresh circumstances we rediscover our aliveness, enthusiasm and creativity. So times of change, crisis and disruption, in which we let go of the past, are to be welcomed, for they are part of our process of growth.

Around the time of the Saturn return, when we are about 30, we have the Jupiter opposition, the mid-point in the Jupiter cycle when we look back at what we've achieved so far in that cycle and compare it with what we'd hoped for. This is a time when we begin to get the results of whatever activities we set in motion at the beginning of the cycle, whether it was one concerned with relationships and the raising of a family, or the development of our career, or the desire not to take on any commitments. Now we have the opportunity to see how this decision has worked out and to make changes which will affect the remainder of this cycle. The opposition coming at this time, when we're still most likely reeling from the effects of the Saturn return, is helpful in that it usually brings with it, in typical Jupiter fashion, hope for the future and thoughts of new opportunities and experiences which may possibly lie ahead. The two contrasting influences, Jupiter and Saturn, are again at work, helping us to evaluate what is going on and to decide what we want for the future. This process continues with the final square of the third Jupiter cycle, when we're about 32 to 33, which brings, as usual, the feeling of wanting to break out and to expand our life, thus helping to pull us out of the chrysalis of the old Saturn cycle which we're leaving behind, towards new opportunities. It was at this final Jupiter square that I was able to make the changes prompted by my Saturn return. The Duchess of York's announcement of her separation from Prince Andrew also took place within a few months of this Jupiter square.

At around the age of 35 to 36 we have a Jupiter return, as the planet gets back to where it was in our birth chart and starts off on its fourth cycle; at about the same time we also get the first square of our second Saturn cycle. As always, the Saturn square forces us to confront issues related to that planet. Saturn is the planet of time and of old age, also of restrictions, limitations and authority figures, so we are likely at this stage to come up against all, or any, of these. At the same time, the new Jupiter cycle is bringing feelings of expansion and a restless urge to do and to achieve. Once again we have in our life the contrasting energies of limiting, solidifying, security-loving Saturn, and expansive, freedom-seeking, outgoing Jupiter. Together these powerful influences explain why 35 is such a significant age for many people. It's the mid-point of what Gail Sheehy calls 'the deadline decade'. The new Jupiter cycle is beginning, prompting ideas of 'what might be', or indeed 'what might have been', while Saturn, the planet of time and of old age, in making its first square of the new cycle, is reminding us that time is moving on. Jupiter brings thoughts of opportunity, Saturn of impending old age. The restlessness and expansiveness of Jupiter makes us acknowledge that there's a great deal we still want to achieve and experience in life, but Saturn also makes us acutely aware of time passing. The combination brings the feeling that this is the last chance to fulfil certain hopes and dreams. For women this urgency is greater because we are conscious of the progressive ticking of our biological clock. If we have not already had a baby, then at 35 we feel this is our last chance, whether or not we are married. We also begin to notice the first wrinkles and grey hairs, to be aware that our bodies are no longer young. Our own mortality may be brought home to us forcibly by the death of a parent. We may start a serious health and fitness regime, which is very much in keeping with the joint influences of Jupiter (sport and exercise) and Saturn (discipline).

As Gail Sheehy says in *Passages*: 'To each of us, our own crossing into midlife is the most dramatic. Women come upon the crossroads earlier than men do. The time pinch around 35 sets off a "my last chance" urgency. What a woman feels it is her "last chance" to do depends on the pattern she has followed so far.' Sheehy also observes that 35 is the most common age of the runaway wife; when the average mother sends her last child off to school; when the average married American woman re-enters the working world after raising a family; the beginning of 'the dangerous age of infidelity – a wife is most likely to be unfaithful, if ever, in her late thirties'.

The mid thirties are certainly a time for taking stock of the first half of our life, looking at what we have achieved so far, and making decisions about what we'd like to do in the time we've got left: a process of re-evaluation and re-balancing. But before this happens, we may feel so depressed and discouraged by the apparent lack of time left that we feel it's not worth starting anything new, or that we cannot break out of the patterns and structures we've already created in order to do what we'd really like to do. For most people, however, this is an illusion; there *is* time, and we *can* make changes, and opportunities *do* lie ahead. There *is* life after 35! At some point, however, either now or later, we have to stop fighting our age and accept it. Once we can do so, and we feel comfortable with our age, we can begin to discover the particular opportunities and advantages which it brings, and express these in our life. We may move more into the Jupiterian role of teacher, as we guide children over the threshold of puberty and into maturity, or, at work, find ourselves in the position of training others. We are becoming mature and moving onwards to the next phase of life, towards the role of the wise person.

As always this new stage calls for a letting-go of certain aspects of our life, certain images. Saturn brings us reality about how things truly are, and an acceptance of them, while Jupiter brings hope and helps us to discover what we really want for ourselves, to move us forward. There is, after all, a Jupiter cycle opening before us, bringing the possibility of a new 12-year period. How are we going to use this? How do we want to expand and develop our life? What has been, or is, stopping us and holding us back? Are we perhaps being held back by Saturnine beliefs that are outworn? An understanding of our birth chart can help us to find an outlet which is particularly relevant and fruitful for us, since many more things than we think are possible. Too often we hold ourselves back by unnecessary fears and beliefs about ourselves, and it's worth remembering that, at his Jupiter return, Richard Branson achieved one of his ambitions, that of winning the Blue Riband trophy for the fastest transatlantic crossing, in *Challenger II*. This took place in January 1986 with Branson's return exact in April 1986. The swashbuckling nature of the event, the huge media coverage which it attracted and Branson's sense of pleasure when, a week later, he celebrated the success by sailing down the Thames in *Challenger II* with the then Prime Minister, Margaret Thatcher, by his side, were all typical of the nature of the planet Jupiter. Jupiter rules sporting events, large ships, long journeys and voyages, publicity and success.

Jupiter is the planet of freedom and widening horizons, and sometimes a Jupiter return can bring exactly these things into our life. It was in 1974, as she was approaching her Jupiter return, and having endured almost two decades of emotional abuse and physical violence, that Tina Turner finally walked out on her husband, Ike, and began the new life which led to her becoming the successful star and fulfilled person she is today. Tina found freedom (Jupiter), but she had to face many difficulties and much hard work (Saturn), too. In *Tina* by Steven Ivory, she is reported as saying: 'It's hard . . . it was hard for me . . . but I think it is possible for us people to deal with more than we know. I believe we have the power to endure a lot. I've gone through a lot in my life, but I've managed to turn it around. All of the times weren't great by any means, but I've learnt something from all of it.' In keeping with Jupiter, which also rules religion, Tina found her Buddhist faith enormously helpful at this time. Again, I quote from Steven Ivory's biography:

> Over and over again in interviews, she has credited Buddhism as the lone force that pulled her from the emotional trenches in which she found herself after her stormy marriage. Today, Tina keeps a small altar in her home. Every morning she is at home, she kneels before it and begins her chant, which, repeated over and over swiftly, sounds not like words, but a droning hum. She continues the ritual on the road. 'I would call it a recharger,' she has said. 'To sit on the floor and chant just before a show or even an important meeting can give you confidence. The confidence comes from the feeling you've plugged into a special energy. You can make it work for you.'

For those who were born in the 1930s, early 1940s and 1970s, the age 35 to 36 either will have been or will be a particularly significant turning-point because they will also experience important Pluto aspects, perhaps at the same time as the Saturn and Jupiter aspects. Those born in the 1930s and early 1940s also experienced the Pluto sextile. This is the aspect which people born in the later decades get in their twenties, and which I described in the last chapter. It shows a time when we may feel deep emotions, but these can lead us forward to a positive new chapter in our lives. Anita Roddick had her Pluto sextile (which also, incidentally, coincided with her Jupiter return) in her mid 30s when her husband went off on a 2-year trip round the world and she started the first Body Shop.

The irregularity of Pluto's orbit means that people born from around the mid 1950s and in the 1960s and 1970s are the first of recent generations to get the Pluto square in their thirties; those born in the early 1940s experienced the square in their early to mid forties, while those born around the 1920s and 1930s might have got it in their mid fifties or late forties respectively. Whenever it occurs, this Pluto square puts us in touch with the deeper, darker depths of ourselves. In fact we need to be able to do this, to face the demons, before we are able to experience our full power and the complete flowering of our potential.

At the time of the Pluto square, something will happen in our

130

lives which cracks the Saturn shell of the ego and puts us in touch with primal feelings, deep, dark emotions which we have not previously wanted to believe we had. Matters which we have not yet faced up to and resolved in the past, perhaps from as far back as our childhood, will resurface with an insistence which cannot be ignored. Parts of ourselves which we have long ago buried deeply in our unconscious and forgotten will re-emerge in a way which forces us to look at them and at the darker side of ourselves. This can lead some people into the depths of depression, or to self-destructive acts such as suicide, accidents or abuse of drink and drugs. We may try to conceal our fears by our lifestyle: those who fear ill-health may throw themselves into vigorous fitness routines; fears of failure or of lack of power may lead to fiercely ambitious actions; doubts about virility in a man, or attractiveness in a woman, may lead to sexual promiscuity; fears about old age and death to an over-emphasis on youthful looks and behaviour.

Now, however, as I explained earlier in the chapter on Pluto, our task is to stop pushing these feelings away and pretending to ourselves they don't belong to us, but to acknowledge and accept them as part of us. Emotions we'd rather not own, such as jealousy, anger, fear and greed, are part of our human legacy, along with selflessness, love, tolerance and self-discipline. They are, however, a lot harder to accept. And while we continue to pretend to ourselves that we do not have them, we are allowing ourselves to be aware of only a part of ourselves. The dark emotions therefore act unconsciously within us. So we may, for instance, stand in the way of someone's progress at work because we are afraid that they will pose a threat to us; or we may subtly undermine a daughter's confidence because we are jealous of her youth and beauty. If, on the other hand, we have owned up to these emotions and accepted them as our own, they cease to have the power to drive us unconsciously. We still experience fear and jealousy and indeed a whole spectrum of human feelings, but we are aware of the fact and so they do not push us into actions 'for someone else's good' or for any other excuse we might like to make in order to justify them. As a result of facing, owning and integrating our shadow side we become stronger, more grounded, wiser, more 'whole'.

The Pluto square and the experiences which it brings can work out in our life in numerous different ways. One woman, who was dominated during her early years first by her mother and then by her husband, went with a friend on a weekend assertiveness course. She went only because her friend wanted someone to accompany her; her husband did not want her to go, but for once she didn't allow him to overrule her. The weekend proved to be a revelation. For the first time she realized the extent to which she was still playing the little girl to both her mother and her husband, and how much of herself she was suppressing in order to 'keep the harmony', as she put it. She also touched the seething anger which lay underneath, and of which she was unaware. After that weekend her life was never the same again. She put her newly acquired assertiveness techniques to good use; she refused to be put down and dominated, and she looked at her life to discover what she really wanted to do, no matter whether other people agreed or not. Her behaviour brought problems in both her marriage and her relationship with her mother, and for a time she sought the help of a counsellor in working through them. She became so interested in the psychological process that she decided to train as a counsellor and became a mature student. In the end her marriage did break up, and her mother, embittered by all the changes in her daughter, blamed 'that feminist course' and said she could no longer talk to her because they had nothing in common and because she had 'become so hard and uncaring'. What the mother failed to see was her daughter's new vibrancy, joy and sense of purpose. She was not being 'hard and uncaring', merely refusing to pander to her self-centred mother's (or husband's) whims any more. She was living her own life fully, and allowing others to do the same.

If we have been fortunate enough to have been brought up by parents who are themselves aware of the shadow and who help us to own our darker side and to express ourselves fully in our life, the time of the Pluto square will not be the first time we have been brought face to face with this aspect. But acknowledging and owning primal emotions is one thing; experiencing them is another. And by some means or other, however well-balanced and aware we are, the Pluto square will take us to uncharted depths. The death of a parent, for instance, may shake us in a completely unexpected way; our partner may walk out after many years of marriage; we may have to face redundancy; we may find ourselves standing helplessly by as a friend wastes away from cancer or AIDS. The human scenarios are as varied and individual as the people experiencing them; the common factor is the Pluto square and the understanding, strength, humanity and depth which it is able to bring to our character.

In a fascinating article which appeared in the *Astrological Journal*, Daniele Patton pointed out the difference between people who have experienced the square of Pluto to its own place in their birth chart, and emerged with a deeper understanding and deeper humanity, and those who have not. Taking a historical perspective, she contrasted the behaviour of those who have experienced the square and those who have not. She was able to do this because of the widely varying ages at which different generations experience the square. So, while at the present time we are experiencing the Pluto square when we are around 40, people born at the beginning of this century did not experience it until they were in their sixties. And, as Daniele Patton pointed out, anyone who lived and died between 1823 and 1914, for example Queen Victoria (1819–1901), did not experience a Pluto square at all. On the other hand, everybody who was 40 at any time between 1740 and 1800, that is the period covering the American and French Revolutions, experienced a Pluto square like our present generation. Patton contrasted the humanity, wisdom and tolerance shown in the drafts of the American and French constitutions and their Declarations of Human Rights, drawn up by people who had experienced their Pluto square, with the behaviour of Robespierre and Danton, who sent Louis XVI to the guillotine and led the French Terror, and also with that of the leaders of the First World War, none of whom had experienced their Pluto square when they launched into war. Had they done so, perhaps history would have been different, for, as Patton noted, 'the Pluto square gives a definite tolerance, acceptance of human weakness and wisdom, to the generations living it'. She emphasized this point further by contrasting the Congress of Vienna, which occurred in 1823, with the Treaty of Versailles, which was drawn up in 1918. At the Congress of Vienna, all the participants except one had experienced their Pluto square and they had the wisdom and maturity not to make the French pay or suffer for Napoleon's follies, merely asking France to go back to its previous borders and settle the lawful king on the throne. However, as Patton pointed out, none of those who drew up the Treaty of Versailles, except for Clemenceau, had experienced the Pluto square, and the treaty is 'historically recognized as having been a disaster; it ruined Germany very quickly, leading to hyperinflation and setting up the conditions for Hitler's rise'.

As I mentioned earlier, we may experience the Pluto square in the next decade, when we're in our forties, depending on our birth date, and I shall look at it again in the next chapter of this book. Either way, however, the square lasts for about 3 years and during that time there may be 3 periods of major intensity as Pluto reaches its position, passes it, then goes backwards and then forwards again. The first Jupiter square of the current cycle, which we experience as we reach the end of our thirties, may get overlooked against the deeper feelings and issues if we're also experiencing the Pluto square. However, in some way or another it will present us with a turning-point, or a chance to make a change, in whatever we started when the Jupiter cycle began, when we were 35 to 36. At this time we will get our first taste of how things are working out. New doors may be opening, and we need to look out for them and to be ready to adapt.

FORTIES

As we enter our forties we may have already experienced or be experiencing the Pluto square, or we may be on the verge of it. In our early forties we also have Neptune squaring its own place, and Uranus, Saturn and Jupiter all opposing their places in our birth chart. Depending on the speed at which they were travelling when you were born, and the speed they're going now, these may all happen in the same year or 18 months, or they may be spaced out over 5 years or more. Either way, there are few people who do not feel their impact and they show the astrological reason for the 'mid-life crisis'.

At 40 we're perhaps half-way through our lives, and the urges and desires we felt during our twenties and thirties, and which helped us create our lifestyle, have changed. Our way of life may not therefore reflect us as we are now, and our inner drives and aspirations may not now have authentic expression. In order to feel comfortable with ourselves, we may need to make changes in our lifestyle, or at least to acknowledge and bring into the open our new feelings. We may find that we have no choice in this because circumstances or other people force us to do so. We may then feel like innocent pawns in a world changing because of other people's whims, desires and ambitions. In either case it is easier to accept the changes if you believe, as I do, that our own unconscious drives are just as much a cause of the changes as the actions of other people. The changes may be giving you the chance to loosen up, to create a new way of life which more truly expresses the person you are now, and which brings you the opportunities you need in order to be more fulfilled in the future.

At this stage of life we have to face ourselves honestly and realize that we're not going to be able to do certain things, and let those hopes go. We may need to allow ourselves to grieve as a result. We may also find ourselves having to re-live stages in our life that we

TABLE 6A   Aspects made by slow planets during years 40 to 50

Age y-m	Period months	Planet	Cycle	Aspect	Strength 1 to 7
40–7	±7	Jupiter	4	1st quincunx	*
41–3	±9	Neptune	1	**1st square**	******
41–7	±7	Jupiter	4	**opposition**	****
41–10	±8	Saturn	2	1st quincunx	***
41–1	±9	Uranus	1	**opposition**	*******
42–7	±7	Jupiter	4	2nd quincunx	*
43–7	±7	Jupiter	4	2nd trine	***
44–3	±8	Saturn	2	**opposition**	******
44–7	±7	Jupiter	4	2nd square	****
45–7	±7	Jupiter	4	2nd sextile	**
46–9	±8	Saturn	2	2nd quincunx	***
47–6	±7	Jupiter	4	**return**	****
49–1	±9	Uranus	1	2nd quincunx	****
49–2	±8	Saturn	2	**2nd trine**	****
49–6	±7	Jupiter	5	1st sextile	**

The aspects printed in **bold** are those described in the text.

The aspects may apply up to three times during the periods shown.

The number of stars shows the approximate strength and importance of the aspect, on a scale of 1 to 7.

The ages in years and months at which Pluto is likely to aspect its natal position for people in this age group are shown for various birth dates in the table below. As usual there will be some variation due to retrograde motion.

TABLE 6B   Aspects made by Pluto during years 40 to 50

Pluto aspect	Year of birth										
	1900 y-m	1910 y-m	1920 y-m	1930 y-m	1940 y-m	1950 y-m	1960 y-m	1970 y-m	1980 y-m	1990 y-m	2000 y-m
sextile	49–6	46	41–3								
square				50–6	45	41–6				44–9	51–6

missed out on the first time around; for instance, if we did not have a proper teenage rebellion, we may find ourselves having one now: psychological growth does not always happen in a tidy, chronological order, although it would be much easier if it did. At the same time, dark feelings may surface which we do not want to acknowledge, let alone own; but as they're faced and accepted we grow in strength and humanity and give ourselves – and others – permission to be ourselves.

In the last chapter I described the Pluto square, and this may be the first of the mid-life influences that you experience. If you were born from the 1960s onwards, it will be. So bear that in mind as I explain the aspects of the other planets, and we'll come back to it later. Remember, too, that you may be coping with two or more aspects at the same time, so there may be more than one thread in the tangle, and it may in fact be helpful, if you can, to disentangle them.

The opposition of Uranus to its own place can hit us any time between the ages of 38 and 42, and nearly always brings change of one kind or another. Uranus is the planet of individuality, and the effect of this opposition is to help us to get a clearer idea of who we are and what we are doing with our life. With Uranus half-way through its cycle, and at the mid-point in our life, we are able, as it were, to look at ourselves, to re-evaluate the past and decide what we want for the future. This process may well come about through some outer event in our lives which brings us up short and forces us to take stock. For one woman on my files, it was the sudden, premature death of her husband, who was also experiencing his Uranus opposition; for a musician, in what he described as 'a dead-end job as a *répétiteur*', coaching and tutoring opera-singers, it was the decision to go freelance, which he considered to be the best thing he ever did; and for one successful marketing man, seeing the firm he'd built up go bust, it was having to sell his house and start again. As a result of this, he became extremely interested in astrology (a Uranian subject if ever there was one), about which previously he'd been fairly sceptical. What these people, and others I've interviewed about the effects of the Uranus opposition, found was that, though the circumstances they faced may have been tough, through them they stopped relying on other people and really took control of their lives. Time and again I've heard people say that at the Uranus opposition they realized that the most important thing was that they should live their life in a way which felt right to them, and do the things which were really important to them. If they felt right within themselves, then what did it matter what other people thought of them? In allowing themselves to be themselves in this way, they also found that they became much more accepting of other people, and of their right to be themselves. People have said to me, on more than one occasion, that when they were going through their most difficult times, the friends who had helped them the most were the ones who, through experiencing pain in their own lives, had found the courage to be themselves.

I think that one of the most important qualities which the Uranus opposition can bring us is, in fact, the courage to be ourselves. Yet many of us realize, at the time of our Uranus opposition, that we hardly know ourselves. For when Uranus opposes itself, we are shown, as if in a mirror, the other side of ourselves, one we hardly recognize. An event, or a revelation, may trigger this process, or it may just happen without us quite realizing why. We may feel bored with our life as it is, and acutely aware of the passing of the years. If we want to do something more exciting with our life we may feel it's now or never. We may measure what we've achieved against our earlier ideals and ambitions and feel disappointed that they don't match up. We may feel deeply unsettled as a result. Increasingly, we realize that we don't feel quite right about ourselves and our lives.

Nearly everyone feels restless and dissatisfied with certain aspects of their life under this Uranus opposition, and many people do make changes. Women, in particular, feel the need for more independence at this time; having spent years caring for children and putting their own needs on one side, they can act in unexpected ways when the Uranus opposition comes along and they feel the surge of independence which it brings. One apparently very conventional woman I know decided, after a twenty-year marriage in which she felt completely unfulfilled sexually, to see what she had been missing and had a string of brief affairs; I also know of an antique dealer in a quiet village who, having spent half his lifetime building up his business, chucked it in to become a locations manager for a film company; and of a woman who decided to leave her home and new job and go to China to study calligraphy, where she subsequently met and married a Chinese man. The successful man who, at this age, finds that the cut-and-thrust of the rat-race begins to pall, and that he wants to spend more time with his family, or enjoying his hobbies, is a well-known stereotype, as is the woman who, having spent a decade or more looking after children, wants the challenge of a job outside the home. Both are examples of this Uranian swing towards the opposite.

People who have been outgoing, ambitious and socially orientated find themselves becoming more introspective; those who have been more introverted feel the urge to break out of their shell and lead a more active life in the world. Men often become more aware of the gentle, imaginative, 'feminine' side of their nature, while women get in touch with their 'masculine' side and become more powerful, independent and outgoing. In keeping with both the opposition aspect, which always puts us in touch with the opposite, and Uranus, which is also the planet of opposites, this can be a time for reversing roles. It's as if our psyche, in trying to find wholeness, is showing us the other half of ourselves and urging us to integrate it, and so become a whole, balanced and powerful person.

This may mean picking up, re-evaluating and owning parts of ourselves or our lives which we've hitherto rejected or kept separate. Jane Fonda's Uranus opposition coincided with her decision to start her own production company, and her feeling that, as Michael Freedland says in his biography, *Jane Fonda*:

> The sense of conflict she had for so long felt between her principles and her work now seemed part of the past. She was working harder at her career than she had for years . . . 'My friends helped persuade me that there was value in acting,' she said, 'and particularly that I could contribute through my film work. That's when I decided not to be so passive any more.'

The strange, exciting, electric feeling of Uranus at work in one's life is difficult to describe, yet you can recognize it immediately once you've experienced it and realized what it is. In fact, you get to recognize the feeling of all the planets once you start being aware of the times when they're at work in your life. One of the difficulties with the Uranian feeling, though, is that it brings with it an urgency and a ruthlessness which are difficult to stem. Uranus is a very compulsive planet. It fills us with ideas which are insistent, urgent, demanding, erratic, eccentric and unconventional. We may be quite obsessed by them. As a result we may make, or want to make, sweeping changes in our lives. Under this influence some people have been known to tear down what they have spent half the Uranus cycle, half a lifetime, building up. It is as if Uranus takes over our mind and feelings for a time, and we may act in a way which is completely out of character – or out of the character which our friends and loved ones *thought* we had, until Uranus gave us the urge to discover our other side! Once the aspect is over, the passions which it arouses go too, as suddenly as they came along. Then, with our old life destroyed, we may find ourselves wondering what kind of madness possessed us, even though at the time there may have seemed to be no other course.

This happened to a friend of mine, who at the age of 40, having never had a satisfactory long-term relationship, exactly at the time of her Uranus opposition fell deeply in love with a man twenty years younger and had a passionate affair. When she realized that he did not feel ready to settle into a committed relationship, she decided, somewhat sadly, to travel round the world while she was still young and free enough. However, her plans had to be changed when, on reaching Hawaii, she began to experience morning sickness and realized, to her amazement, that she was pregnant. She had the baby and is now bringing her up on her own; the father is living with a girl of his own age. After the Uranus opposition which coincided with her affair, she experienced the Neptune and Pluto squares, and the sense of loss, confusion, yearning and primal passions which these arouse in us.

My friend does not regret anything, and believes that her experiences were clearly exactly what she needed to grow and develop. This is, of course, true of everything that happens to us, if you follow this philosophy and, I must say, it's one with which I concur. She says, 'Amy is a complete joy to me, and a lovely little companion, and I wouldn't be without her.' However, she would not deny that she has found her life hard, and completely altered, as a result of what happened during her Uranus opposition. Although I believe that change is frequently positive, I do think that at the time when the Uranian opposition hits us it is helpful to know that we do not *have* to be swept up with it, we do not *have* to tear apart our lives, and that it will pass. It's important at this time, as at any other, to be aware of the possible consequences of our actions, and to be sure that they are what we really want. It certainly isn't good for us to resist strong feelings of change which may be bubbling up and to try to keep all the pieces firmly in place at all costs. Resisting the natural process of change and growth leads to stagnation and rigidity; that's when we give up the vitality of youth and settle into middle or old age. However, the Uranus opposition does not have to bring the break-up of a marriage or lifestyle. It does, though, bring the need for change. That is not to say we have to, or indeed can, change other people. What we can do is change ourselves and the way in which we handle our life, putting into practice assertiveness techniques which enable us to be in control of what is happening instead of being a passive participator or a victim. There are many excellent books on this subject: three which I can recommend are *The Dance of Anger* by Harriet Goldbor Lerner, *Assert Yourself* by Gael Lindfield, and *Feel the Fear and Do It Anyway*, by Susan Jeffers. As all these writers point out, when you start becoming more positive and applying assertiveness techniques, others will react to the change in you.

This will inevitably bring about a shake-up in close relationships. If both partners can participate in these and grow together as a result, then the relationship can survive the changes and become stronger in the process. This was what happened in my own case. I experienced the Uranus opposition and the Neptune and Pluto squares all more or less together, and at the same time took part in a series of workshops on personal growth. Meanwhile my husband also had a Uranus influence in his life, because although he was not being affected by one of the planetary cycles I've been describing, Uranus had reached the Sun in his birth chart. So he, too, was open and ready for change, and in fact he decided to attend the workshops too and we both changed together. We were able to look at our relationship and the aspects of it which we had outgrown. We both became freer and more independent, following our own interests as well as some shared ones, while retaining the loving relationship which we have built up over the years. It may change again – who knows? Relationships, like people, and for that matter, countries and states, have birth charts and need to be able to go through periods of change, but it is great to be able to share the process of change with your partner.

The Uranus opposition can certainly increase our independence and self-reliance; if our partner can accept this, and change too, the relationship can move on into a new and fulfilling phase. If not, it may break up; we may spend a time on our own, or we may move forward into a new relationship, which, hopefully, allows scope for each person to express him- or herself without constraints and manipulation. Jung describes this new approach to relationships, quoted in *The Psychology of C. G. Jung* by Jolande Jacobi:

> Above all we have achieved a real independence and with it, to be sure, a certain isolation. In a sense we are alone, for our 'inner freedom' means that a love relation can no longer fetter us; the other sex has lost its magic power over us, for we have come to know its essential traits in the depths of our own psyche. We shall not easily 'fall in love', for we can no longer lose ourselves in someone else, but we shall be capable of a deeper love, a conscious devotion to the other.

It is a pity that, as Jung also says, 'it takes half a lifetime to arrive at this stage'. What the Uranus opposition is really about is altering ourselves. If we simply end one relationship or way of life because of the restlessness which Uranus brings and then go straight into another, we tend to recreate very similar circumstances. So some counselling or a course on personal growth can be valuable at this time, helping us to understand what is going on within us. If we allow Uranus to shake us up, and to crack the rigid structure of our life, we can emerge from this aspect more alive, more independent, with new ideals and goals for the second half of our life.

Astrologer Sasha Fenton told me that the Uranus opposition was 'the best thing that ever happened to me'. Her husband had always been the main breadwinner while she brought up their family and supplemented the family income through a part-time job. Just before her Uranus opposition, Sasha's husband changed his business and they hit a very difficult time financially. They didn't quite get to the point of having to sell their home to pay their debts, but at one point they thought they might have to. Sasha tried various extra jobs to try and bring in some money, but the only thing which appeared to be really successful seemed to be her astrological and tarot consultations, which she had been doing almost as a hobby before. So she found herself doing more and more of these. Then, seeing the brand new computer and word processor which her husband had rented for his business standing idle, and 'costing us as much as a mortgage each month', Sasha decided to try and write some articles on the tarot. She had planned to send these to a women's magazine, but when a friend saw the first few, she urged Sasha to make them into a book instead. So she did; within a fortnight Sasha had completed the project and submitted her manuscript to the publishers, Thorsons. It was accepted immediately and, to Sasha's amazement, the advance royalty payment was the same, almost to the penny, as the money owed on the word processor. The book was successful, and Sasha's career opened up from that point on.

At around the same time as we are experiencing the Uranus opposition, questioning what we've done with our life so far and shaking our structures, we also get Neptune unsettling and undermining them. Neptune is the planet of the spiritual aspect of life; it's the planet of yearning, imagination, illusion and enchantment. It works through our dreams and longings; we touch something which we cannot explain; it's beyond reason, intangible. Yet it unsettles us. We may feel confused as a result; we don't know quite what we *do* want, but we feel vaguely unhappy and dissatisfied with what we've got. We may feel confused and unable to make a decision; our confidence may be at a low ebb. Sometimes, as in the case of the friend who started to travel round the world and then found she was pregnant, the Neptune square shows the confusion we feel as a result of what happened at the time of the Uranus opposition. The announcement of Princess Anne's separation from Captain Mark Phillips, for example, came on 31 August 1991, more than a year after she had experienced her Uranus opposition which occurred throughout 1990, at the same time as her Pluto square. She then had her Neptune square throughout 1991, which must have been a rather unsettled, confusing time for her. The influences in Elizabeth Taylor's horoscope when her marriage to Richard Burton ended were rather similar, with first the Uranus opposition during 1971–2, then the Neptune square, bringing confusion, illusion and a sense of loss, in operation throughout 1973–4, with the split coming at the end of July 1973. Although the Neptune aspect was widening by October 1975 when they remarried, Alexander Walker in his biography, *Elizabeth*, says that 'within a few weeks, it was clear to both of them that the promises they'd made by the river hadn't really been in the nature of a remarriage, only a short-lived remission'. Or, one final effort to capture the magic of Neptune before it disappeared completely.

What is happening at a psychological level during this Neptune square is that our Saturnine ego-structures are being undermined and dissolved. We will become more open to other people as a result, more aware of the humanity which we share. With everything apparently crumbling before our eyes, we may find that the only thing on which we can rely is our own inner strength, our own essential being. This realization is one of the gifts which this square can give us. Through the pain of loss and muddle which Neptune brings comes freedom, as our ego-barriers are dissolved and we become aware of our own humanity as well as our own power. Tina Turner expressed this when she described how, at the height of her difficulties, she realized that her husband 'wasn't all powerful, he wasn't God, and there is a little piece of God inside each of us – inside of me too – and I could find it and it could set me free'.

The point about the Neptune influence is actually to wash away structures; but our natural reaction is to replace them with new ones, to make us feel secure again. So we feel we should be making plans and being decisive about the future, and yet we just cannot be sure what to do for the best. In fact, I strongly advise anyone to postpone any important decisions while under this powerful Neptune influence. It's much better to let go and accept the insecurity of having no plans, like letting yourself float along with the tide. If you find this difficult, comfort yourself with the thought that if you do try and make plans, they'll most likely go wrong, or need to be changed. I think it's best to accept that Neptune has to take its course, and that as soon as it has done so, miraculously, the mists will clear and you'll be able to see the way ahead. This feeling is well expressed in the following quotation from *Emmanuel's Book*. At one of the Emmanuel workshops, a participant asked: 'I seem to want certainty, but everything seems to be so uncertain. What do I need to look at?' Emmanuel, through the mediumship of Pat Rodegast, replied:

> You need to look at the absolute safety of uncertainty. It is the linear mind that tells you uncertainty isn't safe. There is more safety in uncertainty because there is more *you*. When you are not squeezed into structure, regardless of how it promises predictability and therefore safety, then you are free, and when you are free, you are

empowered; and when you are empowered, what can harm you? You are God: fear tells you uncertainty is chaos. Love will tell you uncertainty is freedom. You must take your choice.

One of the ways in which the influence of Neptune can work out is through our having to accept the loss of something or someone dear to us. We've already seen how this was so in the case of Princess Anne and Elizabeth Taylor; and I have many other examples on my files. One of the saddest was a woman who, having been trapped in a loveless marriage since she was 17, eventually in her forties got divorced and found happiness with someone else. However, this was not to last; they were married for only a brief time before he died, suddenly, of cancer. At the time she was experiencing both her Neptune and Pluto squares.

Even if you do not have to face this kind of pain and trauma, almost everyone experiences a sense of loss in their early forties. It may be the waning of your physical stamina and looks, facing up to the natural ageing process which can no longer be denied. Men may fear the loss of their sex drive, and women have to accept that their childbearing days are now drawing to a close. Even though they may not want to have any more children, this may be a difficult mental adjustment to make. Grief may come, too, through the death of a parent or other loved one; or through having to accept that the 'impossible dream' will never materialize. It's helpful to be aware of these feelings and to allow them to work their way through us so that we are able to let them go. As we accept them they lose their power over us and prepare us for the second half of our life. Grieving is a very important process and brings with it healing and peace. Neptune is the planet concerned with the imagination and this is likely to be active at this time. Some form of artistic or creative expression can be a very helpful outlet for the Neptune energy. Even simply writing down your feelings, your hopes and your fears – for yourself, not for publication – can be enormously helpful. You may not get any answers, but you will get a sense of release.

If we get the Pluto square, which I described in the last chapter, at the same time as the Neptune square and the Uranus opposition, the experiences are considerably more intense and difficult. But even on its own, the Pluto square is a tough one to face. You just cannot plan for this Pluto influence, because you simply do not know what's going to trigger it, nor how it's going to hit you, but its effect is to shake you to the core. It feels as if you are being torn up by your roots and hurled into the darkness of fear and uncertainty. You may experience dark emotions which you thought you never had. You may wonder whether your life will ever be worth living again. It's important not to try and suppress the emotions which Pluto brings. Many people think, 'But I shouldn't be feeling like this.' There is no 'should' or 'shouldn't' about it; a feeling is a feeling, and if you're experiencing it, then it's real and that's all there is to it. But you do not have to *act* on the feelings of hate, jealousy and anger which you may experience; feeling them and accepting that they are there is enough. And each time you do so you discover more about yourself, and about your oneness with the human race, becoming stronger and more whole as you integrate the dark, powerful unconscious side of your nature.

Yoko Ono experienced her Pluto square in 1980, the year in which her husband, John Lennon, was assassinated. President Nixon was going through his Pluto square at the time of Watergate. When Princess Margaret was approaching her Pluto square, from late 1979 to the end of 1980, she had to face the news that her ex-husband Lord Snowdon was getting married again and that his wife was expecting a baby, as well as unpleasant revelations about herself and Roddy Llewellyn which were published in the *News of the World* in January 1980. Joan Collins had her Pluto square between December 1979 and September 1981. On 7 August 1980 her 8-year-old daughter Katy suffered a critical head injury and was in a coma for 42 days. As Joan told *People* magazine in November 1981: 'You cannot envision what it is like to see your child in a coma in an intensive care ward, with her head shaved and tubes coming out of everywhere, eyes closed, not moving at all . . .' During this time Joan discovered inner resources of strength and faith which helped to pull her through and to assist her daughter's recovery. According to Robert Levine's biography, *Joan Collins*: 'For six weeks she and Ron never stopped talking to Katy, never stopped playing music to her, never stopped touching her, never stopped giving her things to smell . . . They provided every stimulus they could. They would not let her die.' Katy did recover, slowly, and in July 1981, before the Pluto square ended,

Joan got a call from her agent asking whether she'd be interested in starring in *Dynasty*. It is interesting how often the Pluto square brings both suffering and success. Another example of this was the filming of *On Golden Pond*, in which Jane Fonda starred with her father, Henry Fonda. Because the story, about the reconciliation of an elderly father and his middle-aged daughter, was so true to life, shooting the film was emotionally draining. As Jane told writer Lois Armstrong: 'I knew that for it to work, we had to be naked, as it were, prepared to reveal ourselves. That is never easy. We would read scenes at the dining room at the house. The moment I opened my mouth the tears came – so much emotion I could hardly control it.' His performance in the film won Henry an Oscar which Jane received on his behalf. Five months later, in the summer of 1982, he was dead. As Michael Freedland says in his biography, *Jane Fonda*: 'Jane's sadness at her father's death was compounded by the inevitable thought: at just the moment she had proved to them both that she had his approval, he was no longer around to bask in that joy.' She said that working with Henry 'had made me confront my own mortality'. Real Pluto stuff, as was the naming of Jane in the *World Almanac 1984* as 'the third most influential woman in the country'.

Someone else for whom the Pluto square coincided with great success was Tina Turner. After all her years of suffering and hard work, in 1984 Tina finally achieved success on her own with her album *Private Dancer*. In January 1985, at the American Music Awards, she won the awards for favourite female vocalist and favourite video performer in the black music categories. A month later, at the Grammys, she was named best female vocalist in both the pop and rock categories, while 'What's Love Got to Do with It?' won the best record category. Afterwards she was mobbed; weeping openly, she said, 'This is the greatest single moment in my career . . . it was totally unexpected. When you win against the people I won against [Bruce Springsteen, Cyndi Lauper], that's really winning . . .' Another 'winner' at the time of her Pluto square was Anita Roddick, who, in 1986, having seen the Body Shop grow from one outlet to a multi-million-pound international company, was voted Business Woman of the Year.

The Saturn opposition takes place when we're 42 to 44, and marks the half-way point in the second Saturn cycle. At this time we reap the results of the decisions and actions we took at the time of the Saturn return, around 14 years ago. This can be a time of success, when we get the benefit of past effort and careful planning. At this time, for instance, one woman I know landed the job of headmistress for which she'd long been hoping and working. Joan Collins achieved her first real success and felt that she'd 'made it' when, in 1977, at the time of her Saturn opposition, she managed to find a backer for a film of her sister Jackie's book, *The Stud*. She also agreed to write her memoirs, a re-evaluation of her life and achievement very much in keeping with the opposition aspect. At the time of his Saturn opposition (and, incidentally, his Uranus opposition and Pluto sextile), Sir Alec Guinness won the Academy Award for best actor for his performance in *Bridge Over the River Kwai*, in 1957.

The Saturn opposition does not, however, by any means always coincide with success. We may discover that we are not particularly happy with the way in which things have worked out since the Saturn return. We may experience disappointment and feel we've reached a dead end. We may be passed over for promotion in our work; we may experience difficulties with someone in authority; we may feel concern over a child, or we may have to cope with the death or dependency of an ageing parent; we may have health problems. Again, there are many ways in which this aspect can work out, but the effect is the same: to make us look at what we've done in our life so far – and particularly since the Saturn return, when we were about 30 – and re-evaluate.

This Saturn opposition can coincide with any of the other aspects I've described, so its influence can be difficult to differentiate among everything else that Uranus, Neptune and Pluto are bringing into our life. In the case of one woman I know, when Saturn opposed its own place, from the eighth house of death, her husband died five days before they and their two children were due to begin travelling round the world. She and the children went anyway, immediately after the funeral, because, having sold their house, they didn't have much option. But she had a testing time, both at a practical level and inwardly, coming to terms with what had happened. This was not an easy time for Princess Margaret, either. At the time of her Saturn opposition, with Saturn in the fourth house of the home opposing its own position in the tenth house, which shows the career and public image, she met and became romantically involved with Roddy Llewellyn. The following spring, in March 1974, he flew out to Mustique to be with her. According to her biography (Nigel Dempster's *HRH The Princess Margaret*) the holiday was perfect, like a honeymoon, but on her return she was met at Heathrow by a grim-faced Lord Snowdon: 'Roddy was the first of Margaret's lovers to get at him and, from that moment, he was determined to get out of the marriage.'

With all the activity from the outer planets, Jupiter's cycle may be overlooked and, indeed, so far I've done just that. However, we have a Jupiter opposition when we are around 41 to 42 and a square when we're about 44. The opposition sometimes brings the need to look at your health and the way in which your physical body is working. If you started a regime of exercise and healthy eating at the beginning of the Jupiter cycle, when you were 35 to 36, then the Jupiter opposition will be bringing results. In any case, this is a time when you may feel the need to make some adjustments in your diet or exercise habits to bring them in line with what your body needs now. The final square of the Jupiter cycle, which happens around the age of 44 to 45, is a time for reassessing what has happened, especially in your health and relationships, during the last cycle and for tying up ends in preparation for the new cycle which will begin when you're around 47 to 48. What you decide at the time of the new Jupiter cycle which begins then will affect you for the next 12 years, and by the end of the cycle you'll be 60, close to retirement. In writing about this, Betty Lundsted, in her book *Planetary Cycles*, advises: 'It's important to listen to what you are thinking during the two months that Jupiter sits on your natal Jupiter [i.e. your Jupiter return] because your inner self will start acting out what you are thinking. Pay attention. Write down your ideas. Listen to yourself.'

This Jupiter cycle is one in which you can expand more into who you really are. With the testing aspects of the early forties behind you, the chances are you'll have a clearer idea of the conditions you want in your life. This may be a time when you wish to look at your spare-time interests and decide what you want to expand in this area; or you may wish to become more involved with other people, through community work or counselling, for instance. In keeping with the symbolism of Jupiter, this is an excellent time to think about courses of education you might like to take; for learning a foreign language or considering some extensive travel; for finding out more about myths, psychology or one of the more open, non-fanatical religions, such as Buddhism. One of the most interesting examples of the effect of this Jupiter return can be seen in the life of Hannah Hauxwell, the Yorkshire farmer who was 'discovered' when Barry Cockcroft of Yorkshire Television filmed her solitary, hard-working life in 1972, at the time of her Jupiter return. The programme, entitled *Too Long a Winter*, was broadcast on 30 January 1973 and the enormous interest which it attracted changed Hannah's life, which expanded in classic Jupiter style. Another interesting example is Bill Clinton, who was elected President of the United States of America in November 1992 as his Jupiter return was approaching exactitude.

I haven't normally considered trines, but I must mention the Saturn trine – a harmonious aspect – which we experience when we are about 49 to 50. This does seem to bring a sense of stability as our forties end. For some people, this trine can mark considerable success and a new boost in their career. The Plymouth artist Beryl Cook held her first public exhibition; and both Ted Heath and Margaret Thatcher were elected leader of the Conservative Party at the time of their Saturn trines, in July 1965 and February 1975 respectively. For nearly everyone it means that having been through one of the most testing times we'll ever experience, we now move towards more tranquil waters with a greater understanding of ourselves and others, more confidence, an appreciation of the preciousness – and brevity – of life and a determination to make the most of it.

FIFTIES

As far as the cycles are concerned, certainly for everyone born after about 1930, this is a much easier decade than the last, with the most challenging aspect, the Saturn return, not occurring until the end, when we're 58 to 59. Until then Jupiter is much to the fore, without the conflicting Saturn influence which so often accompanies it. There are also trines from both Uranus and Neptune and, for those born after 1930, from Pluto, helping us to adapt to circumstances, make some changes, and bringing hope and inspiration for the future. Owing to Pluto's uneven cycle, however, people born before about 1930 experienced their Pluto square in their fifties, except for those born before around 1910, who did not get it until they were 65 – the standard retirement age for many of this generation.

Although, as we've seen, a Pluto square can coincide with considerable success, it is nevertheless difficult at whatever age it occurs, making us confront and integrate unfamiliar aspects of ourselves. The Pluto square was still in operation when, in 1976, Hannah Hauxwell, whom I mentioned in the last chapter, found that she was a celebrity, with television, radio and other public appearances, a best-selling book, and an invitation to attend the Women of the Year luncheon in London. Quite a change from her frugal and hardworking life on a North Yorkshire farm. The Pluto square can be a precursor for significant change – and the emotional and personal upheaval and readjustment which these demand.

I think that the Pluto trine is likely to bring change, too, but so far there have been no examples of people experiencing their Pluto trine in their fifties because the generation who will do so is not old enough yet! The first group to do so, those born in 1940, will be getting their Pluto trine around 1996. Judging by what happened to previous generations at the time of their Pluto trine, which they experienced in their sixties or later, we can guess that for many it is likely to coincide with a period of considerable personal fulfilment, especially as a result of achieving goals and aims. Perhaps in keeping with the acceleration of modern life, success will tend to come earlier for the coming generations. Maybe during the late twentieth century we shall see a decrease in the average age of politicians, successful businessmen and other influential people. It is interesting to note that Bill Clinton, born on 19 August 1946, experiences his Pluto trine in the years 2000–2001, and in November 2000 it coincides with his sixth Jupiter return. When these two cycles – the Pluto trine and the Jupiter return – occur at the same time, they frequently indicate significant achievement and success. In Bill Clinton's case it is particularly interesting since it was his fifth Jupiter cycle which coincided with his election as President of the USA.

The possible Pluto square aside, in terms of the cycles, the period between the ages of 50 and 58 is, for many people, one of the most tranquil and potentially rewarding. If this *is* a difficult period, it is because of planetary influences affecting our own personal chart, or because we stifled the change which was bubbling away at the time of the mid-life crisis in our early forties when these planets were making more difficult aspects.

The first square of our current Jupiter cycle, when we are around the age of 50 to 51, tests the plans we made or the projects we started when the cycle began, when we were about 48. Events will occur which will test our plans and progress, and some adjustments may be made. At a Jupiter square there is usually a feeling of hope and optimism, and the danger is that we will take on more than we can handle in terms of time or resources. As long as we are realistic, however, this can be a helpful influence, building confidence and giving us the courage to take on something which we might otherwise be reluctant to do. And the positive attitude which Jupiter gives us will help our projects to work out well. The next phase of this cycle is the Jupiter opposition which occurs when we're about 53. Halfway through the Jupiter cycle we get the chance to evaluate what we've done, to see where it's leading and to decide where we want to go. The final square of this Jupiter cycle occurs when we're about 56 to 57. As always with the last square of the cycle, this is a time for tying up the ends of the old cycle and preparing for the next one, which will begin when we're about 59.

TABLE 7A   Aspects made by slow planets during years 50 to 60

Age y-m	Period months	Planet	Cycle	Aspect	Strength 1 to 7
50–6	±7	Jupiter	5	**1st square**	***
51–6	±7	Jupiter	5	1st trine	**
51–8	±8	Saturn	2	**2nd square**	****
52–6	±7	Jupiter	5	1st quincunx	*
53–5	±7	Jupiter	5	**opposition**	****
54–1	±8	Saturn	2	2nd sextile	***
54–5	±7	Jupiter	5	2nd quincunx	*
55–0	±9	Neptune	1	**1st trine**	*****
55–5	±7	Jupiter	5	2nd trine	***
56–1	±9	Uranus	1	**2nd trine**	*****
56–5	±7	Jupiter	5	**2nd square**	****
57–5	±7	Jupiter	5	2nd sextile	**
59–0	±8	Saturn	2	**return**	*******
59–5	±7	Jupiter	5	**return**	****

The aspects printed in **bold** are those described in the text.

The aspects may apply up to three times during the periods shown.

The number of stars shows the approximate strength and importance of the aspect, on a scale of 1 to 7.

The ages in years and months at which Pluto is likely to aspect its natal position for people in this age group are shown for various birth dates in the table below. As usual there will be some variation due to retrograde motion.

TABLE 7B   Aspects made by Pluto during years 50 to 60

Pluto aspect	Year of birth										
	1900 y-m	1910 y-m	1920 y-m	1930 y-m	1940 y-m	1950 y-m	1960 y-m	1970 y-m	1980 y-m	1990 y-m	2000 y-m
square		61	55–3	50–6							51–6
trine				62–9	56–9	51–6	50–6	51–9	55–6	65–3	

In her book *Planetary Cycles*, Betty Lundsted describes the Jupiter cycles as being largely about our relationships, and this one, she says, is about learning to receive from other people instead of always being the one to give. She says that we've learnt to be an adult, we've learnt to give, and now we have to relate to the idea of taking:

> The youngster takes life as a matter of course, taking and taking until he or she builds something of value. The parenting stage taught us to consider someone else; then we had to learn to nurture or relate a different way – by teaching and bringing out potential rather than by just taking over. Now it's time to learn how to take again, so that we can move on in the process of being able to receive what we need. If we don't, there is a tendency to become rigid and stubborn, while trying to protect our autonomy. In order to give the most back to society we need to ready ourselves for the philosophical stage. We're not there yet, but we need to prepare. Accepting from others is a part of recognizing the stage we are about to enter. We will have words of wisdom some day soon and we open the door now by avoiding rigidity. This relates to becoming receptive. When you give to others, you stay in control; when you accept from others you can receive. Receptivity relates to spiritual development, for you need to become receptive to the voice within.

For people with children, there are noticeable changes during this period. As the children become further involved with their own lives we may find ourselves in a new role, that of grandparents. During this Jupiter cycle we have to let go of our children in subtle ways, respecting their views about the way in which they are choosing to lead their lives and bring up their children, whether or not we agree with them. Indeed, they may differ radically from our own. With children leading their own lives, if we are still married, we find ourselves in the couple situation again, and there are adjustments to be made here. However, all this may seem relatively easy after the difficult planetary aspects we've been through during our forties.

If we confronted ourselves during our forties and acknowledged our darker side, and perhaps broke away from a way of life which did not feel right for us, we now feel more comfortable with ourselves. We have come to terms with the way we are, our ethics and our morals, and we do not need the approval of others in order to feel good about ourselves. We have reached the state of what Eric H. Erikson, in *Identity, Youth and Crisis*, calls *integrity*, the ability to give a blessing to our own life. This ease within ourselves affects our other relationships at this time. We can forgive our parents for what happened in our childhood; we do not need to compare and measure ourselves against other people; we can respect – indeed, encourage – our children's desire to be themselves; we can accept our partner and love them for what they are, without trying to change them. At the same time, we have a renewed sense of purpose and enthusiasm for our own interests. We experience the warmth and joy of a companionship which allows space for each partner to be themselves and have their own life and interests. Studies have shown a steep rise in satisfaction with marriage for couples who have survived the mid-life traumas together. Equally, since contentment stems from within us, this can be a satisfying time for those who have chosen to be, or find themselves, living alone. As Gail Sheehy puts it in *Passages*: 'People who are alone in middle age may be ready to accept that learning to live alone is not just transitionally good; it can be essentially good.' This may be especially true for those who are experiencing life on their own after a destructive relationship; or who are enjoying the freedom of being on their own for the first time since their teens.

If, during our forties, we kept the lid firmly in position and refused to look at ourselves, especially the shadow side, we will feel dissatisfied with our life, our achievements and, perhaps most of all, the people around us. We will tend to blame other people and circumstances for our own lack of ease; we will try and make other people do what we think they should. Indeed, there will be a lot of 'shoulds' in our life as we try to mould life to fit our requirements and beliefs, rather than accepting it, ourselves, and other people, and flowing with the current, rather than against it. It is never too late to begin the exciting and rewarding process of self-awareness. But the starting-point is a readiness to look at yourself and realize that the outer personality is not the real 'you'; to stop pretending to yourself and acknowledge and own that you have deep, dark passions, fears of failure, loss and pain, and the desire to give love and to be loved, like everyone else.

The trines of both Uranus and Neptune, and also, for those born between 1940 and 1980, Pluto, affect us in our early to mid fifties (late fifties for the Pluto trine for some people, as I explained earlier). It's tempting to dwell on the negative effects of the ageing process, but the fact that both Uranus and Neptune make important harmonious aspects – trines – during this period means that if we are prepared to change and grow we will find that life still holds many opportunities and much that is positive. We have considerable experience behind us and we have a good idea of our strengths and weaknesses, so we are in a good position to know what we can undertake and what, indeed, we would really like to do. The Uranus trine reminds us of our own uniqueness and individuality which we now have the courage to express without worrying about what others may think or say. The Uranus trine brings a wonderful opportunity to try something completely different, perhaps something we've always wanted to do but, until now, have never dared try. The Neptune trine shows that this can be a time during which we can gain much pleasure from art or music, and develop an increasing awareness of a more spiritual dimension to our being.

The time of our Uranus trine can be dynamic. It was at this time, in May 1979, that Margaret Thatcher was elected the first woman Prime Minister of Great Britain. She was also under the influence of the Uranus trine when she went on, the following November, to secure from the EEC a large rebate for Britain. At the time of her Uranus trine, Elizabeth Taylor experienced the death, from AIDS, of her old friend Rock Hudson, in the summer of 1985. Then, as she came under the influence of her Neptune trine, she became publicly identified with the AIDS campaign, becoming chairwoman of the American Federation for AIDS Research on 3 March 1987. Neptune, you'll remember, symbolizes hospitals and sacrifice, and brings out the qualities of compassion, concern for, and empathy with, other people. Interestingly, since Neptune also rules drugs, during the span of her Neptune trine Elizabeth Taylor went to the Betty Ford clinic for medication abuse and was able to get to grips with a Neptunian problem. At the time of her Neptune trine, Margaret Thatcher was celebrating Britain's victory over Argentina in the Falklands conflict. Again, the symbolism is precise: Neptune is the planet of the sea and the navy (as well as of the sacrifice of lives), and in Margaret Thatcher's birth chart it is in the ninth house of foreign affairs.

In the chart of another woman I know, the Neptune trine also brought contact with a distant country. Having lived all her life in Britain, the woman decided to return to the land of her birth, South Africa. Another example of the connection of the sea with the Neptune trine is Sir Alec Rose, who at the time was preparing for his single-handed transatlantic race, which he started on 23 May 1964, at the age of 56. Since Neptune is the planet of the imagination, the trine is also a superb time for artistic expression of any kind; this is a wonderful opportunity to develop that gift which you've had hidden away for more than half a lifetime. This is a time to fill your life with vibrant colour or music; to find yourself through a drama or choral group. One friend of mine began to paint at this period in her life and discovered a real talent, as well as an enthralling passion. The Neptune trine can also bring love and romance. One woman, having been widowed in her early forties at the time of her Uranus opposition, was swept off her feet at the time of her Neptune trine by a man some ten years younger than herself: *he* was experiencing *his* Uranus opposition at the time! They married and are still very happy: she is now in her mid eighties!

One of the problems about getting older is our stereotyped view of old age. As living conditions and health-care have improved, and life-expectancy has risen during this century, so our idea of when middle and old age begin has changed. For instance, not many years ago the menopause was considered to be a very difficult time for most women, and a precursor to old age. Now most women take it in their stride, use HRT if they wish, and look on it as the transition to a vigorous and active second half of their life. Women like Kate O'Mara and Joan Collins have proved that it is possible for a woman still to be glamorous, sexy and attractive well into her fifties and beyond. On the other hand, a woman in her fifties has the confidence to feel that she can now, at last, truly be herself. If she wants to look glamorous and sexy she has this option, but if she does not, then she need not. This is a time when both men and women can be themselves. Middle life is definitely a time to have a healthy respect for eccentricity. This is only possible when we overcome the habit of trying to please everyone, which seems to be a late development for many women. Dr Estelle Ramey, a robust physiologist nearing 60, with grown children and a long-standing marriage, is now of that frame of mind: 'I find I'm telling the truth more often. I didn't realize I was lying. I just thought I had good, ladylike manners. The one thing in the world I always wanted was to have everybody like me. Now I don't give a damn. I want *some people to like me, and I'll settle*.' Or, as Gail Sheehy succinctly put it in *Passages*, it's a time when we say 'no more bullshit'.

How we will make the transition into old age is, like many other things in our life, affected by our thoughts and beliefs. If we expect to be ill, weak and useless, then we are inviting these very conditions. I like the quote in Richard Bach's book *Illusions*: 'Argue for your limitations, and sure enough, they're yours.' Carla Lane, the writer of such successful television series as *Butterflies* and *Bread*, and now in her mid fifties, said in an interview in the *Vegetarian*: 'I am a great believer in mind over matter. I think if you tell yourself you are old or start counting how many summers you have left, it starts to show in your face. At this moment I feel 17. I am not 17, of course, but I have that sort of energy. Also I am doing something I love and I get well paid for it. I have not been without trauma and despair and I still have them, but basically to be able to do what you love is very lucky.'

This is certainly a good time for looking at your beliefs and noticing the ways in which these may be affecting your attitude to getting older. The combined influences of Jupiter, Uranus and Neptune during one's fifties are helpful for this, and, indeed, for any philosophical interests and development. It's important not to be limited by negative attitudes to old age; on the other hand, fighting the ageing process and almost pretending that it isn't happening is not helpful, either. We have to accept our age without either resisting it or becoming unnecessarily limited by it. As Carla Lane says, work that we love to do is very helpful, and this is an excellent time to think about interests or skills which you could develop. With retirement on the horizon for most people – and this can happen as early as 55 – the time of the Uranus and Neptune trines is ideal for developing interests apart from work. This is the time both to plan for retirement and to begin enjoying doing those things you've always wanted to do, and with which you can enrich your later years.

As we reach the end of our fifties we experience another of the major aspects in the astrological cycles: Saturn's second return to the place where it was when we were born. When we experienced this for the first time, around the age of 28 to 30, we were just setting out on our life. At that time we had to look at our lives and judge whether they were an honest expression of our beliefs and aims. We made important decisions about the kind of life we wanted to lead, the goals we wanted to achieve. Now, 30 years on, we reach the same point in the astrological cycle again, and we can look back and see how it has worked out. Many people may feel sad, depressed and regretful as a result. This is quite natural; at the time of his second Saturn return in 1915 George Bernard Shaw said that he was attempting to keep from falling into 'the bottomless pit of an utterly discouraging pessimism'. For him, the First World War had been the obvious trigger for this, but it could just as well have been something else. At the time of our Saturn return, something brings us up short and makes us confront ourselves, our fears and insecurities, our mortality. It may be the death of a parent, retirement or impending retirement, ill-health, or cutting the final links with a much-loved child.

If a parent has a child at the time of their first Saturn return, when they are about 29 years old, they will be going through their second Saturn return at the time when their child is experiencing his first. This can lead to some interesting situations as the child finds the strength to live his life in the way which he thinks right but which may go against the parent's views, hopes and principles, and the parent has to learn to let go and respect the child's freedom to make his own decisions. This can be difficult and painful for them both, particularly if the issue concerned is something about which the parent feels passionately, possibly deeply held religious beliefs or moral values. Since Saturn's position in our birth chart shows an area of our life where we feel the most vulnerable, the parent was most likely facing up to some kind of testing situation around the time of the child's birth; then, at the second Saturn return, the issues have to be faced again, in a slightly different form, through the child. In one case the child was born after the mother had lost a previous baby, and the relationship between mother and baby was extremely close until the time of the joint Saturn return, when the child had to break away and have more space to find himself. With real acceptance and love on both sides, though, this crisis can be overcome and both the parent and the child can grow, and probably become closer, as a result.

One of the issues which come up for many people at the time of the Saturn return is that of work. Most people are facing retirement at this time, with subsequent loss of status and a reduction in their income. If they have identified strongly with their work, and measured their success as a person by their position and salary, loss of these can seem like a negation of themselves. They may feel useless and disorientated as a result. A public demonstration of the way in which the Saturn return can coincide with loss of status can be seen in the life of the former British Prime Minister Edward Heath. In February 1974, after his power struggle with the miners which led to power cuts throughout the country and the 3-day working week, he lost the General Election. He then went on to lose his leadership of the Conservative Party early in 1975. Others, too, have to accept that they are no longer participating in the running of affairs; they've given their contribution, and now they have to let go and let others have their chance. They have to realize that they are not their work. Then what are they? they may ask. What, indeed, are any of us? Reading philosophical books can be helpful and enlightening when pondering such issues, as can meditation. Some useful books are suggested in the Bibliography (page 236), but there are plenty of others. Those who are really determined to explore this issue may well take up a path of training through a religious organization or a transpersonal psychology group. Eastern religions such as Buddhism have a long history of helping people to discover themselves. For people who have faced and come to terms with themselves and their feelings, the second Saturn return brings clarity. They are able to accept themselves and others exactly as they are; and they are also able to accept the circumstances of their life. So there is a sense of peace which brings its own joy and contentment.

It is important to realize that the Saturn return represents both the ending of one cycle and the beginning of a new one. As we let the past go we can move on to a new life. One person who did this in a particularly dramatic way was a woman who, at the time of her Saturn return, decided she was not going to put up with a boring, unfulfilling life with her husband any longer. So she divorced him, moved to London and got a part-time job so that she could support herself and enjoy going out with her many lively friends. I think we need to be open to the different options and possibilities ahead of us. As at the first Saturn return, we need a way of life which allows us to be truly ourselves; and this is of course different for each individual. Some people may want to continue to work for longer, and they may be able to do so, with, if necessary, a change of job. Some people may want to develop spare-time interests to the full, others to spend the winters in Spain. One man I met recently told me that since he had been retired early (at the time of his Saturn return) he had taken a part-time job in his local supermarket. He and his wife had moved to a small house with low outgoings, and with the money he was earning from his job he and his wife were taking long holidays travelling the world: something he had wanted to do all his life.

Saturn is also, however, the planet of limitation, and at the Saturn return we have to face the restrictions which getting older may bring: less energy or slower reactions and, for many, less money. Freeing oneself of financial burdens and mundane tasks by getting rid of things we no longer need and streamlining our lives materially can have an enlivening effect at any age, particularly at the Saturn return. A move to a smaller home, with fewer possessions and outgoing expenses, in a place where you can continue to be a member of a community of mixed ages, is also practical and sensible, and much in keeping with the positive side of Saturn. Putting less worry and effort into material matters will give you more time and energy for doing the things you really enjoy. The same applies to sensible health-care. Saturn rules the body, and at the second Saturn return demands that we pay attention to our health. Regular exercise such as walking or swimming, some yoga to keep the body flexible, a good healthy diet perhaps supplemented with extra vitamins, can do much to enable us to see our third Saturn return, happy and healthy! In being realistic about the future, though, I do feel there is a fine line between accepting reality and creating limitations for ourselves by our beliefs about old people and old age. This is where reading books such as *You Can Heal Your Life*, by Louise L. Hay, can help. One nice example of this is given by Philip Bristow in the introduction to his book, *Famous Ways to Grow Old*:

> We stood on the bridge at St Jean-de-Losne and watched our 81-year-old friends move out of the lock into the Canal de Bourgogne. They looked back to us and we waved goodbye as they set off on the long cruise home. On returning to our own boat we found an

161

English couple standing enviously alongside, attracted by our flag. He volunteered the information that he would have loved to cruise the inland waterways of France, but felt it was too late to consider it now. We enquired whether he had been ill, but this was apparently not the case at all; it was merely that he and his wife were both over 60 years of age . . .

While being positive about the future, we do need to allow ourselves time for reflection. We need to acknowledge and if necessary mourn for the aims we haven't achieved, the hopes we haven't realized, the things we haven't done. We need to face the thought that our life is going to end; to allow ourselves to mourn the passing of our vitality, power and strength; the loss of our youthful body. All this is hard to face, and it's not surprising that people need quiet periods on their own in order to do so. In Eastern cultures it was traditional for the older person to leave their home, family and possessions and go off to the forest to meditate on hidden things. At the time of his second Saturn return, in July 1967, Sir Alec Rose did this by sailing out of Portsmouth harbour at the start of his lone voyage round the world. In November 1967 he reached an all-time low when the boat was almost dismasted, but he managed to cope and: 'I went on my hands and knees and thanked God for helping me and giving me the strength to do it. I tidied up on deck and we finished up minus one staysail halyard and one topping lift. It was a very lucky escape.'

Sir Alec Rose's lone struggle against the wind and waves seems to me a nice metaphor for the inner struggles which many people feel at the time of their second Saturn return. I find it very interesting, too, that it was in 1533–4, at the time of his Saturn return, that Michelangelo was painting his fresco of the *Last Judgement* in the Sistine Chapel in Rome. I like to think that while doing so he confronted the issues of his own Saturn return, in a way which would leave inspiration and hope for future generations. Those who can do that are rare indeed, but, at the time of our Saturn return, anyone can take comfort from looking at great works of art, listening to music which gladdens their heart and uplifts them, reading inspiring books. Or we can cheer ourselves with simple pleasures: a walk in the countryside, some fragrant flowers, making time to do the things we enjoy. The present is rich, and every experience is of value for itself without reference to anything that might happen.

Margaret Thatcher, at the time of her second Saturn return in October 1984, experienced the trauma of the Brighton bomb attack on the hotel where she and most of the top Tories were staying during the party conference. Three people were killed and more than 30 were injured, but Margaret Thatcher herself escaped unharmed. Although not many people come face to face with death in such a graphic way at the Saturn return, there can be few who do not contemplate it. It's not morbid, however, at this time, or, for that matter, at any point in our life, to think about death and perhaps to read books about death and dying. Death, or the leaving of the physical body, is an event which happens to us all, so why not read about it and prepare for it as for any other major event in life? Books such as *Life After Life* by Raymond A. Moody, about people who have been on the point of death but have come back to life and described their experiences, are inspiring and helpful, as are those written by Elisabeth Kubler-Ross, who has spent a large part of her life caring for the terminally ill. In the foreword to Dr Moody's book, Elisabeth Kubler-Ross wrote:

> Since I have worked with terminally ill patients over the last two decades, I have become more and more preoccupied with looking into the phenomenon of death itself. We have learned a lot about the process of dying, but we still have many questions with regard to the moment of death and to the experience our patients have when they are pronounced medically dead.
>
> It is research such as Dr Moody presents in his book that will enlighten many and will confirm what we have been taught for two thousand years – that there is life after death. Though he does not claim to have studied death itself, it is evident from his findings that the dying patient continues to have a conscious awareness of his environment after being pronounced clinically dead. This very much coincides with my own research, which has used the accounts of patients who have died and made a comeback ... All of these patients have experienced a floating out of their physical bodies, associated with a great sense of peace and wholeness. Most were aware of another person who helped them in their transition to another plane of existence. Most were greeted by loved ones who

had died before them, or by a religious figure who was significant in their life and who coincided, naturally, with their own religious beliefs.

Thinking about dying, reflecting on our life, making peace with ourselves and with our loved ones is a natural part of our development during this decade.

At around the time of the Saturn return we also have a Jupiter return, as Jupiter finishes one cycle and begins a new one. It was this Jupiter return, incidentally, which I think helped protect Margaret Thatcher at the time of the Brighton bomb. The Jupiter return intensifies the feeling of chapters ending, but at the same time brings a feeling of hope for the future and of possibilities opening up. So, as Saturn brings the need for us to contract in certain areas of our life, and the ending of the Jupiter cycle brings the need for re-evaluation, especially in the area of relationships, it also brings the chance to begin something new, to start a fresh 12-year cycle. This could be in the sphere of relationships, or it may be to do with a hobby or spare-time interest, or second career.

This Jupiter return can be the starting-point of a more philosophical period of life; or one in which new, Jupiterian subjects are studied. Philosophy, religion, study and travel all come under Jupiter, and so this is an excellent time to make plans for any of these in case they crop up over the Jupiter cycle which lies ahead.

SIXTIES

When we reach the age of 60, we are most probably still experiencing the effects of the Saturn return which was exact when we were 58 or 59. Like the first Saturn return at the end of our twenties, the impact may be pronounced. We may make changes in our life as a result of circumstances which arose at the time of the Saturn return, and these will be further encouraged by the square of Uranus to its own place which occurs when we're 61 to 62. This is the same aspect that we experience when we are about 21. At that juncture it coincides with our pulling up roots, becoming independent and finding out who we are in our own right, apart from our parents. Now this aspect again forces us to make changes and to discover who we really are. For some people this aspect coincides with retirement from work, or, for some women, the impact which their husband's retirement can have on their lives. Both of those events demand considerable adaptation and need to be prepared for in advance. Retirement is challenging, but it offers great opportunities too. For some people the loss of structure in their lives which retirement brings, and the loss of the identity which they gained from their position at work, are very unsettling. And there may be other circumstances which come into our life at this time and require a change in our lifestyle or outlook. If we clamped down on the urge for change which the Uranus opposition brought in our mid forties, this Uranus aspect may now demand extensive changes in our outlook. Our true individuality is again bursting to get through the structures of our life.

New interests and experiences may come along with this aspect and it can be invigorating, helping us to find what really matters to us in our life and to make the time and opportunity for this. We can be more truly ourselves without regard to what others think, and, for many people, without the restriction of work; or we may become involved in a second career, perhaps on a freelance basis. The Uranus changes at this time can be extremely positive, with as much opportunity inherent in them as the first Uranus square brought – but now we are wiser and more able to enjoy them! It's important to do things that you really want to do; interests that you feel passionate about, not things that you feel you ought to do. This is a time for feeling free and invigorated by life and by what you do. Partners need to feel able to follow separate activities which bring interest into the relationship without threatening the companionship and mutual support which it offers.

Changes which happen as a result of the Saturn return, and the Uranus square which follows it so closely, may be ones which are forced on us, such as retirement, and its repercussions, as I've already mentioned. Or they may be changes which we instigate ourselves, especially if we did not make the changes we wanted to when we were in our early forties. There is often pain with the ending of one stage, as we leave behind that which is familiar and well loved. But if we don't alter, we don't grow, and we don't get the chance to experience new delights. I've always liked the quote, 'What the caterpillar sees as the end of the world we call a butterfly.' Life goes on, and so must we. As astrologer Patric Walker says:

> Everything changes, nothing remains the same. And letting go of the way things are, anticipating instead what they might become, frees us to live each moment more fully. Time marches on, and our destiny marches with it. There is a purpose in how our lives unfold; the ups and downs serve our growth. We must neither resent the doldrums nor savour too long the elation. Giving too much attention to either state interferes with our awareness of the present. And the present has come to teach us.

The Jupiter square which happens around the same time as the Uranus square brings hope and helps us to look ahead as we make the Uranus changes. The Jupiter and Uranus squares were the two aspects in operation in Margaret Thatcher's chart when she won her third General Election in June 1987, which she described as 'a fantastic triumph'. She became the first Prime Minister for a century to achieve a third consecutive term in office, backed by a massive majority. President Bush became President of the USA on a Jupiter aspect, in his case the one following the square, the opposition; and

TABLE 8A   Aspects made by slow planets during years 60 to 70

Age y-m	Period months	Planet	Cycle	Aspect	Strength 1 to 7
61–4	±7	Jupiter	6	1st sextile	**
62–4	±7	Jupiter	6	**1st square**	****
63–1	±9	Uranus	1	**2nd square**	******
63–4	±7	Jupiter	6	1st trine	***
63–11	±8	Saturn	3	1st sextile	***
64–4	±7	Jupiter	6	1st quincunx	*
65–4	±7	Jupiter	6	**opposition**	****
66–4	±8	Saturn	3	**1st square**	*****
66–4	±7	Jupiter	6	2nd quincunx	*
67–3	±7	Jupiter	6	2nd trine	***
68–3	±7	Jupiter	6	**2nd square**	****
68–9	±9	Neptune	1	1st quincunx	****
68–10	±8	Saturn	3	1st trine	****
69–3	±7	Jupiter	6	2nd sextile	**

The aspects printed in **bold** are those described in the text.

The aspects may apply up to three times during the periods shown.

The number of stars shows the approximate strength and importance of the aspect, on a scale of 1 to 7.

The ages in years and months at which Pluto is likely to aspect its natal position for people in this age group are shown for various birth dates in the table below. As usual there will be some variation due to retrograde motion.

TABLE 8B   Aspects made by Pluto during years 60 to 70

Pluto aspect	Year of birth										
	1900 y-m	1910 y-m	1920 y-m	1930 y-m	1940 y-m	1950 y-m	1960 y-m	1970 y-m	1980 y-m	1990 y-m	2000 y-m
trine		73	67	62–9	56–9				55–6	65–3	77–3
1st quincunx				72–9	69–6	67–9	66–6	70–3			

this Jupiter opposition, along with the Saturn square, was also in operation when Sir Winston Churchill became Prime Minister in May 1940, at the age of 65. So the combination of influences can coincide with success and achievement.

This Saturn square, which happens when we're around 65, as always brings issues which force us to confront ourselves. The decisions which we made at the time of the Saturn return when we were 58 to 59 may be tested at this time, or there may be further repercussions or issues to be faced. Once again we may come up against authority; we may have to face fears about getting old; we may chafe against the restrictions imposed on us by our waning vitality, or the need to take extra care of our health. We may be resisting old age. It's important to realize that we may not like old people because we fear the old person which we will become. One of the problems of old age is that we tend to think of all old people as a group. We need to remember that older people, like any other age group, are individuals, and that they have much to enjoy and much to contribute.

How much we will get out of this stage of our life depends to a large extent on us, and in what we place our values. Certainly, if we prize physical strength and activities, and the acquisition of power and of worldly goods, above all else, then this will indeed be a sterile and empty time. If, however, we can appreciate what we have – the capacity to love, the time to reflect on life and its mysteries – life can be truly rich and satisfying. When we have the courage to let go of each stage of our life as it becomes outgrown and outworn, and to move on and be receptive to the joy which the next can bring, we will find that each phase thus becomes full of vitality. The ability to make it so is within each one of us.

Those born between about 1910 and 1930 will get a Pluto trine sometime in their sixties, while those who were born in the first decade of this century or earlier experienced their first Pluto square in their sixties. Sir Harold Macmillan was, at the age of 69, experiencing his Pluto square in 1962–3, at the time of the Profumo affair, during which he accepted Profumo's denial of any impropriety between himself and Christine Keeler, who was also having a liaison with a Soviet naval attaché. In October 1963 Macmillan resigned as

Prime Minister, making his announcement from his hospital bed, where he was recovering from a prostate operation.

Sir Laurence Olivier had the Pluto square in 1968–9, when he was 61. During this time, Olivier found himself 'violently at odds for the first time with Peter Brook' in an argument about the Seneca *Oedipus* at the National Theatre, which left him feeling 'alone naked in my misery'. Peter wanted to end the production with the brutal unveiling of a 6-foot high monolith which turned out to be a huge phallus. Olivier says in *Confessions of an Actor*:

> Peter was adamant; in my deepest conscience I believed I too had to be adamant. I was alone in my convictions. Ken Tynan and Frank Dunlop clearly did not share them and, obviously dying to bring matters to a close, when Peter left us for a moment, they immediately started to persuade me to give in. Ken produced a cunning little ace: 'You know what will happen if you persist in refusing him? Peter will go straight down to Fleet Street and report that Stratford and the National are at open war.' I felt weak, I was weak; and weakly I gave in . . . Peter had, in fact, dealt a shrewder blow to my *amour propre* than he could have known, not that any victor broods to excess over the fate of the one defeated; but, like a defeated boxer, I knew I should remember it as the punch that started my undoing; that little inner voice squeaked, 'You're only allowed three like that, you know.' Well, there were two more to come then.

I've quoted Olivier at length because the situation, and his description, seem to me to be so much of the nature of Pluto. When we come face-to-face with this planet we experience power, either through feeling power*ful* or power*less* – they are both sides of the same coin. His feeling of being naked, and of having been dealt a severe blow, not to mention that the incident revolved around a phallus (Pluto is the planet which is very much concerned with our sexuality), are also typical of Pluto. Shortly after this incident Olivier, still under the influence of the Pluto square, underwent treatment for cancer of the prostate, received news of the death of first wife, Vivien Leigh, 'with whom I had shared a life that had resembled nothing so much as an express lift skying you upwards and throwing you downwards in insanely non-stop fashion', and had an emergency appendectomy.

As I've said before, any strong Pluto aspect coincides with events which put us in touch with our deep feelings and make us confront Pluto issues: power (which, as we've seen, can mean we experience its loss), sex, death. The Pluto square is generally more challenging than the trine, and I think it's interesting that, as the age at which we experience the square has decreased, so has the age at which most people retire. For those born in the 1900s, retirement age was most likely to be 65, the time of their Pluto square. Now, the age at which we retire has become more flexible, so 65 is not such a landmark and no longer coincides with the Pluto square.

The Pluto trine, which people born in the 1920s and 1930s experienced, or will experience, in their sixties, brings us in touch with the usual Pluto issues, but usually in a way which is easier to handle. Margaret Thatcher's Pluto trine, for instance, occurred in 1988; that April, following her massive election victory the previous June, she celebrated the achievement of being Britain's longest continuously serving Prime Minister. Both Ronald Reagan and George Bush were experiencing their Pluto trine when they became President of the USA, Reagan in 1980 at the age of 69, and Bush in 1988, when he was 65. For Reagan, it brought not only presidential success, but an attempt on his life, in March 1981.

As we reach the end of this decade, we experience the final square of our Jupiter cycle, followed by a Jupiter return when we're around 70. So this is a time for tidying up loose ends in interests and activities, as well as in relationships, so that we can make a fresh start with our new Jupiter cycle, which will take us through our seventies and into our eighties. For most people, these Jupiter aspects, and the Jupiter return which we experience as we leave this decade and enter our seventies, help us to adapt in our relationships as we become less in command, learning how to receive from others instead of always giving. The Jupiter aspects, as always, bring opportunities for widening our scope, applying the Jupiter principle of expansion to our interests and our mental capacities. We may take up new interests, learn new skills. There is a wealth of study open to us, and there is no age limit with the Open University and on courses run by local authorities. These can bring new enthusiasms, new friends, new opportunities. In *Older Students in Europe*, a survey of older students in four European countries, it states:

We need . . . a new view of retirement and old age. Our survey has shown that fit, active, elderly people can continue vigorous mental and often physical activity well beyond 60; many have some 20 years of active life before them; they are the so-called 'younger old' and not the 'older old' who may be less active and in need of care. The generation to which our respondents belong is better educated than in the past, highly motivated, capable of learning and of participating in society.

The course results show that there is no difference between the over 60s and the under 60s in the overall pass rate for courses; but closer analysis reveals one important difference: older students do slightly better on continuous assessment and slightly worse in examination. In addition, analysis of course results by age shows that those aged 60 to 64 are among the most successful of all OU students.

There are some stereotypes which associate age with loss of memory, and powers of concentration. These negative images of older people tiring quickly and unable to think or work for more than a very short time span are not supported by older student responses to a question about their ability to undertake concentrated study.

As one student said: 'I do the work for my own pleasure and delight, and it is wholly pleasurable and delightful.' Another said: 'I find study fascinating. It is not a pastime for me – it fulfils a deep interest. It educates one intellectually and morally; it teaches me to think and understand myself, other people, the world . . .' Yet another mature OU student, Pauline McClelland, who began by obtaining an honours degree in combined arts, is now, in her late sixties, using her knowledge of history and social issues to write historical novels for Mills & Boon. Her first was published in 1990 when she was 67 and she has already written ten more, which will appear at regular intervals in Britain, Canada and the USA. Reflecting on her success, Pauline is full of gratitude for 'the discipline and encouragement of completing a degree in middle life. My life would have been very different without it. Perhaps what I have achieved may serve to inspire others that it is never too late to start again.'

As well as bringing success and expansion, the aspects which we experience during this decade can help us to let go of some of our excess baggage, both material and mental; to streamline our lives and to travel lighter. At the same time, they can help us to become more aware of our own individuality and to find a sense of peace and detachment. If, through the earlier experiences of our life, we have been able to face and embrace our own dark side, and have accepted our weaknesses and fallibilities, we will have found an inner peace and strength which will grow in this decade. With this inner security we are no longer dependent on the approval of others. By releasing ourselves from material attachments we are freer to live in the way which feels right to us; to speak from our heart with complete honesty. We have less to lose, no reason to persuade another to do anything they don't want to or to be anything other than who they are. So we are in a sense detached, but not in a cold, unloving way. On the contrary, because our ego is not getting in the way (we have no vested interest, are not trying to manipulate people for any reason), we can be more truly there for people. People who, in the latter part of their life, reach this state – the images which come to mind are those of the wise old woman or man, the male or female 'crone' – can bring a healing presence to the world and to the lives of others; they exude an energy which has a transforming effect on everyone around them.

SEVENTIES

At the beginning of our seventies, we experience the sextile of Uranus, on its return to the position it was at when we were born, which happens in our early eighties. The last time we experienced the Uranus sextile was when we were around 14. At that time, we were just discovering our individuality and feeling the urge to become more independent. Now, nearly six decades later, we feel the Uranian energy in our lives again. So, for many people, this is another good time for making changes and, indeed, for starting new interests and activities. Most of all, however, it is a time for tuning in to ourselves; for becoming aware of who we are at this stage in our lives, and of how we wish to spend our remaining years. There are, of course, many different ways to live this decade. For some people, life continues to be very active; they may continue to work, or they may find their hours occupied with an absorbing hobby. Others may choose a more contemplative path; some may just want to relax, with few demands and commitments. The important thing is for us to be able to live in a way which feels right for us: the seventies, of all ages, are a time when we need to be able to be ourselves without reference to anyone else.

Of course our choice of lifestyle will be influenced by practical factors, such as the condition of our physical body, our energy level and our income. These Saturnine facts of life are with us throughout life, and will certainly affect the way we live in our seventies. We haven't been able to fight Saturn before in our life, and we're unable to do so now. We may have to face physical frailty and disabilities; less vitality; perhaps even pain. We have to accept these, and the natural changes which this decade brings. As always, we have to be ready to adapt and change; to know when it's time to let go of one way of life and move on.

Apart from the Uranus sextile, and a Pluto trine for those who were born from 1900 to about 1915, the major influences in this decade all come from the planets Jupiter and Saturn, which is quite in keeping with astrological tradition, since these planets have always been associated with old age. The first of these aspects, the Jupiter return, occurs when we're about 71, sometimes at the same time as the Uranus sextile. This can be a dynamic combination of influences and may explain to some extent the great burst of creativity which some people experience at this point. After this come the square and trine of Jupiter at the ages of 74 and 75, the opposition at 76 to 77 and the second trine at 78 to 79. And from Saturn we get the opposition when we're around 73, and the trine when we're 78. So this is a period of our life which begins with the possibility of change, or new experience, and then brings a combination of expansion from Jupiter, and paring-down from Saturn. As usual the forces of Jupiter and Saturn are contradictory, with expansion always followed by contraction, joy by pain. But that's the way life is; the astrological cycles reflect this. Peace of mind comes through accepting this; enjoying the good times fully while they last, but realizing that they will end and not trying to cling on to them or to re-live them; and, equally, realizing that the bad times, too, will pass. Everything changes; but we can be at peace within. This law of impermanence is part of the Buddhist teaching and, I think, helpful and practical at any stage of life, but perhaps especially as we grow older.

In their seventies, many people experience the influence of Jupiter through mental and cultural interests, which Jupiter rules. In his book, *Modern Man in Search of a Soul*, C. G. Jung says:

A human being would certainly not grow to be seventy or eighty years if this longevity had no meaning for the species to which he belongs. The afternoon of human life must also have a significance of its own and cannot be merely a pitiful appendage to life's morning . . . Could by any chance culture be the meaning and purpose of the second half of life?

This is also a time when Jupiter's other activities – travelling and teaching – may be to the fore. Freed from work and family responsibilities, we at last have the chance to visit other places, other countries. We also have a wealth of experience, both in our own field of work and in life, which we may be able to pass on to others. It does seem sad to me that the experience of older people is not more

TABLE 9A   Aspects made by slow planets during years 70 to 80

Age y-m	Period months	Planet	Cycle	Aspect	Strength 1 to 7
70–1	±9	Uranus	1	**2nd sextile**	****
71–3	±8	Saturn	3	1st quincunx	***
71–3	±7	Jupiter	6	**return**	****
73–3	±7	Jupiter	7	1st sextile	**
73–9	±8	Saturn	3	**opposition**	******
74–2	±7	Jupiter	7	**1st square**	****
75–2	±7	Jupiter	7	**1st trine**	***
76–2	±8	Saturn	3	2nd quincunx	***
76–2	±7	Jupiter	7	1st quincunx	*
77–2	±7	Jupiter	7	**opposition**	****
78–2	±7	Jupiter	7	2nd quincunx	*
78–8	±8	Saturn	3	**2nd trine**	****
79–2	±7	Jupiter	7	**2nd trine**	***

The aspects printed in **bold** are those described in the text.

The aspects may apply up to three times during the periods shown.

The number of stars shows the approximate strength and importance of the aspect, on a scale of 1 to 7.

The ages in years and months at which Pluto is likely to aspect its natal position for people in this age group are shown for various birth dates in the table below. As usual there will be some variation due to retrograde motion.

TABLE 9B   Aspects made by Pluto during years 70 to 80

Pluto aspect	Year of birth										
	1900 y-m	1910 y-m	1920 y-m	1930 y-m	1940 y-m	1950 y-m	1960 y-m	1970 y-m	1980 y-m	1990 y-m	2000 y-m
trine	78–9	73	67							65–3	77–3
1st quincunx		84–9	79	72–9	69–6		66–6	70–3	78–9	92	

valued in this country. Because we do not want to get old ourselves, we project our fear on to older people and do not, in general, value them. This is a loss for all concerned, and a situation which I hope will improve in the future.

I think it is interesting to contrast the way in which we treat old people in the West with the Eastern approach. In her book *Ancient Futures*, about the life of the people of Ladakh in the Western Himalayas, Helena Norberg-Hodge describes how the older people remain valued members of the community until the day they die. Because life there is unhurried, they can perform useful tasks at their own pace and have a particular role to play in the care and upbringing of the young, which in itself helps them to keep youthful in their outlook. Because they believe in reincarnation and see life and death as two aspects of a recurring process, the people of Ladakh fear neither the passing of the years nor death itself. Their attitude is one of acceptance, which, I am convinced, is a vital key to peace, and, dare I say it, happiness throughout life.

This attitude is movingly described in *The Snow Leopard*, in which Peter Matthiessen, a student of Zen Buddhism, describes his expedition to Nepal to search for the elusive snow leopard and to make a personal pilgrimage of spiritual exploration. Having endured great difficulty getting to the very high, isolated mountains, he was able to visit the abbot of a small, isolated and almost empty monastery. In fact the abbot was now living in an even more remote retreat on a mountainside, with a single companion. He found it very difficult to walk and the writer tentatively asked him how he felt about the prospect of never leaving his remote hermitage. He says:

The Lama of the Crystal Monastery appears to be a very happy man, and yet I wonder how he feels about his isolation in the silences of Tsakang, which he has not left in eight years now, and, because of his legs, may never leave again. Since Jang-bu [the interpreter] seems uncomfortable with the Lama, or perhaps with himself or perhaps with us, I tell him not to inquire on this point if it seems to him impertinent, but after a moment Jang-bu does so. And this holy man of great directness and simplicity, big white teeth shining, laughs out loud in an infectious way at Jang-bu's question. Indicating his twisted legs without a trace of self-pity or bitterness, as if they belonged to all of us, he casts his arms wide to

176

the sky and the snow mountains, the high sun and dancing sheep, and cries, 'Of course I am happy here! It's wonderful! *Especially* when I have no choice!'

In its wholehearted acceptance of *what is*, this is just what Soen Roshi might have said: I feel as if he had struck me in the chest. I thank him, bow, go softly down the mountain: under my parka, the folded prayer flag glows. Butter tea and wind pictures, the Crystal Mountain, and blue sheep dancing on the snow – it's quite enough!

'Have you seen the snow leopard?'

'No, isn't that wonderful?'

With its realism and practicality, the planet Saturn helps us to acknowledge and accept the condition of our life as it is. If we fail to do so, then at the time of Saturn's major aspects a situation comes into our life which helps – or forces – us to. As Jung said to the Baroness Vera von der Heydt, 'If you can't take the hint, life hits you.' Saturn is the planet of paring-down and streamlining, and this process needs to continue throughout its third cycle, which we began as we entered our sixties. Now, in our seventies, the opposition, which happens when we're about 73, encourages us to continue this process, to discard, to simplify. This is a time for getting rid of excess baggage, both physical and mental. Now we can let the past go, physically and mentally; throw out everything we no longer need, both possessions and outworn beliefs about ourselves, others, and life itself. At the same time, we can use the Saturn influence positively to plan our lives so that they have some structure. In her book *Pathfinders*, Gail Sheehy comments that one of the conditions present in the lives of those who were the happiest and most fulfilled in their sixties and seventies was a sense of structure, or routine. This was one of the things which Margaret Thatcher seemed to miss so much when she suddenly found herself no longer Prime Minister. In an interview with the US magazine *Vanity Fair*, in May 1991, she was quoted as saying: 'The pattern of my life was fractured. Sometimes I say "Which day is it?" I never said that at No 10.' The structure of Margaret Thatcher's life disappeared, along with her job, just as it does for many of us on retirement. Gradually we need to replace this, not so that we become trapped in a rigid routine which cannot be altered, but so that we have the security of some kind of framework for our days.

For those who are healthy and who choose an active, outgoing lifestyle, the seventies can be a busy, productive decade, as fulfilling as any other. And for some, it can be particularly demanding. Golda Meir, for instance, wasn't elected Prime Minister of Israel until this Jupiter return, in 1969, when she was rising 71. She was a widowed grandmother, and she was suffering from leukaemia, although this was not generally known at the time. Ronald Reagan was rising 70 when he was elected President of the USA in 1980, at the time of his Jupiter return and his Uranus sextile, and he held this office until January 1989, when he was almost 78. My own mother is in her late seventies and is still working full time, lecturing and writing books and articles. This year she has already travelled to Florence, Denmark and Sweden, and is shortly going to Texas. She attributes her vitality partly to her daily practice of yoga, which she has been doing since the time of her Neptune trine, in her fifties. There is no doubt that being fit and healthy during this decade enables people to enjoy life more, and the regular practice of yoga is one way of helping to keep the body in good working order as we grow older. The great yoga teacher B. K. S. Iyengar, now in his early seventies, is still in perfect shape, teaching yoga all over the world. One of his pupils, Vanda Scaravelli, has written her own yoga book, *Awakening the Spine*, based on Iyengar's principles. In this inspiring book there are photographs of Signora Scaravelli at the age of 83, performing some of the *asanas*. She says:

> To die is all right, we all have to die sooner or later, but what we must do is not allow the body to degenerate while living. By doing yoga in the proper way, we should be able to maintain its purity to the end.
>
> There is no age limit, one can start yoga when 70 or 80 years old and no damage will occur if the movements originate from the spine. People feel elated and it gives them comfort and encouragement to discover that it is possible for them to control and modify their bodies. To talk about old age as an impediment is an excuse to be lazy. A lady of seventy was delighted to follow the movement along her back saying 'It feels like being young again.'
>
> A different life begins and the body expresses a happiness never felt before. These are not just words, it actually happens.

If we want to take up yoga, then the Jupiter return, at the beginning of our seventies, is a good time for doing so, or, indeed, for starting any new interest or course. The novelist Mary Wesley had her first adult novel, *Jumping the Queue*, published at this time, in 1982, and has been writing productively ever since, becoming increasingly successful. For established writers, musicians and artists, the years between 70 and 80 do seem to bring the possibility of great creativity. Verdi wrote his tragic masterpiece *Otello* in his seventy-fourth year; Goethe was working on *Faust* during his seventies; Toscanini was conducting, with intensity and vigour; Picasso was painting; the great cellist, Pablo Casals, was composing, conducting and teaching; Arthur Rubinstein, the distinguished pianist, was giving concerts and making recordings. These are just a few examples; there are many more. At this age, to be able to spend your days doing something you really enjoy, and to get paid for it, is indeed a great blessing, and, in all honesty, exceptional. However, as I've mentioned earlier, the Open University has many success stories of people who have begun to study for, and have obtained, degrees in their seventies (and in their eighties, for that matter). These show that it is certainly not too late to take up, or start developing, an interest at this age; in doing so you may revitalize your life.

When we're 73 to 74 we experience the midway point of our Saturn cycle, when Saturn opposes its own place in our birth chart. It was during this time that Golda Meir was struggling with the divisions in her party which led to her resignation in April 1974. This, as I've already mentioned, is a time in the cycle, and in life, when it's natural to think about paring down and simplifying life, especially the practical aspects, so that energy can be saved for the things we really enjoy doing. For Ronald Reagan, the Saturn opposition came in 1983 when he was deciding whether to run for a second term as President. According to Joan Quigley, the Reagans' astrologer, 'the Reagans had deliberated for months about his running for a second term. Their children, Ron and Patti, were against it. In the fall of 1983 Nancy told me that she and Ronnie had decided to enter the Presidential race.' The fact that this had not been an easy decision fits in with the nature of the Saturn opposition, which brings the need for reflection and re-evaluation. It makes us look back on what has happened since our Saturn return, at the end of our fifties, and allows us to look forward, too. Saturn helps us – indeed, forces us – to be realistic and practical. It forces us to accept limitations which we can no longer ignore; but, on the positive side, it brings patience, acceptance and the ability to plan well for the future. Again, at this Saturn opposition, we may need to make changes; and the ability to keep open to circumstances and to other people, and to change, is one of the keys to happiness and serenity at this time of life. We have to live for now, and not hark back to the past.

The Jupiter square when we are about 74 gives us the opportunity to look at the way in which our interests, and whatever we began at the Jupiter return when we were 70, are developing, and to make adjustments if necessary. And when we are about 77 the Jupiter opposition marks the half-way point in the cycle, and we can look back and see what we've achieved. Around this time we also experience the second trine of our third Saturn cycle. This can be a time for realistic planning and also a time of achievement. It was at the time of her Saturn trine, in 1984, that Dame Peggy Ashcroft won an Academy Award for best supporting actress in the film *A Passage to India*. Her performance at this time in the television production *The Jewel in the Crown* was also widely acclaimed. President Reagan made his farewell speech to the American nation at the time of his Saturn trine, which also coincided with his Pluto trine. In fact the Pluto trine often marks a time of fruition, when we reap the rewards and acknowledgement for our past effort. This is nicely demonstrated in the life of Barbara McClintock, 'unquestionably one of the most original scientists of this century', according to Neville Symonds's obituary. At the time of her Pluto sextile, in 1950–51, Barbara McClintock published and presented the results of several years of genetic research, together with her original theory as to what these meant. The response to her work was negative, the uniform reaction from distinguished geneticists being that her interpretation was wrong. However, in the mid-1970s, when she herself was in her early seventies, Barbara McClintock's ideas were proved to be correct and, according to her obituary: 'Belated recognition was soon showered on her. She received numerous awards, culminating in the Nobel Prize, and was named American Woman of the Year, an accolade which gave her much innocent pleasure.' This period of recognition coincided with her Pluto trine, which became exact at the end of 1978. For people born in the early years of this century, the Pluto trine can indeed mark a high point in their seventies.

The keys to fulfilment during this decade and indeed the next would seem to be good health; for many, plenty of interests, mental or more active, for which we feel a real enthusiasm; an openness to other people and to change, which comes about through facing, acknowledging and accepting ourselves and our feelings. We also need to be able to live happily without depending on other people, or circumstances, to 'make' us happy. It's helpful to have this kind of real self-sufficiency at any age, but we'll especially feel the benefit of it as we get older. It comes down, really, to loving and accepting ourselves; if we can do that, then we'll end this decade with a sense of contentment and satisfaction.

EIGHTIES PLUS

In our eighties, and, indeed, in our nineties, there is, as always, the familiar interplay of Jupiter and Saturn aspects, with their contrasting principles of optimism and pessimism, expansion and contraction. There are also, especially in the eighties, a number of important and challenging aspects: the Uranus return, when Uranus gets back to the place it was when we were born; the Saturn return, when Saturn does the same for the third time in our life; and the Neptune opposition, which is the last major Neptune aspect we experience in a normal life-span. For some people there are also Pluto aspects; those born between about 1930 and 1970 will get the Pluto opposition in their eighties, while those born in the 1920s and 1970s will get it in their nineties. People who were born in the latter part of the last century, between about 1880 and 1900, got their Pluto trine in their late eighties or nineties, while those born in the 1870s experienced their Pluto square in their eighties. Whatever the outer circumstances and events with which Pluto aspects occur, their effect on us is the same: to stir in us deep feelings. And, no matter at what age these occur, if we can face these fears, insecurities and dark emotions they will lose their power over us. Experiences which recur with Pluto time and again in different guises are those of power, and of new chapters or phases in our life, with the consequent need to let go of the old one; also, situations to do with Pluto's process of life – sex, birth and death.

The experience of power may come through success, as we've seen in previous decades. For my grandmother, Grace Cooke, the Pluto trine, which she experienced when she was 82, coincided with what she felt was the culmination of her life's work with the completion and opening in 1974 of the temple of the White Eagle Lodge, a charitable religious trust which she founded in 1936. The Pluto trine also brought the celebrated and much-loved pianist Arthur

Rubinstein 'unexpected honours', as he modestly put it, when he received notification in 1971 that the French Republic had promoted him to the grade of Grand Officer of the Légion d'Honneur and, 2 months later, that the Italian government had bestowed on him that country's equivalent. The Dutch government then appointed him Commander of the high order of Orange-Nassau, and also created a new tulip, named 'Arthur Rubinstein'. For both Arthur Rubinstein and my grandmother, the Pluto trine coincided with the Jupiter return. As we've seen before, both these aspects can signify success and celebration, so when they occur together they are a powerful indication that these will follow. People alive today will, however, experience the Pluto trine much earlier than their eighties, and it may or may not coincide with an earlier Jupiter return: people born in the 1930s might get the Pluto trine at the same time as the seventh Jupiter return, when they're around 60; those born in the 1950s, 1960s and 1970s might get it at the same time as the sixth Jupiter return, around the age of 48, while people born in the 1940s and 1980s could get the Pluto trine coinciding with the Jupiter opposition, which occurs around the age of 53 and is, as we've seen before, another signifier of success.

Success is, one would think, a pleasant enough way to learn about the power of Pluto; where are the deep, dark feelings which Pluto usually stirs? They are probably very much in evidence. With success may have come a different way of life, with all the adjustment which this entails; and with success come the inevitable fears of losing it, or of not being able to live up to it. The Buddhist philosophy, that everything changes, and that happy times are as much a part of life as sad ones, is very helpful here. In accepting this we can allow ourselves to enjoy the success fully, while not clinging to it, or spoiling our joy worrying about if and when it will end.

Sometimes our experience of Pluto's power comes through having to face the opposites: loss of our power and the need to submit to a greater one. In our eighties and nineties, we could experience this through, for instance, giving up an independent life and thus putting ourselves very much in the power of other people. With this, of course, comes the other Pluto experience of the ending of a chapter. And at this age we may have to face a succession of closing chapters, one of the most painful being the loss of friends

TABLE 10A Aspects made by slow planets during years 80 to 90

Age y-m	Period months	Planet	Cycle	Aspect	Strength 1 to 7
80–2	±7	Jupiter	7	**2nd square**	****
81–1	±8	Saturn	3	**2nd square**	*****
81–2	±7	Jupiter	7	2nd sextile	**
82–6	±9	Neptune	1	**opposition**	*******
83–1	±7	Jupiter	7	**return**	****
83–7	±8	Saturn	3	2nd sextile	***
84–1	±9	Uranus	1	**return**	*******
85–1	±7	Jupiter	8	1st sextile	**
86–1	±7	Jupiter	8	**1st square**	****
87–1	±7	Jupiter	8	1st trine	***
88–1	±7	Jupiter	8	1st quincunx	*
88–6	±8	Saturn	3	**return**	*******
88–12	±7	Jupiter	8	**opposition**	****
89–12	±7	Jupiter	8	2nd quincunx	*

The aspects printed in **bold** are those described in the text.

The aspects may apply up to three times during the periods shown.

The number of stars shows the approximate strength and importance of the aspect, on a scale of 1 to 7.

The ages in years and months at which Pluto is likely to aspect its natal position for people in this age group are shown for various birth dates in the table below. As usual there will be some variation due to retrograde motion.

TABLE 10B Aspects made by Pluto during years 80 to 90

Pluto aspect	Year of birth										
	1900 y-m	1910 y-m	1920 y-m	1930 y-m	1940 y-m	1950 y-m	1960 y-m	1970 y-m	1980 y-m	1990 y-m	2000 y-m
1st quincunx	90–9	84–9	79						78–9	92	
opposition			92–3	89	85–3	84–9	86–9	93–9			

TABLE 11A Aspects made by slow planets during years 90 to 100

Age y-m	Period months	Planet	Cycle	Aspect	Strength 1 to 7
90–11	±8	Saturn	4	**1st semi-sextile**	**
91–0	±7	Jupiter	8	2nd trine	***
91–1	±9	Uranus	2	**1st semi-sextile**	***
92–0	±7	Jupiter	8	**2nd square**	****
93–0	±7	Jupiter	8	2nd sextile	**
93–4	±8	Saturn	4	1st sextile	***
95–0	±7	Jupiter	8	**return**	****
95–10	±8	Saturn	4	**1st square**	*****
96–3	±9	Neptune	1	**2nd quincunx**	****
96–11	±7	Jupiter	9	1st sextile	**
97–11	±7	Jupiter	9	**1st square**	****
98–1	±9	Uranus	2	**1st sextile**	****
98–3	±8	Saturn	4	**1st trine**	****
98–11	±7	Jupiter	9	**1st trine**	***
99–11	±7	Jupiter	9	1st quincunx	*

The aspects printed in **bold** are those described in the text.

The aspects may apply up to three times during the periods shown.

The number of stars shows the approximate strength and importance of the aspect, on a scale of 1 to 7.

The ages in years and months at which Pluto is likely to aspect its natal position for people in this age group are shown for various birth dates in the table below. As usual there will be some variation due to retrograde motion.

TABLE 11B Aspects made by Pluto during years 90 to 100

Pluto aspect	Year of birth										
	1900 y-m	1910 y-m	1920 y-m	1930 y-m	1940 y-m	1950 y-m	1960 y-m	1970 y-m	1980 y-m	1990 y-m	2000 y-m
1st quincunx	90–9	84–9							78–9	92	
opposition	100–9	97	92–3	89			86–9	93–9	106		

185

TABLE 12A Aspects made by slow planets during years 100 to 110

Age y-m	Period months	Planet	Cycle	Aspect	Strength 1 to 7
100–9	±8	Saturn	4	1st quincunx	***
100–11	±7	Jupiter	9	opposition	****
101–11	±7	Jupiter	9	2nd quincunx	*
102–10	±7	Jupiter	9	2nd trine	***
103–2	±8	Saturn	4	**opposition**	******
103–10	±7	Jupiter	9	2nd square	****
104–10	±7	Jupiter	9	2nd sextile	**
105–1	±9	Uranus	2	**1st square**	******
105–8	±8	Saturn	4	2nd quincunx	***
106–10	±7	Jupiter	9	return	****
108–1	±8	Saturn	4	2nd trine	****
108–10	±7	Jupiter	10	1st sextile	**
109–9	±7	Jupiter	10	1st square	****
109–11	±9	Neptune	1	2nd trine	*****

The aspects printed in **bold** are those described in the text.

The aspects may apply up to three times during the periods shown.

The number of stars shows the approximate strength and importance of the aspect, on a scale of 1 to 7.

The ages in years and months at which Pluto is likely to aspect its natal position for people in this age group are shown for various birth dates in the table below. As usual there will be some variation due to retrograde motion.

TABLE 12B Aspects made by Pluto during years 100 to 110

Pluto aspect	Year of birth										
	1900 y-m	1910 y-m	1920 y-m	1930 y-m	1940 y-m	1950 y-m	1960 y-m	1970 y-m	1980 y-m	1990 y-m	2000 y-m
opposition	100–9	97						93–9	106		
2nd quincunx		112	108–3	106	103–3	107–9	111–6				

and loved ones, which puts us in touch with Pluto's other domain, death. It's not easy saying 'goodbye', especially to those we've known the best part of a lifetime.

Pluto is most painful when we resist the process of change which it brings. So letting go, in faith and trust, really is the answer, although this is always challenging, and especially so at this age. Repeating an affirmation such as 'I am willing to let go; I let go; I am at peace with myself and the process of life', I am safe', or something similar, could be helpful.

The Buddhist practice of mindfulness – that is, of giving ourselves completely to whatever we are doing at each moment, with no thoughts of the past or worries about the future – is, I think, an extremely helpful one at any age, but particularly when one is going through a difficult period. If you put your attention wholly on what you are doing, you experience it fully and have no room for negative thoughts. Perhaps beauty becomes more poignant at this age. As the writer and Jungian analyst Marion Woodman said in an interview with Barbara Goodrich-Dunn, entitled 'The Conscious Feminine', published in *Common Boundary*, a US magazine, in March/April 1989:

> Sentimental people feel sorry for people who really feel. Sentimentality looks down on life being fully lived. It's afraid of real feeling. Real feeling, on the other hand, blasts away sentimentality. Sentimentality cheapens the culture and betrays friendships. People who are terrified of suffering don't allow themselves to experience reality. They suffer neurotically, but they don't live the real conflict. And they're afraid to die so they're stuck ... If you are in reality, yes, you suffer, but you also experience the joy of reality; the sheer happiness of walking out and seeing that tree, that fantastic tree right there. Look at it, it's just a marvel! You know you're here, present in the moment! And with people, the same is true. You're giving energy; you're receiving energy. There's continual flow.
>
> So when you face death, when you know you've lived life, lived it to the fullest, you're ready to go on with a new chapter. If you haven't lived it, if you've never been here, never been present, I'm sure you'll be terrified of death, because your whole life has been an absence. You've missed it. Well, by heaven, I don't intend to miss mine.

If the Neptune opposition happens to occur at the same time as one of these Pluto aspects this can help us in the process of acceptance and surrender, for these are principles of Neptune. The Neptune opposition can occur any time between the ages of 80 and 85. We last experienced a major aspect in the Neptune cycle when it trined its own place, in our mid fifties, and before that there was the Neptune square to its own place in our early forties. Now we experience this influence again.

Neptune, you will remember, dissolves boundaries, loosens fixed structures and brings the need for acceptance. Neptune is the planet of loss and of sacrifice; also of escape, illusion and delusion. Under this influence we may have to accept that the time has come to withdraw from some of our activities; or such change may be forced on us by circumstances. It was at the time of his Neptune opposition that the pianist Arthur Rubinstein lost the sight of one of his eyes, although he made light of it and continued to give concerts, make recordings and travel for more than a decade afterwards. Sir Winston Churchill, experiencing the Neptune opposition in 1959, resigned the premiership of the Conservative Party. He was then 80, and described as 'frail but indomitable'. At the time of her Neptune opposition, which also coincided with her Uranus return, the writer Elizabeth Longford damaged her spine while decorating a Christmas tree and spent 6 weeks in hospital following an operation. Afterwards, in a reply to a request from Philip Bristow for a quote about old age, to appear in his book, *Famous Ways to Grow Old*, she wrote:

I should have written to you quite differently if I had seized my pen a few months ago. Up till last Christmas I was a hale and hearty 82-year-old. I walked fast, weeded my garden, carried heavy water cans. My problem was to realize how old I was and not to go on behaving like a skittish 50-year-old.

You may ask, why try? Because you can't reap the full benefits of old age if you go on too long aping the features of youth. And what are those benefits? More time for thought, reading, companionship, remembering, appreciating the gifts that still come one's way. The bliss of not having to bother about superficial things; not having to traipse from shop to shop indecisive and disappointed by the failure of all those dresses to please. Instead, mail orders deserve the order of merit for services to the old. No one will love

188

you less for wearing old favourites more. I am lucky in having seven children, twenty-six grandchildren and one great-grandchild in whom to renew my own sense of youth. But even without one's 'own' children, there are always ways of using one's years in the service of the young. They all love stories about the past. The way things were in, say, George V's days seem stranger to them than fiction. Or write them letters; you will get some surprising answers.

If you are handicapped as well as old, cling on for dear life to your remaining independence and relics of youth. Dress better than before, never miss a hair-do, accept all invitations despite the effort. This cheers your family. Then, to cheer yourself, take up something new. For instance, thousands of people were rather good at painting when at school, and then dropped it. It's one of the best things to pick up again. And something to start, or re-start, is a diary.

I've quoted Elizabeth Longford at length because she makes several remarks which are relevant to the Neptune opposition: the need for acceptance, which Neptune both brings and helps us to achieve, and the fact that acceptance doesn't mean collapse, which is a negative manifestation of the planet; also, that in giving up certain things, we can free ourselves for others, especially those which make use of one of Neptune's gifts: our imagination. Neptune can lift our consciousness, making this a natural time for reading, listening to music, and, as Elizabeth Longford suggests, more creative activities such as painting and writing, if we feel like them. Neptune loosens the ego's grip and makes us more receptive to the unconscious at any age, but perhaps particularly at this late time in life. Neptune helps to dissolve the boundaries between people, and we may at this time experience circumstances which force us to do this. We experience our own humanity and that of others, we can let go of the ego and of barriers erected through fear and become more truly ourselves: open, willing both to receive help graciously and to give it where we can.

Jung, who experienced the Neptune opposition in 1957–8, could have been describing the effects of it when he wrote the following passage, which appears in his last work, *Memories, Dreams, Reflections*:

When people say I am wise, or a sage, I cannot accept it . . . The difference between most people and myself is that for me the 'dividing walls' are transparent. This is my peculiarity. Others find these walls so opaque that they see nothing behind them and therefore think nothing is there. To some extent I perceive the processes going on in the background, and that gives me an inner certainty. People who see nothing have no inner certainties and can draw no conclusions – or do not trust them even if they do. I do not know what started me off perceiving the stream of life. Probably the unconscious itself. Or perhaps my early dreams. They determined my course from the beginning.

When Lao-tzu says: 'All are clear, I alone am clouded', he is expressing what I now feel in advanced old age. Lao-tzu is the example of a man with superior insight who has seen and experienced worth and worthlessness, and who at the end of his life desires to return into his own being, into the eternal unknowable meaning. The archetype of the old man who has seen enough is eternally true. At every level of intelligence this type appears, and its lineaments are always the same, whether it be an old peasant or a great philosopher like Lao-tzu. This is old age, and a limitation. Yet there is so much that fills me: plants, animals, clouds, day and night, and the eternal in man. The more uncertain I have felt about myself, the more there has grown up in me a feeling of kinship with all things. In fact it seems to me as if the alienation which so long separated me from the world has become transferred into my own inner world and has revealed to me an unexpected unfamiliarity with myself.

The time of his Neptune opposition, which was exact between November 1956 and September 1957, proved to be an extraordinary one for the great composer and cellist, Pablo Casals. In April 1957 he suffered a heart attack while rehearsing in Puerto Rico, and at about the same time his divorce from his wife, whom he had not seen for nearly thirty years, became finalized. So the Neptunian factors, hospitals and dissolution, were brought into his life. But there were other Neptunian forces at work, too. He and a young student, Marta (Martita) Montañez, who was sixty years younger than Casals, had, according to his biographer H. L. Kirk,

> fallen mutually and profoundly in love, and Casals felt he had discovered happiness for the first time in his life. If love should have neither limit nor boundary, wide differences in age or the opinion

of others need not affect a great love between two people . . . Marta and Casals were married in San Juan on August 3, 1957 . . . 'I was aware at the time that some people noted a certain discrepancy in our ages,' Casals said for publication some years later, 'a bridegroom, of course, is not usually thirty years older than his father-in-law. But Martita and I were not concerned about what others thought; it was, after all, we who were getting married – not they. If some had misgivings, I can only say with joy that our love has deepened in the intervening years.'

Marta was to remain Casals's inseparable companion for the rest of his life. Again I quote from H. L. Kirk: 'Those who came to know the couple best, accepted, and in time knew they were in the presence of, a great love between two extraordinary people that enriched and enhanced both. Casals said unequivocally that Martita had given him life; every evidence suggests that he spoke the truth.'

Pablo Casals's experience is exceptional, but it shows the extra-ordinary way in which the planetary cycles can sometimes work, though always according to the symbolism of the planet involved.

To get back to the realm of more everyday happenings, the first aspect which many people experience as they enter their eighties is a square from Jupiter. This is the final one in the seventh cycle, so, in general terms, it is a time for tying up ends and completing unfinished business in preparation for the Jupiter return, which happens when we're around 83. This Jupiter can be a time of rejoicing: for Arthur Rubinstein it was 'great news! My first Rubinstein grandson, named Jason, was born . . .' And at the time of his Jupiter square, which he experienced at the same time as the Saturn and Pluto squares, Ralph Vaughan Williams composed his *Romance for Harmonica and Orchestra*.

The Saturn square is also the final one of a cycle, in this case, the third, and the average age for it to happen is 81. With it, as always with Saturn, comes the need to face up to practical matters and possibly our own limitations, to be realistic; perhaps to make changes as a result. We may need to help ourselves to be independent by looking at ways in which we can make life as stress-free as possible at a practical level. Clothes which are simple to slip on and to wash, comfortable and relaxing to wear; labour-saving devices, as the budget allows, to make life easier.

The Uranus return, which happens when we're in our early eighties, means that we have completed a whole cycle which began when we were born. Now we can look back and reflect – and begin a new cycle. At any age in life Uranus brings issues of freedom and independence; also new ideas, breakthroughs and inspiration, as well as sudden and unexpected events. So we may experience one or more of these. In addition, the Uranus return is often a time of fruition: when Arthur Rubinstein received his 'unexpected honours' for his life's work, and when my grandmother completed the building of her Temple, the Uranus return was in operation as well as the Pluto trine and the Jupiter conjunction which I've already mentioned.

At the time of his Uranus return, in November 1958, Pablo Casals was invited to play before the United Nations at a ceremony commemorating the thirteenth anniversary of its formation. In his *Reflections*, Casals, whose life was dedicated to the ideal of world peace, as well as to music, says of the event that he:

> gratefully welcomed the opportunity to use my music in that cause. The concert on that occasion was the most extraordinary event. It was transmitted by television and radio to seventy-four nations throughout the world. Never before had a message of music reached an audience of so many human beings . . . I had written a message for the occasion, which was distributed among the audience at the General Assembly Hall before I played. 'If at my age I come here for this day,' I stated, 'it is not because anything has changed in my moral attitude or in the restrictions I have imposed upon myself and my career as an artist for all these years, but because all else becomes secondary in comparison to the great and perhaps moral danger threatening all humanity.'

How appropriate that this event, taking place at the time of Casals's Uranus return, should be so widely transmitted by radio and television, both of which are ruled by Uranus. The United Nations ceremony marked both a culmination for Casals and the beginning of a new period in his life. As he says in his book:

> In the immediately ensuing years I used every meaningful opportunity to raise my voice in the cause of peace, and I joined the

boards of several organizations – like the Committee for a Sane Nuclear Policy – which were working to arouse people to the menace of atomic warfare. But I was not satisfied with these words of mine. I felt the need to act with deeds, not words. All my life, music had been my only weapon. How then, I asked myself, could I best use this weapon now? A plan took form in my mind. It revolved around my oratorio *El Pessebre*, 'The Manger', for which I had composed the music in Prades during the war. Since the message of this work was peace and the brotherhood of man, what better vehicle had I for acting at this urgent hour? I decided to take the oratorio anywhere in the world that I could and conduct it as a personal message in the cause of international understanding and world peace.

The story of the Nativity had always had a special meaning for Casals; one of the first compositions on which he worked, when he was 6 or 7, at the time of the very first of the cyclic Uranus aspects, the semi-sextile, was the music which he and his father composed for a performance of *Els Pastorets*, 'The Adoration of the Shepherds'. Now, over 70 years later, at the time of his Uranus return, he was using this to bring a message of peace and brotherhood to the world. Some of his friends tried to persuade him that he was too old to be undertaking such an arduous task. Casals replied:

I am a man first, an artist second . . . As a man my first obligation is to the welfare of my fellow men. I will endeavour to meet this obligation through music – the means which God has given me – since it transcends language, politics and national boundaries. My contribution to world peace may be small. But at least I will have given all I can to an ideal I hold sacred.

At the time of his Uranus return, Carl Jung was writing his autobiography, *Memories, Dreams, Reflections*, looking back over his life, meditating, evaluating: following exactly the process initiated by the Uranus return and also by the Neptune opposition, which he had at the same time. As Aniela Jaffe, his friend and assistant of many years' standing, with whom he was working on the book, said:

During the years when the book was taking shape [during the time of Jung's Uranus return and Neptune opposition] a process of transformation and objectiveness was taking place in Jung. With each succeeding chapter he moved, as it were, further away from himself, until at last he was able to see himself as well as the significance of his life and work from a distance. 'If I ask the value of my life, I can only measure myself against the centuries and then I must say, Yes it means something. Measured by the ideas of today, it means nothing.'

Sometimes the inner and outer process of completion is so full that life finishes at the Uranus return. In this context, I am reminded of the quotation in *Illusions* by Richard Bach: 'Here is a test to find whether your mission on earth is finished: If you're alive, it isn't.' Someone I knew whose mission clearly had finished began to feel unwell around the time of her Uranus return. She had previously been very healthy and vigorous and neither she nor her friends were particularly worried about her. After a week or so, however, she went to her doctor. It was discovered that she had advanced cancer of the liver, and she died, peacefully, within 6 weeks. Another woman experienced death at the time of her Uranus return, but in her case it was the death of her husband. It had not been a very good marriage, but she had nursed her husband at home for a number of years before he died. When he died she felt mixed feelings of sorrow, relief, guilt; as well as the challenging prospect of facing the future on her own. So for her the return brought up Uranian issues of independence and freedom, as well as a natural need to reflect on the past 82-year cycle as she faced the beginning of a new one.

The Uranus return can signify inspiration, especially if it comes at the same time as the Neptune opposition. I've already mentioned Jung's writing during this period. Goethe was writing *Faust* at the time of his Uranus return; Michelangelo was painting the dome of St Peter's in Rome; Pablo Casals and Arthur Rubinstein were both continuing to make brilliant recordings and to give concerts internationally; and there are many other examples. People who have an enthralling career or hobby which they can continue to the Uranus return and beyond seem to be especially able to withstand the effects of the years and, indeed, creativity may be intensified by them. Sir Michael Tippett was still composing well into his eighties, and the composer Havergal Brian wrote twenty of his thirty-two symphonies after he was 80! He continued to live an active life throughout his eighties, and retained his youthful mind and all his faculties into his nineties.

Throughout his eighties, Dr D. T. Suzuki, who unlocked the mysteries of Mahayana Buddhism for Westerners, and is especially remembered for his lucid expositions of Zen Buddhism, was travelling and lecturing widely. In his biography, A. Irwin Switzer III says of this period, which, incidentally, began at the time of Suzuki's Pluto square, in 1949:

> Now having reached the advanced age of 79, Suzuki wished only to remain quietly in Kamakura enjoying the pleasures of study and having time to watch the seasons change. However, quite the opposite was to happen. The demands of the outside world for the benefits of his unique wisdom would draw him into the limelight rather than allow him to slip into the tranquil obscurity towards which he inclined. The year 1949 may have started quietly enough, but it was to herald the beginning of ten years of intensive activity upon three continents, years during which Suzuki would be continually moving about, rarely staying in one place for more than six months at a time.

When, at the age of 85, at the time of his Uranus return, he was asked why he continued to lecture rather than write, he replied: 'The lectures take much time, but they make me think, and stimulate me to careful preparation.'

The Uranus return is followed by the first square of the eighth Jupiter cycle, when we're around 86, and then the opposition, which happens when we're about 89. Both of these, however, are overshadowed by another major cyclic aspect, which happens at around the same time, the third Saturn return. Saturn is the planet of discipline, limitation, restriction, responsibility, also of paring down; and it rules the body in general, and the bones, skin and teeth in particular. Each time the Saturn return occurs it marks a time of change, of pruning away the inessentials, getting rid of that which we have outgrown in our life: a time when we shed a skin, to allow ourselves to grow and become freer, to express more truly ourselves. This process often comes about through our having to face one of Saturn's restrictions. These can never be avoided; they are often painful and mean limitation, and they force us to take a realistic look at our life, to take stock, and to make changes accordingly.

At the time of his Saturn return in June 1962, Sir Winston Churchill broke his left thigh, and this led him, nearly a year later, in May 1963, to announce his retirement from the House of Commons, at the age of 88. For Arthur Rubinstein the Saturn return coincided with further sudden serious deterioration in his sight. He was no longer able to give concerts, or to read. He says of this time:

> I suddenly found myself with such a wealth of time on my hands. The long, long hours I had spent reading – mornings, afternoons, and late in bed, all through my life and often to the detriment of my pianistic activities – had to be filled with a new way of living. My wife taught me to listen to the radio, which I had always refused to do, she put an apparatus on my table and made me become a reluctant novice, but by and by, I became like the rest of my family, an obedient servant of this diabolical intruder into our privacy. But still, I was trying desperately to find other possible occupations.

He soon succeeded, and began dictating his memoirs, continuing where he had left off previously, when he had written *My Young Years*. He found unexpected pleasure in this task, which he completed around the time of his ninetieth birthday. At that time he wrote:

> Since then I have been living the happiest time of my life. My excellent gramophone, my wealth of records, allow me to hear the most divine music from morning until night, while previously my concert tours hardly let me hear a sprinkling of recitals and here and there a good orchestral performance. My partial blindness has deepened my love of life. My feeling for music, my thoughts and ideas have become clearer and my dear *deus ex machina* has provided me with the most beautiful last years of my life.

Arthur Rubinstein demonstrates how, once we have accepted Saturn's constraints, they can, paradoxically, be surprisingly freeing. At his third Saturn return, Humphrey Blake moved from the house which had been his home for over 50 years to a retirement home. His son, Christopher Blake, writes in his biography, *Times and Seasons*, 'It was . . . a relief that, for the first time in nearly thirty years, the domestic side of things was being taken care of by others.' Another man reluctantly realized, at his Saturn return, that it was time to give up driving his car. He found the decision difficult, because he felt that this meant an end to his independence. However, he and his wife began to use their local taxi service instead. Once he was able to get used to this, he found that he began to enjoy being driven by someone else; he could relax and enjoy the drive with no worries about parking. To his surprise he found that although he was able to take taxis whenever he wanted to, it actually worked out cheaper than running his car. Saturn's changes, like any others, are most painful if we resist them and fight against them. If we can accept them and look for the positive side of whatever they are bringing us, and be prepared to change with them, then they can work out for our benefit.

Some people do still have enormous spirit and stamina in their late eighties. Around the time of her Saturn return, Barbara Cartland wrote the following letter to Philip Bristow for his book, *Famous Ways to Grow Old*:

> I shall be eighty-eight on the 9th of July this year [1989] and many people ask me how I am managing to do so much work – ten books already this year – and as you know, I am the best-selling author in the world. I will tell you my secret. The answer is quite simply because I believe in my vitamins and take a great number of them. I am also quite convinced that the older one gets, to feel young and remain young, one must keep working. I do not mean a nine-to-five job. What I mean is what they call in America 'Go, go, go!' all day!
>
> We have the terrible habit in this country of pushing people, soon after they are fifty, into Old People's Homes, giving them nothing to do, and sitting them down in front of the television until they die. This means they are not using their brains, and the brain gradually atrophies. Then they become really senile long before they should do so. My mother, who kept going all the time, lived until she was ninety-eight, and drove her car until she was ninety-five.

The next decade opens with the last square of the Jupiter cycle and a semi-sextile from Uranus, the first aspect of the new cycle, which is likely to coincide with the Uranian qualities of change, independence, the need to adapt. For Humphrey Blake this aspect coincided with the death of his wife after over 65 years of marriage.

The eighth Jupiter return takes place when we are around 94, followed at 95 by the first square of the fourth Saturn cycle. For Humphrey Blake the Saturn square coincided with a series of falls, of which he said, 'Fortunately I always fall on my head, so do not break any bones'. He kept his memory until the end of his life, and around the time of his ninety-eighth birthday, in October 1986, he was invited to take part in a BBC regional radio programme about young people's modes and manners. This, appropriately, in view of Uranus's connection with radio, coincided with his Uranus sextile. Humphrey Blake died 3 months before his hundredth birthday, at the time of his Jupiter opposition, which freed him from his physical body. His life, like the others I have mentioned in this chapter, expressed the truth of the words which Longfellow wrote in his *Morituri Salutamus*:

> It is too late! Ah nothing is too late
> Till the tired heart shall cease to palpitate.
> Cato learned Greek at eighty; Sophocles
> Wrote his grand Oedipus, and Simonides
> Bore off the prize of verse from his compeers,
> When each had numbered more than fourscore years,
> And Theophrastus, at fourscore and ten,
> Had but begun his Characters of Men.
> Chaucer, at Woodstock with the nightingales,
> At sixty wrote The Canterbury Tales;
> Goethe at Weimar, toiling to the last,
> Completed Faust when eighty years were past.
> These are indeed exceptions; but they show
> How far the gulf-stream of our youth may flow
> Into the arctic regions of our lives,
> Where little else than life itself survives.
> For age is opportunity no less
> Than youth itself, though in another dress,
> And as the evening twilight fades away
> The sky is filled with stars, invisible by day.

PART THREE

How to Work Out Your Cycles

LOOKING UP
YOUR PLANETS AND
THEIR CYCLES

You can look up the positions of your planets from Jupiter to Pluto and plot your cycles by turning the book and using the following graphs for the years 1900 to 2020. The horizontal scale at the bottom of each graph shows the signs of the zodiac in sequence. The sign of Aries is shown on the left, followed by Taurus, Gemini and so on to Pisces on the right. (For a key to the symbols, see page 202.) The years are shown on the left-hand axis with horizontal lines marking the dates every 3 months. Because the actual zodiac is round and the page is flat, the graphs disappear off the page on the right and reappear on the left of the next page.

It is very easy from the graphs to see when the paths of the planets cross each other. For instance, if you look at the years 1980 to 1999 you will see how the planet Saturn crosses first Pluto in 1982, then Uranus in 1988 and Neptune in 1989. And also how Uranus and Neptune cross in 1993.

You will see clearly how the yearly motion of the Earth makes the position of each planet appear to wobble. This is what makes it difficult to give accurate estimates for the exact lengths of the cycles and why it is good to calculate them properly for your own date of birth.

First look up your birthday for the year of your birth, and as carefully as you can draw a line across the graph at that point. (You might like to photocopy the graphs if you want to work out the cycles for several people, or if you don't want to mark your book.) Next take a piece of paper and place it so the left edge is on the left-hand axis of the graph, and the top edge is along the date line you have drawn. Now draw clear marks on the paper where the paths of the five planets cross the line you have drawn. Label each mark with the appropriate planet. Use this pattern to mark the top and bottom of each graph following your birth page with the position of your natal planets, making sure that you line up the left-hand edge carefully each time, then draw vertical lines joining the marks. You should be able to make an approximate estimate of the degree each planet makes in its sign by reading the scale at the bottom of the graph. Each sign is divided into three divisions of 10 degrees, with 0 degrees on the left and 30 degrees on the right. Label the lines you have drawn with the planets' symbols. The page should now look like the graph in the diagram opposite, showing the Princess of Wales's chart from 1990 to 2002.

You should now be able to see at a glance where the faster planets cross their own natal position, and you can find the other aspects if you take the aspect rule and, keeping the conjunction line on the natal line you have just drawn, slide the rule up or down the page. You should be able to see clearly where the paths of the planets cross the various aspects marked on the rule, and from the scale on the left judge the dates on which these aspects occur. You can use either end of the marker, depending on whether the transiting planet is to the left or right of the natal planet. You might like to write out a list of the main dates showing the planets and the aspects formed, or photocopy the list of aspects and cycles and add your own dates.

The Planets		The Signs	
SYMBOL	PLANET	SYMBOL	SIGN
☉	Sun	♈	Aries
☽	Moon	♉	Taurus
☿	Mercury	♊	Gemini
♀	Venus	♋	Cancer
♂	Mars	♌	Leo
♃	Jupiter	♍	Virgo
♄	Saturn	♎	Libra
♅	Uranus	♏	Scorpio
♆	Neptune	♐	Sagittarius
♇	Pluto	♑	Capricorn
		♒	Aquarius
		♓	Pisces

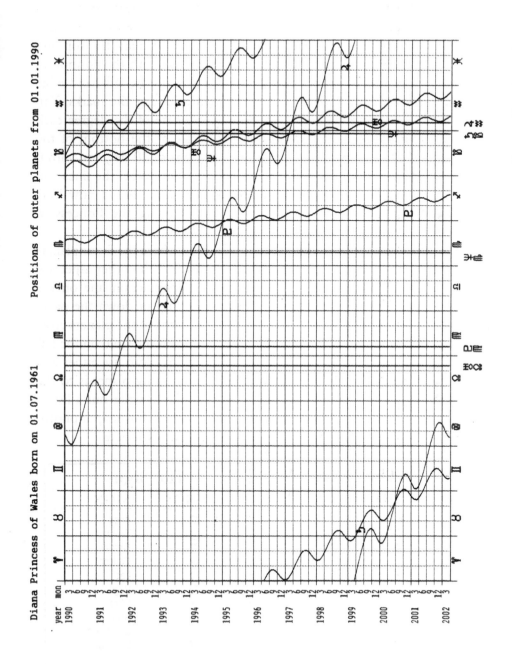

Diana Princess of Wales born on 01.07.1961   Positions of outer planets from 01.01.1990

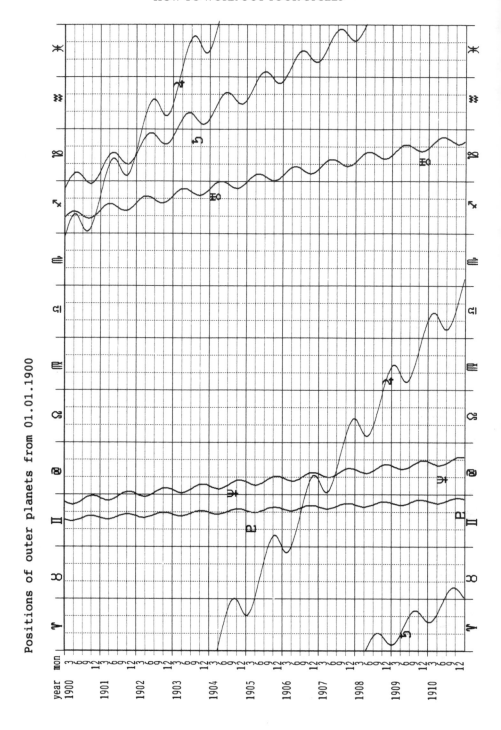

Positions of outer planets from 01.01.1900

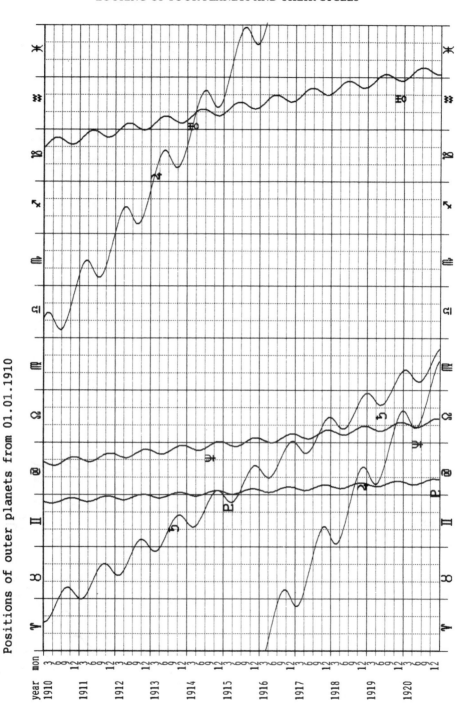

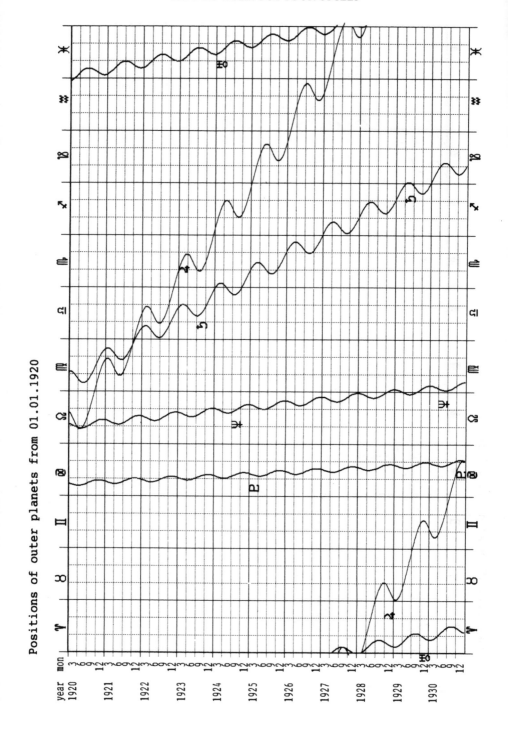

Positions of outer planets from 01.01.1920

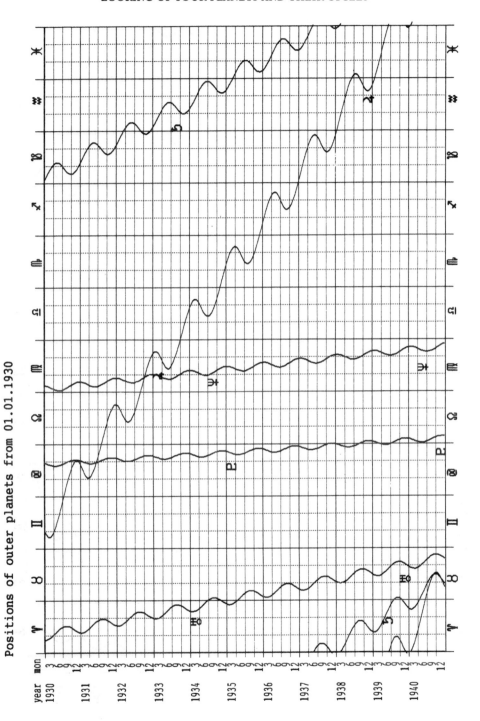

Positions of outer planets from 01.01.1930

Positions of outer planets from 01.01.1940

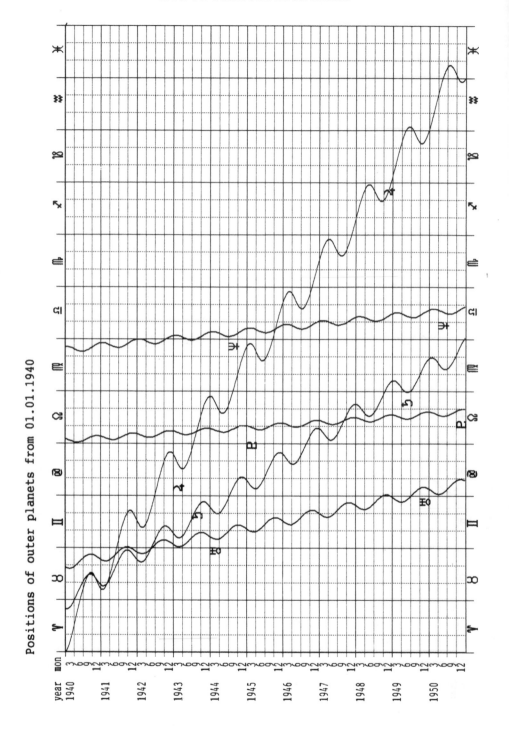

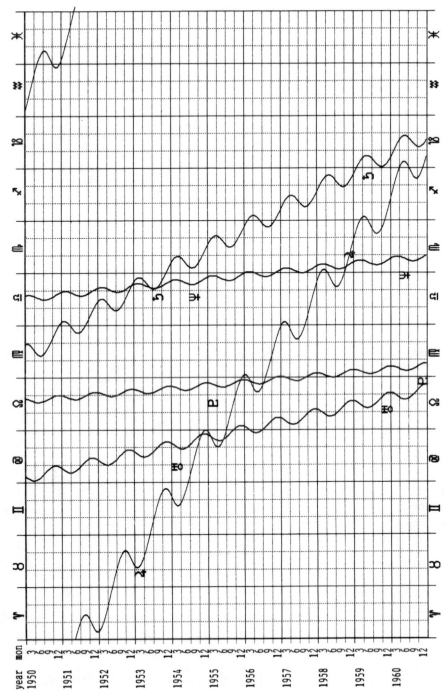

Positions of outer planets from 01.01.1950

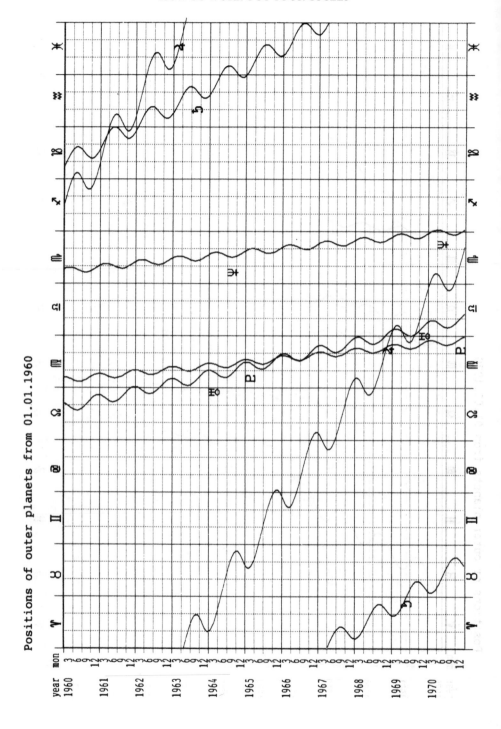

Positions of outer planets from 01.01.1960

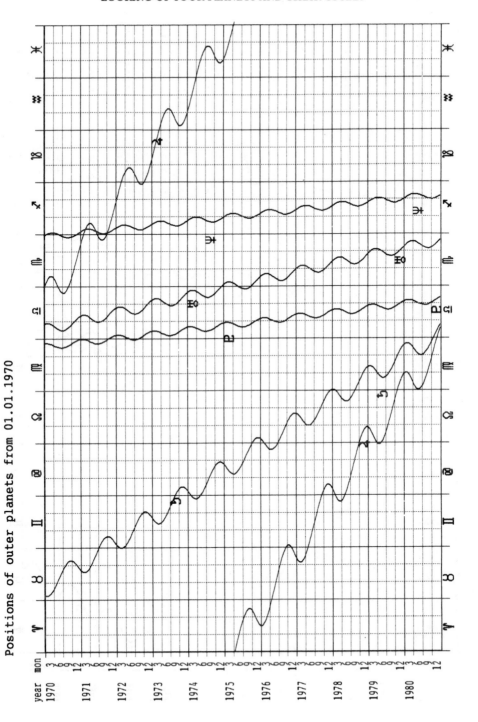

Positions of outer planets from 01.01.1970

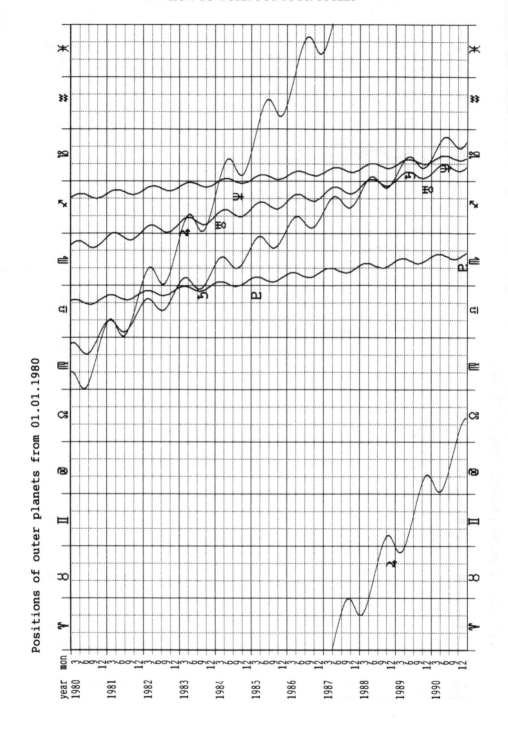

Positions of outer planets from 01.01.1980

Positions of outer planets from 01.01.1990

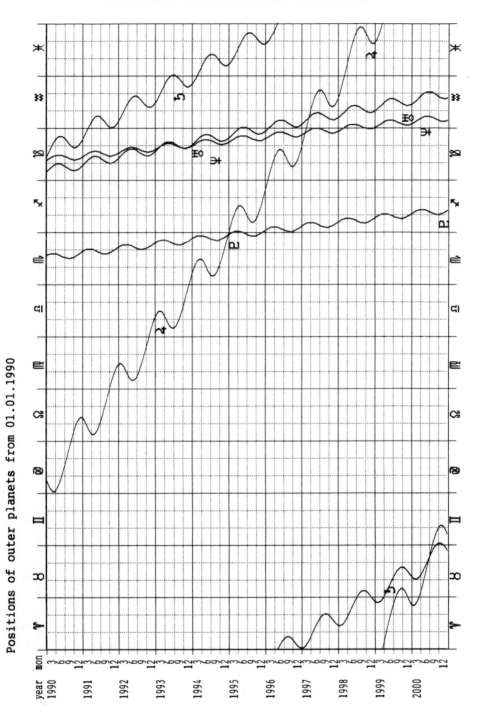

213

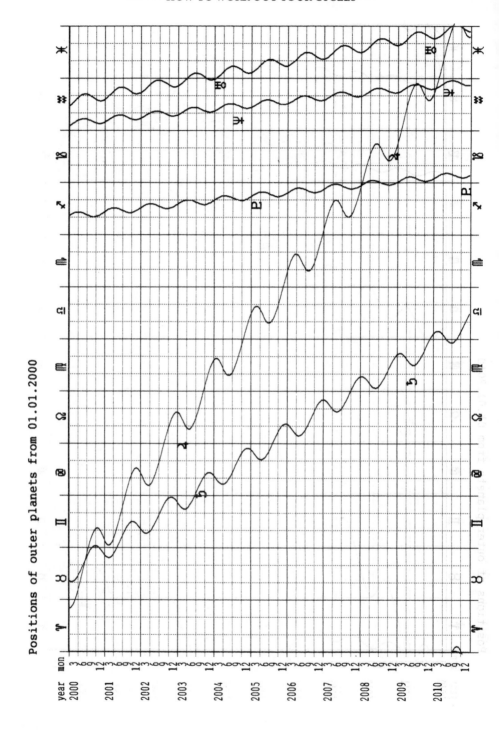

Positions of outer planets from 01.01.2000

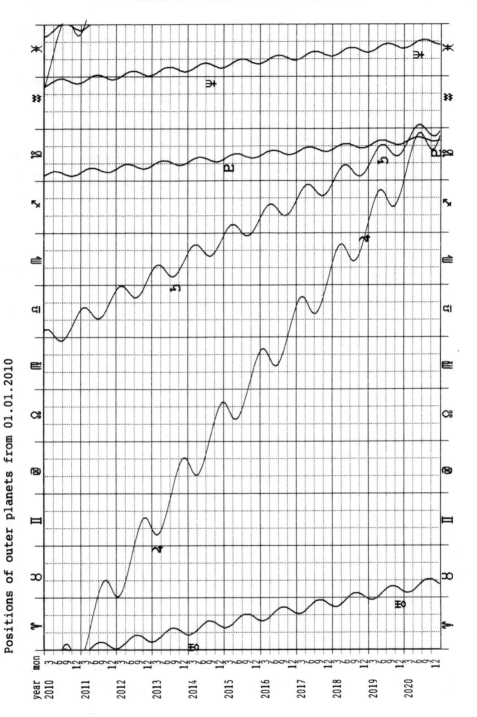

Positions of outer planets from 01.01.2010

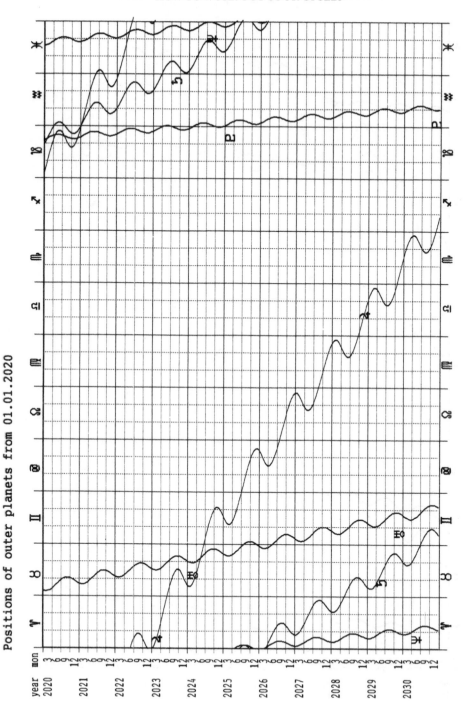

Positions of outer planets from 01.01.2020

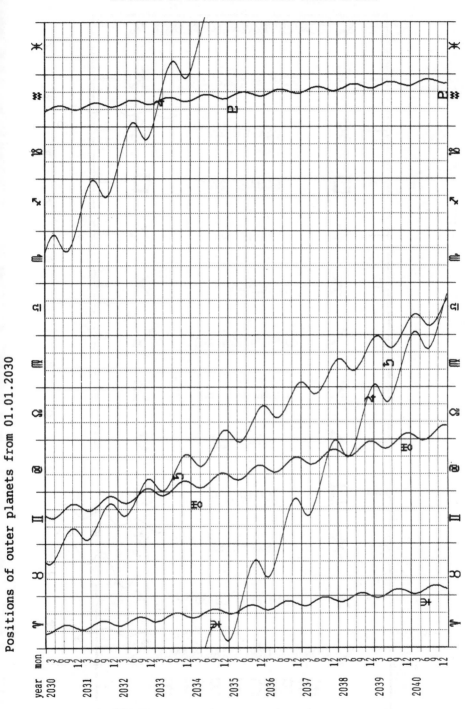

Positions of outer planets from 01.01.2030

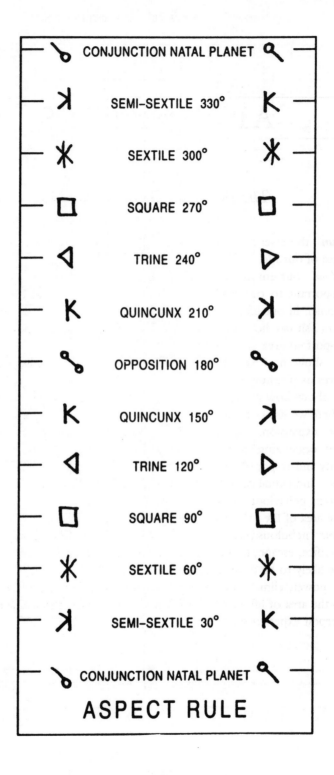

ASPECT RULE

APPENDICES

The Planets – Basic Meanings

The Sun   the essential personality; house position shows a very important area of our life.

The Moon   our emotions, feelings; sign and house position shows what is important to our emotional security; our mother and the important women in our life; home and family life.

Mercury   shows how we learn and communicate; house position shows important area of communication.

Venus   shows how we love and relate to others; house position shows what gives us pleasure.

Mars   shows how we take action and get things done; house position shows where we use our energy and initiative and what makes us angry.

Jupiter   expansion, opportunities; house position shows where these lie.

Saturn   organizing ability; house position shows our main area of limitation, duty and responsibility.

Uranus   individuality, independence, change, rebellion, unconventionality, erratic behaviour, sudden and unexpected events; house position shows the area of life in which these are most likely to occur.

Neptune   nebulousness, impressionability, imagination, dissolution, self-sacrifice, escape; house position shows the area of our life in which we are likely to be most inspired – and deluded.

Pluto   power, elimination, renewal, regeneration; house position is a clue to the area of life in which we'll have power-struggles and some of our deepest experiences.

The Signs of the Zodiac – Basic Meanings

Aries (fire)   assertive, energetic, seeking the new.

Taurus (earth)   possessive, practical, sensual.

Gemini (air)   versatile, communicative, changeable.

Cancer (water)   sensitive, caring, responsive, home-loving, conventional.

Leo (fire)   proud, dramatic, passionate, generous.

Virgo (earth)   critical, intelligent, realistic, with attention to detail.

Libra (air)   harmony-loving, balanced, companionable, fair.

Scorpio (water)   passionate, secretive, intense, with great determination.

Sagittarius (fire)   freedom-loving, enthusiastic, optimistic.

Capricorn (earth)   prudent, cool, ambitious, calculating, with high standards and respect for tradition.

Aquarius (air)   detached but friendly, quirky, erratic.

Pisces (water)   imaginative, gentle, kind, sometimes confused and deceptive.

Compatible and Incompatible Signs

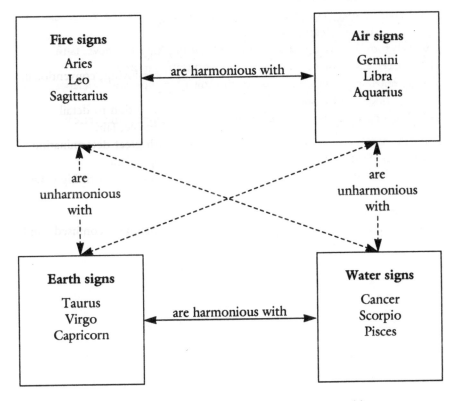

Signs linked by solid lines are naturally compatible.
Signs linked by broken lines are not naturally compatible.

The Houses – Basic Meanings

1. Outward personality; self-expression; physical appearance.
2. Money, possessions, our sense of values, including our self-worth.
3. Attitude and approach to communication, study, writing and correspondence; short journeys; immediate environment; brothers, sisters, cousins and neighbours.
4. Home, father, base, security.
5. Creativity, fun, pleasure; attitude towards children and love.
6. Work and daily routine; health.

7. Marriage and close one-to-one relationships, including rivals and open enemies; the public.
8. Financial matters involving other people; contracts and wills; sexuality; birth and death; medical matters.
9. Wisdom, knowledge and further education; long journeys; faith.
10. Career and achievement; authority and status; mother.
11. Friends and unformalized relationships; groups and societies; aims, hopes and wishes.
12. The unconscious; secret enemies; prisons, hospitals and retreats.

The Planetary Rulerships

planet	rules	exalted	detriment	fall
Sun	Leo	Aries	Aquarius	Libra
Moon	Cancer	Taurus	Capricorn	Scorpio
Mercury	Gemini and Virgo	Virgo	Sagittarius and Pisces	Pisces
Venus	Taurus and Libra	Pisces	Scorpio and Aries	Virgo
Mars	Aries and Scorpio	Capricorn	Libra and Taurus	Cancer
Jupiter	Sagittarius and Pisces	Cancer	Gemini and Virgo	Capricorn
Saturn	Capricorn and Aquarius	Libra	Cancer and Leo	Aries
Uranus	co-rules Aquarius			
Neptune	co-rules Pisces			
Pluto	co-rules Scorpio			

Ruler is the term used to describe the special affinity or connection between a planet and a sign. Traditionally, the Sun and Moon each ruled one sign – Leo and Cancer respectively – and the rest of the known planets – Mercury, Venus, Mars, Jupiter and Saturn – each ruled two signs. Since Uranus, Neptune and Pluto have been discovered, astrologers have noticed that they have an affinity with certain signs, which many astrologers consider that they co-rule, along with the traditional ruler. A planet can manifest strongly when it is placed in its own sign.

Detriment is the term used when a planet is in the sign which is opposite in the zodiac to the one which it rules. So the Sun, which rules Leo, is in its detriment in the sign opposite to Leo, Aquarius; Mars, which rules Aries, is in its detriment in the sign opposite to Aries, Libra. The planets cannot function so strongly when in the sign of their detriment.

Exaltation is the term used when a planet is placed in a sign in which it is traditionally known to manifest at its best.

223

Fall is the term used when a planet is placed in the sign opposite to the one in which it is exalted. The planet is said to be 'debilitated' or weakened when it is in the sign of its fall.

The Planetary Aspects

degrees apart	aspect	nature
0 (usually same sign)	conjunction	blends influences
30 (1 sign)	semi-sextile	mildly harmonious
45 (11/2 signs)	semi-square	tense
60 (2 signs)	sextile	cooperating influences
90 (3 signs)	square	conflicting influences
120 (4 signs)	trine	cooperating influences
150 (5 signs)	quincunx	tense
180 (opposite signs)	opposition	opposing influences

The Aspects in the Birth Chart and What They Mean

Aspect	Angular separation of the two planets			Significance in the birth chart
	degs	orbs	signs	
Conjunction	0	8	0	blends influences
Semi-sextile	30	2	1	mildly harmonious
Semi-square	45	2	1.5	tense
Sextile	60	4	2	cooperating influences
Square	90	6	3	conflicting influences
Trine	120	6	4	cooperating influences
Quincunx	150	2	5	tense
Opposition	180	8	6	opposing influences

The closer the angle between the planets to the figure given in the 'degs' column, the stronger the effect of the aspect. The aspect is considered to be effective when the planets are within the exactitude of the figure shown in the column marked 'orbs'; e.g. a trine will be effective from the time the planets are 114 degrees apart until they are 126 degrees apart.

The Aspects in the Cycles and What They Mean

Aspect	Angular separation of the two planets			Significance in the planetary cycles
	degs	*orbs*	*signs*	
Conjunction	0	1	0	Ending of one cycle, beginning of another; intensification of planet's influence
Semi-sextile	30	1	1	Minor intensification of planet's influence
Semi-square	45	1	1.5	Tension
Sextile	60	1	2	Time of opportunity, opening out, beginning a venture
Square	90	1	3	Plans are tested and may need to be changed; challenging conditions
Trine	120	1	4	Stable, harmonious, expansive conditions
Quincunx	150	1	5	Usually a weak influence, but can show tension, confusion, separation
Opposition	180	1	6	A time of re-evaluation, possibly as a result of change; separation or difficulty

The effect of the aspects in the cycles will be felt both when the aspect is plus the orb and when it is minus.

GLOSSARY

AFFIRMATIONS Positive statements which are frequently repeated to oneself to change negative beliefs and views, and help to bring about a desired condition, e.g. 'All things are working together for good in my life.'

AIR SIGNS Signs of the zodiac which are of the element air: Gemini, Libra and Aquarius. Air emphasizes the faculties of the mind and communication and affects ideas and social activities rather than practical matters, enthusiasm or emotion.

AQUARIUS Fixed air sign whose main characteristics are detachment, friendliness, quirkiness, inventiveness.

ARIES Cardinal fire sign, the first sign of the zodiac, whose main characteristics are assertiveness, energy, innovation.

ASCENDANT The sign and degree of the zodiac which is rising above the eastern horizon at a given time. In a birth chart it is very important and forms the starting-point for the twelve houses, or divisions, of the chart which are numbered anticlockwise starting at 1. The sign on the ascendant, also called the rising sign, is important in terms of character.

ASPECT Describes the situation when two or more planets are a set number of degrees apart. The list of aspects and the degrees are given on page 224. The influences of the planets blend either harmoniously or inharmoniously.

BIRTH CHART The chart which maps the positions of the planets at the time of birth; sometimes called a horoscope or natal chart.

CANCER Cardinal water sign whose main characteristics are sensitivity, caring, responsiveness, love of home and family.

CAPRICORN Cardinal earth sign whose main characteristics are prudence, coolness, ambition, high standards, respect for tradition.

CARDINAL SIGNS Signs which all have the quality of being outgoing, active and with initiative; they are Aries, Cancer, Libra and Capricorn.

COLLECTIVE UNCONSCIOUS A term used by Carl Jung to describe

227

the areas in the unconscious which appear to be a source of material common to groups of people.

CONJUNCTION Aspect formed when two planets are 0–8 degrees apart; their influences blend.

CUSP The boundary between two houses or two signs. People who are born around the time when the Sun changes from one sign to another have their Sun on the cusp of the two signs. The influences tend to blend, but usually with a bias towards the new sign or house.

CYCLE The complete orbit of a planet around the Sun during which it is seen to move through all twelve signs of the zodiac.

EARTH SIGNS Signs of the element earth, which have to do with practical matters rather than abstract ideas, enthusiasm or emotion: Taurus, Virgo and Capricorn.

ECLIPSE When one heavenly body disappears behind another. A lunar eclipse occurs when the orb of the Earth interposes itself between the light of the Sun and the Moon; and a solar eclipse happens when the orb of the Moon interposes itself between the Earth and the light of the Sun. Both, but particularly the solar eclipse, can coincide with important events if they occur close to significant degrees in the birth chart.

ECLIPTIC The path in the sky along which the planets appear to travel. The path of one point can be seen by the movement of the Sun across the sky from sunrise to sunset, but this is misleading because the full ecliptic extends beyond that trajectory. Thus, in winter, the Sun, in Capricorn, has a low trajectory, but the full Moon, in Gemini, appears high in the sky.

EGO That part of ourselves which we recognize consciously. It contains all the thoughts, ideas, beliefs and fears we have about ourselves. It acts as a controller to enable us to function effectively in the world, but has the disadvantage of filtering out much of our experience of the unconscious, particularly if that would cause the ego self-image to be threatened. The ego is a product of the mind and according to some philosophies has no real substance. The ego is always trying to protect itself from pain, particularly from the fear that it does not in fact exist.

EGO BOUNDARY The mental boundary the ego constructs between what it considers to be 'self' and 'other'. In some states of consciousness this boundary dissolves, often leading to states of great joy and a sense of freedom.

EGO IMAGE This is the picture we hold about ourselves in our heads. It has usually been built up over a long time so we tend to feel comfortable about it, even when it contains diminishing ideas and beliefs. The prospect of having to change this self-image can initially cause great pain and stress, though the result of doing so can be most uplifting and releasing. It is important to realize that the limitations of the ego image are self-imposed and to try to work beyond them. This is the principle behind many sporting and other achievements.

EIGHTH HOUSE   The eighth division of the birth chart which stands for financial matters involving other people; contracts and wills; sexuality; birth and death; medical matters.

ELEMENTS   A division of the signs of the zodiac into four basic types which describe their essential nature. They are fire, earth, air and water.

ELEVENTH HOUSE   The eleventh division of the birth chart which stands for friends and unformalized relationships; groups and societies; aims, hopes and wishes.

ESSENTIAL BEING   The life essence which is at the heart of our being. It is beyond ego and selfishness; it appears to have qualities which are above those of the personal. Many people experience this essential being at some time in their lives, often with religious or mystical associations. See also **Transpersonal Self**.

FIFTH HOUSE   The fifth section of the birth chart, which stands for creativity, fun, pleasure; attitude towards children, and love.

FIRE SIGNS   Signs of the element air, which are enthusiastic and outgoing rather than practical or to do with abstract ideas or emotion: Aries, Leo, Sagittarius.

FIRST HOUSE   The first division of the birth chart, which stands for the outward personality; self-expression; physical appearance. The cusp of the first house is the ascendant or rising sign.

FIXED SIGNS   Signs which all have the quality of being stable and persevering: they are Taurus, Leo, Scorpio and Aquarius.

FOURTH HOUSE   The fourth section of the birth chart, which stands for the home, father, base, security.

GEMINI   Mutable air sign, whose main characteristics are versatility, communication, changeability.

HOROSCOPE   The chart on which are mapped the positions of the planets at the time of birth; often referred to as a birth chart by modern astrologers.

HOUSE   One of twelve sections into which the circle of the birth chart is divided. Each house stands for a certain area of life such as finance, relationships, career and so on.

HOUSE SYSTEM   A method of dividing the circle of the birth chart into twelve sections. There are various house systems, the simplest being the

229

Equal House System, in which the divisions each consist of 30 degrees, starting with the ascendant. Other systems also start with the ascendant, but have different ways of dividing up the space between the ascendant and its opposite point, the descendant, and the mid-heaven and its opposite point. The house system which we have used for the charts in this book is called the Topocentric, which is very similar to the Placidus House System.

IMUM COELI Known also as IC. The lowest degree of the ecliptic, opposite to the culminating degree the *medium coeli*, or mid-heaven. It symbolizes our base, our home and foundation.

JUPITER The largest of the planets which, in the birth chart, symbolizes, among other things, expansion, opportunities, good fortune, travel, publishing, the law, the Church, higher education.

LEO Fixed fire sign whose main characteristics are pride, love of drama, passion and generosity.

LIBRA Cardinal air sign whose main characteristics are love of harmony, balance, fairness, companionability.

MARS Planet between the Earth and Venus which in the birth chart symbolizes, among other things, energy, action, initiative, young men, courage, challenge.

MERCURY Planet nearest the Sun which in the birth chart symbolizes, among other things, communication, letters, short journeys.

MID-HEAVEN The culminating degree of the ecliptic, sometimes called the *medium coeli* and abbreviated to MC. It symbolizes our career, activities in the world and success. The opposite point is the *imum coeli*, usually shortened to IC.

MOON The Earth's satellite, which, by astrological convention, is known as a planet. In the birth chart it symbolizes, among other things, the home, the mother, women, changeability and emotions.

MUTABLE SIGNS These signs all have the quality of being versatile and changeable: they are Gemini, Virgo, Sagittarius and Pisces.

NEGATIVE SIGNS The alternate signs from Taurus to Pisces inclusive, which belong to the earth and water elements. These signs are all essentially introvert in nature.

NEPTUNE One of the outer planets which in the birth chart symbolizes, among other things, imagination, nebulousness, inspiration, the sea, alcohol and drugs.

NEW MOON In astronomical and astrological terms, this is when the Sun and the Moon are in conjunction. If the new Moon occurs close to a sensitive degree in the birth chart it can coincide with a significant event or change.

NINTH HOUSE The ninth section of the birth chart, which stands for wisdom, knowledge and further education; long journeys and religion.

OPPOSITION Aspect formed when two planets are 180 degrees apart; their influences oppose or balance each other.

ORB The angular separation allowed when calculating if aspects are effective. This varies according to the strength of the planet and the aspect. For instance, for a conjunction an orb of 8 degrees is usually allowed (or sometimes 10 degrees if the aspect involves the Sun and Moon), whereas a maximum of only 2 degrees would be allowed for a minor aspect such as a semi-sextile.

PISCES Mutable water sign whose main characteristics are imaginativeness, gentleness, kindness, tendency to confusion.

PLANET Astronomically this is the term applied to all celestial bodies (with the exception of comets and meteors) which revolve around the Sun of our solar system. In astrology the Sun and Moon are also called planets, although the term 'lights' can be used for them.

PLUTO Outermost of the known planets, which in the birth chart symbolizes, among other things, power, elimination, renewal, regeneration, sexuality, birth and death.

POSITIVE SIGNS The alternate signs from Aries to Aquarius inclusive, which belong to the fire and air elements. These signs are all essentially extrovert in nature.

PRECESSION OF THE EQUINOXES Although the signs of the zodiac have the same names as constellations in the heavens, they are actually slowly separating from them. In astrology the signs are measured relative to the 0 degrees Aries point, which is taken as the position of the Sun as it crosses the equator on the first day of spring. Because the Earth wobbles on its axis, over approximately 26,000 years this vernal equinox now occurs against different stars from those 2000 years ago, after which the signs were named. This indicates that astrology is more linked to the activity of the solar system than to the outside universe.

PROGRESSION A system of plotting forward the planets in the birth chart according to various methods and thereby predicting future events.

PROJECTION The process by which we project facets of our unconscious on to someone or something else. Because the facet is in the unconscious we are normally unaware of it, but the energy will emerge when something occurs to trigger it. The event or person who acts as the trigger will then be blamed for the experience of emotion which is felt.

This process is often the cause of irrational likes and dislikes, and occurs in large groups as well as in individuals, e.g. irrational racial prejudice. It can be used positively if we monitor our reactions and then seek out the cause of the emotion inside ourselves. If you feel a great deal of emotion about someone or something, either positive or negative, projection is almost certainly involved.

QUALITY A division of the signs of the zodiac into three groups which describe the ways in which they act. They are cardinal, fixed and mutable.

QUINCUNX Aspect formed when two planets are 150 degrees apart; their influences work together tensely.

REPRESSION An activity of the ego to put uncomfortable thoughts, feelings and emotions into the unconscious. We are then unaware of them, but the tension associated with the emotion is still there and will block the free flow of activity and energy. The ego will be uneasy about any action which threatens to unveil the repressed emotions. Release of repressed emotions can be very stimulating and invigorating because the energy which was being used to suppress them is then available to be used elsewhere.

RETROGRADE The apparent backward motion of a planet due to the relative motion of the planet and the Earth revolving round the Sun.

RETURN When a planet completes a circuit of the ecliptic and returns to the degree and sign in which it was in the birth chart. It is the end of one cycle and the start of the next.

RISING SIGN The sign of the zodiac rising above the eastern horizon at the moment for which an astrological chart is cast, usually the moment of birth. Also called the ascendant.

RULER The planet traditionally linked with a particular sign of the zodiac; for instance, the Sun rules Leo. See **The Planetary Rulerships**, page 223.

RULING PLANET The planet which rules the rising sign; for example, if you have Gemini rising, Mercury is your ruling planet, and the influence of this planet, and that of the sign in which it is placed, are particularly important.

SAGITTARIUS Mutable fire sign whose main characteristics are love of freedom, enthusiasm, optimism.

SATURN Planet between Jupiter and Uranus which in the birth chart symbolizes, among other things, limitation, duty and responsibility, bones, old people.

SCORPIO Fixed water sign whose main characteristics are passion, secretiveness, intensity, determination.

SECOND HOUSE   Second section of the birth chart, which has to do with money, possessions, our sense of values.

SELF   See **Essential Being** and **Transpersonal Self**.

SELF-DEVELOPMENT   Processes and activities leading to better understanding of the workings of our own ego, so unravelling the self-diminishing beliefs and emotional blocks, and leading to a truer understanding of one's own nature. Ironically, if taken far enough it leads to the diminution of 'I', the separate self, and more awareness of the transpersonal self.

SEMI-SEXTILE   Aspect formed when two planets are 30 degrees apart; their influences blend in a mildly harmonious way.

SEMI-SQUARE   Aspect formed when two planets are 45 degrees apart; their influences work together in a tense way.

SEVENTH HOUSE   Seventh section of the birth chart, which stands for marriage and close one-to-one relationships including rivals and open enemies; the public.

SEXTILE   Aspect formed when two planets are 60 degrees apart; their influences blend together harmoniously.

SHADOW   Those beliefs, characteristics and patterns which the ego considers to be unacceptable, and are relegated to the unconscious. Wherever there is a strong desire to have certain characteristics there will be an unconscious fear of not having them. So strong conscious attributes and qualities, such as generosity and courage, can also lead to a strong shadow. Both the positive and negative aspects of the personality need to be acknowledged and integrated in order to acquire wholeness. We need to recognize our own fears, angers and weaknesses with love and understanding, to heal the split between the conscious and the unconscious.

SHIELD   This is the façade we put up to the world to hide our inner feelings of insecurity, fear, worthlessness, etc. It tends to appear to be rather false and lacks integrity with our true nature.

SIGN   This term refers to the 30-degree arcs of the zodiac which have the same names as the constellations in the heavens. In astrology they are measured relative to the 0 degrees Aries point, which is taken as the position of the Sun as it crosses the equator on the first day of spring.

SIXTH HOUSE   Sixth section of the birth chart, which stands for work and daily routine; health.

SQUARE   Aspect formed when two planets are 90 degrees apart; their influences conflict.

SUN   The star at the centre of our solar system which by astrological convention is known as a planet: In the birth chart it symbolizes, among other things, the heart, the father, men, royalty, the person in control. Its sign position tells us a great deal about a person's character.

SUPER-EGO This is the name given to the part of our ego which is built up from all the injunctions we received in childhood about the dos and don'ts of life. It tends to be very critical both of itself and others, and to be rather domineering and self-important, and may appear to be outside the self, rather like a stern God or father figure. It can, however, be distinguished from the transpersonal or higher self by observing the quality of the thoughts and words used. For example, the super-ego tends to use the words 'should' and 'ought', and to be very judgemental, whereas the transpersonal self is accepting, tolerant and loving.

TAURUS Fixed earth sign whose main characteristics are possessiveness, practicality, sensuality.

TENTH HOUSE Tenth section of the birth chart, which stands for the career and achievement; authority and status; mother.

THIRD HOUSE Third section of the birth chart, which stands for our attitude and approach to communication, study, writing and correspondence; short journeys; immediate environment; brothers, sisters, cousins and neighbours.

TRANSIT The passage of a planet in the sky over a sensitive degree in the birth chart.

TRANSPERSONAL SELF Also called the real self or higher self or essential being, it is that part of ourselves which connects with the highest source of our being. We are not normally conscious of this real aspect of self, so when we do occasionally become aware of it we may think it is outside ourselves and call it God or some other name. It is outside the realms of ego, but the ego would like to acquire its qualities, and tries to imitate it to boost its own image. Only when the neurotic aspect of ego is finally seen through and set aside can the full splendour of the transpersonal self manifest in the life. This is summed up in the words of Jesus – 'My Father and I are one.'

TRINE Aspect formed when two planets are 120 degrees apart; their influences cooperate.

TWELFTH HOUSE The twelfth section of the birth chart, which stands for the unconscious; secret enemies; prisons, hospitals and retreats.

UNCONSCIOUS This refers to the large part of our nature which is beneath the level of our consciousness. Sometimes this barrier is breached in dreams, meditation or waking visions. Often the ego tries to stop unconscious material from emerging because it could threaten the existing ego image, or the material could contain painful or emotional memories. This protection can be bypassed using methods which don't allow the ego knowledge of the material, e.g. analysis, word association, painting, dance, psycho-drama or body-work, or by giving the ego reassurance that the release is actually beneficial. The unconscious is divided into the personal unconscious, which contains personal memories and experiences, and the collective unconscious, which touches long-standing group memories from the past. The energies in the collective unconscious can be of very powerful archetypal forces.

URANUS Planet between Saturn and Neptune which in the birth chart symbolizes the new and exciting; the unusual; change, revolution, electronic equipment, computers.

VENUS Planet between the Earth and Mercury which in the birth chart symbolizes, among other things, love, relationships, young women, beauty, pleasure, money.

VIRGO Mutable earth sign whose main characteristics are critical ability, intelligence, realism, attention to detail.

VISUALIZATION A process in which the person deliberately imagines or visualizes situations or symbols in their heads. This act of creation can stimulate activity so that the actual situation is resolved positively, or releases emotional blocks so that the situation is perceived in a different light.

WATER SIGNS Signs which are concerned with emotion and feelings, rather than abstract ideas, enthusiasm and practicality: Cancer, Scorpio, Pisces.

BIBLIOGRAPHY

Preface: About This Book

Howell, Alice O., *Jungian Synchronicity in Astrological Signs and Ages*, Quest Books, 1990.

Introduction: Astrology and the Planetary Cycles

Morrow, Ann, *Princess*, Chapmans, 1991.
Ptolemy, *Tetrabiblos*, Loeb Classical Library, Harvard Heinemann, 1980.

The Sun

Elwell, Dennis, 'How Far Can the Future Be Predicted?' article in *Astrological Journal*, Nov./Dec. 1987.
Lilly, William, *Christian Astrology*, Regulus Publishing Co. Ltd, 1985.

Mercury

Hay, Louise L., *You Can Heal Your Life*, Eden Grove Editions, 1984.
Sri Ramana Maharshi, *The Teachings of Sri Ramana Maharshi*, ed. David Godman, Arkana, 1985.

Venus

Gawain, Shakti, *Living in the Light*, Whatever Publishing, 1986.
Hay, Louise L., *You Can Heal Your Life*, Eden Grove Editions, 1984.
Ray, Sondra, *Loving Relationships*, Celestial Arts, 1984.
Vaughan, Frances, *The Inward Arc*, Shambhala, 1986.

Mars

Lerner, Harriet Goldbor, *The Dance of Anger*, Hartnolls, 1990.

Saturn

Bach, Richard, *Illusions*, Pan Books, 1978.
Greene, Liz, *Saturn*, Aquarian Press, 1976.
Jeffers, Susan, *Feel the Fear and Do It Anyway*, Random Century, 1987.

Pluto

Goodrich-Dunn, Barbara, interview with Marion Woodman entitled 'The Conscious Feminine', published in *Common Boundary*, US, March/April 1989.

Childhood

Peck, M. Scott, *The Road Less Travelled*, Rider, 1978.
Wickes, Frances G., *The Inner World of Childhood*, Coventure, 1977.
Faber, Adele, and Maglish, Elaine *How to talk so kids will listen and listen so kids will talk*, Avon Books, New York, 1980

Teens

Peck, M. Scott, *The Road Less Travelled*, Rider, 1978.
Sheehy, Gail, *Passages*, Bantam, 1976.

Twenties

Davies, Nicholas, *Diana: A Princess and Her Troubled Marriage*, 1992.
Dempster, Nigel, *HRH The Princess Margaret*, Quartet Books, 1981.
Morrow, Ann, *Princess*, Chapman, 1991.
Morton, Andrew, *Diana, Her True Story*, Michael O'Mara, 1992.
Sheehy, Gail, *Passages*, Bantam, 1976.
Walker, Alexander, *Elizabeth*, George Weidenfeld and Nicolson, 1990.

Thirties

Brown, Mick, *Richard Branson, the Inside Story*, Headline, 1988, 1992.
Freedland, Michael, *Jane Fonda*, Fontana/Collins, 1989.
Patton, Daniele, 'The Pluto Return Generation II', *Astrological Journal*, November/December 1990.
Sheehy, Gail, *Passages*, Bantam, 1976.

Forties

Accurso, Linda, 1989, 'Tina Turner', from *Astrology – Your Daily Horoscope*, US, December 1989.
Dempster, Nigel, *HRH The Princess Margaret*, Quartet Books, 1981.
Freedland, Michael, *Jane Fonda*, Fontana/Collins, 1989.
Ivory, Steven, *Tina*, Bantam, 1986.
Jacobi, Jolande, *The Psychology of C. G. Jung*, New Haven, Yale University Press, 1973.
Levine, Robert, *Joan Collins*, Virgin Books, 1985.
Lundsted, Betty, *Planetary Cycles*, Samuel Weiser, Inc., 1984.
Rodegast, Pam, and Stanton, Judith, *Emmanuel's Book*, Bantam, 1985.
Sheehy, Gail, *Passages*, Bantam, 1976.
Walker, Alexander, *Elizabeth*, George Weidenfeld & Nicolson, 1990.

Fifties

Bancroft, Anne, *Zen*, Thames & Hudson, 1979.
Bristow, Philip, *Famous Ways to Grow Old*, Age Concern, 1989.
Hay, Louise L., *You Can Heal Your Life*, Eden Grove Editions, 1984.
Lundsted, Betty, *Planetary Cycles*, Samuel Weiser, Inc., 1984.
Moody, Raymond A., Jr, MD, *Life After Life*, Bantam, 1976.
Rose, Sir Alec, *My Lively Lady*, Nautical Publishing Company, 1969.
Sasportas, Howard, *The Gods of Change*, Arkana, 1989.
Scott, David, interview with Carla Lane in *The Vegetarian*, July/August 1992.
Sheehy, Gail, *Passages*, Bantam, 1976.
Walker, Alexander, *Elizabeth*, George Weidenfeld & Nicolson, 1990.

Sixties

Clennell, Stephanie (ed.), *Older Students in Europe*, The Open University, 1990.

Goodrich-Dunn, Barbara, interview with Marion Woodman entitled 'The Conscious Feminine', published in *Common Boundary*, US, March/April 1989.

Olivier, Sir Laurence, *Confessions of an Actor*, Weidenfeld and Nicolson, 1982.

Open Graduate, The, no. 003.

Sheehy, Gail, *Passages*, Bantam, 1976.

Seventies

Guardian, obituary of Barbara McClintock by Neville Symonds, 5 September 1992.

Jung, C. G., *Modern Man in Search of a Soul*, Routledge & Kegan Paul, 1961.

Matthiessen, Peter, *The Snow Leopard*, Collins Harvill, 1989.

Norberg-Hodge, Helena, *Ancient Futures*, Rider, 1991.

Quigley, Joan, *What Does Joan Say?*, Birch Lane Press, 1990.

Scaravelli, Vanda, *Awakening the Spine*, Aquarian Press, 1991.

Vanity Fair, US, May 1991.

Eighties Plus

Blake, Christopher, *Times and Seasons*, Mendip Publishing, 1989.

Bristow, Philip, *Famous Ways to Grow Old*, Age Concern, 1989.

Casals, Pablo, as told to Albert E. Kahn, *Reflections, Joys and Sorrows*, Macdonald, 1970.

Goodrich-Dunn, Barbara, interview with Marion Woodman entitled 'The Conscious Feminine', published in *Common Boundary*, US, March/April 1989.

Jung, C. G., *Memories, Dreams, Reflections*, Collins and Routledge, Kegan Paul, 1963.

Kirk, H. L., *Pablo Casals, a Biography*, Hutchinson, 1974.

Rubinstein, Arthur, *My Many Years*, Hamish Hamilton, 1980.

Switzer III, A. Irwin, *D. T. Suzuki*, The Buddhist Society, 1985.